New Directions for International Relations

Innovations in the Study of World Politics

Series Editor
Zeev Maoz, Tel-Aviv University

Advisory Board
Michael Barnett, University of Wisconsin, Madison
Deborah Larson, UCLA
Brett Ashley Leeds, Rice University
Jack Levy, Rutgers University

This series provides a forum for the publication of original theoretical, empirical, and conceptual studies that seek to chart new frontiers in the field of international relations. The key emphasis is on innovation and change. Books in the series will offer insights on and approaches to a broad range of issues facing the modern world, in an effort to revolution-ize how contemporary world politics are studied, taught, and practiced.

Forgetting Ourselves: Secession and the (Im)possibility of Territorial Identity
By Linda S. Bishai

Multiple Paths to Knowledge in International Relations: Methodology in the Study of Conflict Management and Conflict Resolution
Edited by Zeev Maoz, Alex Mintz, T. Clifton Morgan, Glenn Palmer, and Richard J. Stoll

New Directions for International Relations: Confronting the Method-of-Analysis Problem
Edited by Alex Mintz and Bruce Russett

New Directions for International Relations

Confronting the Method-of-Analysis Problem

Edited by
Alex Mintz and Bruce Russett

LEXINGTON BOOKS
Lanham • Boulder • New York • Toronto • Oxford

LEXINGTON BOOKS

Published in the United States of America
by Lexington Books
An imprint of The Rowman & Littlefield Publishing Group, Inc.
4501 Forbes Boulevard, Suite 200, Lanham, Maryland 20706

PO Box 317
Oxford
OX2 9RU, UK

British Library Cataloguing in Publication Information Available

Library of Congress Cataloging-in-Publication Data

New directions for international relations : confronting the method-of-analysis problem /
edited by Alex Mintz and Bruce Russett.
    p. cm. — (Innovations in the study of world politics)
  Chiefly papers presented at a Feb. 2003 conference held at the Yale University Center
for the Study of Globalization.
  Includes bibliographical references.
  ISBN 0-7391-0848-4 (cloth : alk. paper) — ISBN 0-7391-0849-2 (pbk. : alk. paper)
  1. International relations—Methodology—Congresses. I. Mintz, Alex, 1953- II.
Russett, Bruce M. III. Series.
JZ43.Y3N49 2004
327.1'01—dc22

                                                                              2004018395

Printed in the United States of America

⊗™ The paper used in this publication meets the minimum requirements of American
National Standard for Information Sciences—Permanence of Paper for Printed Library
Materials, ANSI/NISO Z39.48-1992.

Contents

Acknowledgments

This volume grew out of a February 2003 conference at the Yale University Center for the Study of Globalization. The conference was funded by the Gilman Foundation and organized by the Curiel Center for International Studies, Tel Aviv University in cooperation with United Nations Studies at Yale University and the Program in Foreign Policy Decision Making at Texas A&M University. We thank these organizations for their support of this project and Susan Hennigan for an excellent job preparing the volume for publication.

Authors of quantitative empirical chapters have made their material available on a website provided by Lexington books for this purpose: www.yale.edu/usny/newdirections/data

It provided all data, specialized computer programs, program recodes, and an explanatory file describing what is included and how to reproduce the published results.

1

INTRODUCTION

1

The Method-of-Analysis Problem in International Relations

Alex Mintz

I introduce the method-of-analysis problem in international relations: inconsistent, even contradictory, results are often obtained depending on the method of analysis used. In turn this leads to a credibility problem: policy makers, the business community, and other "outsiders" seldom utilize our results, as they often are inconclusive, even conflicting. Consequently, IR research has limited impact on policy makers. The method-of-analysis problem also hinders the accumulation of knowledge and scientific advancement. The lack of scholarly consensus on findings and their implications is one reason for the limited effect of IR research on the policy community. When a consensus emerges (e.g., as on the democratic peace result), policy makers often adopt IR results. I document contradictory results in IR, and offer two potential solutions: (1) greater use of robustness tests, and (2) multiple tests of the same research question using multiple methods of inquiry. Just as we strive to obtain results that are robust across levels of analysis, so should we seek to report results that are robust across methods of analysis and various specifications.

PUZZLES IN INTERNATIONAL RELATIONS

The field of international relations addresses an impressive array of important questions and intriguing puzzles. Fundamental questions include:

1. Why don't democracies fight each other but fight other regimes?
2. What causes an arms race? Is there an action-reaction process in armament?
3. Do arms races lead to war? Under what conditions?

3

4. What factors influence the calculus of deterrence of potential attackers and defenders? How? What makes deterrence work (or fail)?
5. Under what conditions do rebels initiate, escalate, and/or terminate civil war?
6. Do presidents and other chief executives use force to divert attention from difficult domestic and economic conditions?
7. Do leaders follow the bureaucratic politics model of governance or poliheuristic decision rules when making peace and war decisions? Do they maximize or satisfice utility in making foreign policy and national security decisions?
8. Are state leaders risk-acceptant in the domain of loss and risk-averse in the domain of gain? Does the framing of policy options influence choice?
9. How do alliances influence war initiation, escalation and termination?
10. What is the nature of the interrelation between trade and conflict? Does interstate trade promote peace? Does conflict limit trade?
11. Do "guns" come at the expense of "butter"? What are the effects of increases or decreases in defense expenditures on economic growth and welfare spending?
12. What is the impact of policy advisors on foreign policy decision making? How do leaders aggregate individual advice into choice?
13. Where do policy preferences, choice sets, and dimension sets come from?
14. How do international networks affect interstate conflict and cooperation?
15. Under what conditions do enduring rivalries terminate? Continue? Under what conditions does cooperation occur in the international system?
16. Is it the balance of power or power transition that causes wars in the international system?
17. Are there long cycles of war in the international system?

These and other puzzles have been analyzed using the case study approach (e.g., Astorino-Courtois and Trusty 2000, Larson 2003), statistical analysis (e.g., Huth and Russett 1984; Mintz 1989; Mintz and Ward 1989), formal models (e.g., Brams 1985, Bueno de Mesquita and Lalman 1992), and experimentation/simulation/computational modeling (e.g., Taber 2004, Schrodt 2004, Mintz et al. 1997).

Although great progress has been made in the international relations (IR) field over the past two decades (Elman and Elman 2003), and puzzles and questions tackled by scholars of international relations are important and interesting, there is a basic problem in international relations: results are often dependent on the method employed. Furthermore, numerous results are inconsistent and sometimes contradictory (see Table 1.1). Often, even replications with the same designs do not generate identical results. This reduces the confidence policy makers, the policy and business communities, and even our students have in our findings, and creates a credibility problem for IR. It makes findings not too useful for the policy community. It also impedes scientific progress in our field.

The method-of-analysis (MoA) problem is not unique to international relations or political science. It is very common in the social sciences to obtain divergent results based on the use of different methods and/or designs. Social science is probabilistic. The data are often poor. Methods are evolving rapidly, and often last year's model produces results that are subsequently superceded and corrected. It also takes a long time to sort out consensus. For example, macroeconomic models are inaccurate in many of their forecasts and economists have difficulty reaching a consensus (e.g., on the economic

Table 1.1. Conflicting Findings in IR: Examples

Arms races lead to war (Wallace 1979, 1982; Morrow 1989).
Arms races do not lead to war (Diehl 1983; Weede 1980; Altfeld 1983).
Guns come at the expense of butter (Hartman 1973; Wilensky 1975; Mintz and Huang 1990).
Guns do not come at the expense of butter (Domke, Eichenberg and Kelleher 1983).
Alliances lead to war (Levy 1981; Singer and Small 1966; Wayman 1984).
Alliances do not lead to war (Bueno de Mesquita and Lalman 1988; Weede 1989).
Nuclear deterrence works (Schelling 1960; Waltz 1981; Mearsheimer 1990).
Nuclear deterrence does not work (Achen and Snidal 1989; Powell 1987; Huth and Russett 1984).
Leaders maximize utility when making decisions (Bueno de Mesquita 1981; Bueno de Mesquita and Lalman 1992; Zagare 1990).
Leaders do not maximize utility when making decisions (Mintz 1993; Nincic 1997; Ostrom and Job 1986).
Leaders use force to divert attention from domestic problems (Ostrom and Job 1986; James and Oneal 1991; DeRouen 2000; Fordham 1998a).
Leaders do not use force to divert attention from domestic problems (Meernik 1994, 2000; Gowa 1998).
A balance of power in the international system prevents wars (Waltz 1979; Deutsch and Singer 1964; Mansfield 1988).
A balance of power in the international system encourages wars (Gilpin 1981; Thompson 1986; Spiezio 1990).
Long cycles of war occur (Modelski 1981; Thompson 1988; Goldstein 1985; Sayrs 1993)
Long cycles of war do not occur (Beck 1991; Singer and Cusack 1981)
Trade promotes peace (Russett and Oneal 2001; Polachek 1997; Oneal and Ray 1997).
Trade does not promote peace (Barbieri 1996; Barbieri and Levy 1999).

effects of tax cuts). Similarly, sociologists have difficulty agreeing on the effectiveness of various educational reforms. There are ways, however, to minimize the method-of analysis problem in IR as will be explained below.

As J. David Singer pointed out decades ago (1969): "we have as great a right and responsibility to take public stands in our area of special competence as the engineer, medical researcher, lobbyist, sales manager, planner, or land speculator have in theirs." However, four decades later, international relations is still a field with too little consensus and too much inconsistency in results. This resembles where cosmology (the study of the universe as a whole) was in the 1970s.

Cosmology, however, has experienced an explosive progress over the past two decades and has become "a rigorous, quantitative branch of astrophysics with a strong theoretical foundation backed by abundant data" (Strauss 2004). A major reason for this progress has been the *multiple* observations verifying and confirming the *same findings*, such as the exciting finding about cosmic acceleration. According to a recent report in *Scientific American* (Strauss 2004), cosmologists can now go to "the next level and claim an understanding of the formation of structures in the universe." To move to the next level in international relations, IR scholars should recognize and address the method-of-analysis problem. Specifically, just as we strive to obtain results that are robust across levels of analysis, so we should also aim at reporting results that are robust across methods of analysis and various specifications.

THE METHOD-OF-ANALYSIS PROBLEM
IN INTERNATIONAL RELATIONS

The method-of-analysis problem in international relations can be stated as follows: the use of different methods, designs, datasets, and techniques produces inconsistent, often conflicting results. The MoA problem consists of (*a*) *the inconsistency of findings problem*, (*b*) *the lack of consensus on results and their implications*, and (*c*) *the resultant credibility problem in IR*. The *inconsistency problem* can be stated as: depending on the method selected for analysis, the dataset used, the time frame studied, etc., one often gets conflicting results. The *lack of consensus on results and their implications* leads to a *credibility problem* in international relations: policy makers, the business community, and other "outsiders" do not seem to utilize many of our results. The choice of the research method often determines the results of the study, as different methods lead us down different paths and produce different results.

In the natural sciences, getting the same result through the use of multiple methods is generally considered the norm and a prerequisite for the verification of any really novel result. Similarly, one would not imagine accepting findings that aspirin reduces fever and another study that claims that aspirin raises fever (although it is a fact that it took the medical community decades to establish—against huge vested interests—that smoking causes cancer). But this is what we currently have in the field of international relations. If the medical/pharmaceutical expert would only report some results (e.g., only the significant ones) without conducting any sensitivity tests for the indirect effects and the side effects and/or tests for sensitivity for the inclusion/exclusion of additional variables on the impacts of the medicine under question—people could die (and unfortunately, they often do due to such mistakes)! Yet, in international relations, where there are typically no such directly verifiable consequences and implications for our findings (although it can be claimed that politics kills people all the time, for example, in the allocation of health benefits), we scholars allow ourselves to report findings that might at best be viewed as unstable, tentative, and shaky. If the IR community wants to produce *robust* findings and *credible* policy guidelines and recommendations, it needs to address this problem.

It is as legitimate to ask whether our theories and findings are useful and policy relevant as it is to ask whether they are innovative. Hiding behind the argument that our theories are still much too "underdeveloped" does not help policy makers gain confidence in our results. No wonder policy makers, civil servants, and strategists typically do not take IR findings too seriously. Many of our prominent theorists are still using seventeenth-century theory (e.g., Hobbes, which is like using Newton without Einstein for nuclear physics), and political leaders often defend entrenched political interests that are resistant to change.

Some would contend that theories do not have to be useful or policy relevant. My point is that generating conflicting results without understanding the conditions under which such results are obtained hinders theory development and the accumulation of knowledge in our field.

THE LACK OF CONSENSUS ON FINDINGS AND ITS IMPLICATIONS

As table 1.1 above shows, scholars of international relations have claimed that arms races lead to war, that arms races do not lead to war, that "guns" come at the expense of "butter," that "guns" do not come at the expense of "butter," that leaders use force to divert attention from domestic problems, that leaders do not use force to divert attention from domestic problems, that alliances lead to war and that they do not lead to war, that

Alex Mintz

power transition leads to war and that it prevents war, that nuclear deterrence works (deters) and does not work (fails to deter), that long cycles of war occur and do not occur, that interstate trade promotes peace and does not promote peace, and so on. If we cannot agree on whether arms races lead to war, whether the balance of power in the international system increases or decreases the likelihood of war, whether leaders maximize or satisfice utility, whether alliances contribute to war initiation, escalation, and termination, or whether "guns" come at the expense of "butter," then why would others take us seriously?

When there is a greater consensus on findings, such as on the democratic peace result, the results have often been noticed, recognized, and even utilized by policy makers. For example, a recent report published by the Rand Corporation states that "one of the major tenets of U.S. foreign policy is the encouragement and support of democratization in the world. At the core of this argument is a national security objective of a less war-prone world. The linkage between a more peaceful world and more states with democratic political systems is the belief that democratic states are unlikely to fight wars against each other"—the democratic peace result (Szayna et al. 2001, 147). The research program on democratic peace has been subjected to numerous tests using multiple methods (formal, statistical, experimental, case study), and the key to its "acceptance" by the policy community has been the consistent and relevant empirical finding that democracies rarely fight other democracies while they fight other regimes. Another reason for its success has been the numerous robustness tests of the theory (see e.g., Maoz and Abdolali 1989; Maoz and Russett 1992) and the fact that, while there is a dissenting minority that does not accept this finding, there is a wide consensus in the IR literature that democracies rarely (if at all) fight each other. As studies in political marketing have shown (Wolfsfeld 1997), elite consensus is often a prerequisite for support of a policy by the media in the United States and many other countries. Similarly, scholarly consensus over results is more likely to lead policy makers and the business community to adopt such results, as experience with the democratic peace result has shown.

Conversely, a lack of robust, consistent findings leads to low-level and often shaky generalizations which make the whole scientific enterprise in international relations less useful and not too credible. It leads policy makers and academicians from other disciplines often to doubt and ignore findings of scholars of international relations. Some of the causes of this problem are the divisions across methodological approaches and techniques in international relations and the overspecialization of many scholars in a particular method.

Conflicting results are often obtained not only by using different methodologies but also *within* the same methodological orientation (i.e., across different statistical methods, various experimental analyses, case studies, etc.) and even in attempting to replicate the same results with the same design. Statistical studies utilizing multiple regression often produce results that are different from those generated while employing Logit or Probit. Similarly, computerized process-tracing experiments often produce results different from "pencil and paper" experiments. Comparative case studies may yield different results, of course, than analysis based on an individual case. While the rationale for utilizing each of the four methods of analysis naturally varies and depends, of course, on our theories, the policy maker who does not care much about the research method utilized is confused by conflicting findings. Again, this problem is not unique to international relations. However, the lack, in many instances, of stable, robust, and valid results limits the usefulness of our findings for the policy community.

The method-of-analysis phenomenon is not only problematic because IR research often produces inconsistent results that typically have minimal use for policy makers, but also because it hinders the accumulation of knowledge and scientific advancement in international relations. International relations is on the verge of "making it." It addresses important questions; it uses sophisticated methodologies and techniques; it has advanced greatly since the early days of "the scientific revolution." However, in order to "cross the chasm," so to speak, in terms of the applicability of our work to the policy community, decision makers, the business community, other segments of the academic community, and the public at large, we need a critical mass of stable, robust, verifiable empirical findings. We cannot ignore conflicting results in the study of the same phenomenon or the same research question. It is mainly a research design issue, although it is partly an empirical question and partly an epistemological issue.

Disappointment with what IR offers, and criticism of political science research in general and of IR in particular as being less than useful and even confusing, abound. Consequently, IR does not seem to have the same impact on the policy community as demography, statistics, marketing, finance, criminology, or public health. Rosenfeld (2004), for example, pointed out that the criminology research community "has reached a consensus on the basic contours of the 1990s crime decline—the who, what, when, and where" of the drop in U.S. crime rates. Consequently, the findings have received a lot of attention in the policy community.

The following section introduces several *potential solutions* for the method-of-analysis problem in international relations.

POTENTIAL SOLUTIONS FOR THE
METHOD-OF-ANALYSIS PROBLEM

In this section, I offer several solutions to the method-of-analysis problem in international relations. These solutions call for a greater use of sensitivity analysis (SA) through: (*a*) a greater use of robustness tests, and (*b*) combining multiple methods of inquiry to test IR theories. Sensitivity analysis is typically used to increase the confidence in the model and its results and predictions, by providing an understanding of how the model's dependent variables "respond to changes in the inputs (model structure, data, or the model's independent variables," European Commission, N.D). Sensitivity analysis is the study of "how the variation in the output of a model (numerical or otherwise) can be apportioned, qualitatively or quantitatively to different sources of variation" (ibid). Sensitivity analysis aims to ascertain "how the model depends upon the information fed into it, upon its structure" and upon its assumptions (ibid). Originally, sensitivity analysis was created to deal simply with uncertainties in the input variables and model parameters. Over the course of time, "the ideas have been extended to incorporate model conceptual uncertainty, i.e., uncertainty in model structures, assumptions and specifications" (ibid).

Sensitivity analysis can help produce more credible results and recommendations (both theoretically relevant and policy relevant). Such an analysis can be conducted in several ways:

1. by varying elements of the research design (model specification, data sources, time frames, samples, etc)—i.e., by greater use of robustness tests to determine how changing a variable, data source, or time frame affects results;
2. by combining methods of inquiry (case study, formal, statistical, and experimental); and
3. by devoting time, effort, journal space, and conference time to replicating research and reporting why divergent results emerge in the first place.

The goal is to produce less "unstable" and more robust and consistent findings that will be less vulnerable to challenges based on the use of different methodologies, different data sources, different samples, or different time frames in the study of the same phenomenon. This should be a standard in our field. We should educate our students to aspire to meet this standard.

We should also devote considerably more journal space to identifying and understanding *why* differences across studies of the same research problem produce different results. This is essential for the growth of scientific knowledge. For example, it will be useful to identify (based on multiple studies using different designs and different methodologies, quantitative and qualitative), the conditions under which armament leads to war, the conditions under which armament leads to peace, and those that are insignificant. Whereas sensitivity analysis will not resolve the method-of-analysis problem completely, it can greatly reduce and minimize it to the point where our findings are more stable and credible.

Greater Use of Robustness Tests

Results are naturally sensitive to the use of different designs. A familiar situation is when an IR scholar (or for that matter any social scientist) removes or adds a variable or a set of variables to a model or relaxes an assumption and gets different (sometimes even contradictory) results. Also common is the situation in which we extend the temporal domain and number of observations we study (or change the unit of analysis from annual observations to quarterly observations) and get different results than originally reported.

We typically defend differences in results by claiming that they represent different theories (and this is in most cases true). We often note that the use of different variables or measures and/or different data sources, and/or methods, comes down to differences of (implicit or explicit) theory. While it is indeed the case that different designs often reflect variations in theory, this rationalization is of no value to the policy analyst, the business executive, or the policy maker who wants to know whether or not A leads to B and the conditions under which it does or does not, and who is less interested in how we arrived at our findings. Policy makers do need to know the limits (boundaries) of our explanations. More replications using the same research designs, and robustness tests using different specifications, different indicators, various data sources, different samples, and methods of inquiry can help minimize the method-of-analysis problem. None of this will help, of course, if the models are poorly specified—which is a matter not only of method, but also of theory.

Sensitivity Analysis Through the Use of Multiple Methods of Inquiry

The use of a multimethod approach (MMA) in the study of puzzles in international relations is rare—but see Maoz et al. (2004) in the context of conflict management and conflict resolution, and Bueno de Mesquita et al.'s (2003) use of formal, statistical, and historical case studies in the analysis of the causes and consequences of political survival.

Table 1.2.   Some Sources of Variations in Results Across Studies of the Same Research Question

Use of different variables and/or measures across studies
Use of different data sources
Use of different temporal domains
Use of different geographical domains
Use of different methods of inquiry
Poor execution

Stoll (2004) argued that research that relies on any one approach is usually inferior to research that makes use of several methods. Scholars should use a box of tools (methods), rather than employ a single tool. It is rare when "one method is so superior that the others can safely be ignored" (Stoll, ibid). In research on democratic peace, for example, scholars have used formal, statistical, and experimental analyses and case studies of this popular subject. However, there is not enough comparative assessment of results obtained from different studies across different methodologies even on this popular topic. This is different from a standard literature review that surveys relevant literature.

As pointed out above, it is as legitimate to ask whether our findings are functional as it is to ask whether the method we use is novel. Referring to forecasting accuracy, for example, Armstrong (1989) recommended that to improve accuracy, one should "combine forecasts derived from methods that differ substantially and draw from different sources of information." According to Armstrong, combining forecasts is especially useful when one "is uncertain about the situation, uncertain about which method is most accurate, and when you want to avoid large errors." Armstrong calculated that compared with errors of an individual forecast, *combining methods reduces errors* (the emphasis is mine). According to Armstrong (ibid.), "in 30 empirical comparisons, the reduction in ex ante errors for equally weighted combined forecasts averaged about 12.5% and ranged from 3 to 24 percent." Combining methods in IR research by using a multimethod perspective may likewise reduce errors in explaining and forecasting international politics.

All four methods of analyses typically used in IR (case studies, formal models, statistical analyses, and experiments) have strengths and weaknesses. These have been summarized and discussed elsewhere (see King, Keohane, and Verba 1994; Morton 1999; and Stoll 2004). The method-of-analysis problem is not a by-product of the use of different research methods and methodologies in studying international relations (this should actually be encouraged). It results from obtaining unstable, divergent (often contradictory) results based on the method we choose to employ. Multiple methods of inquiry supplement each other: for example, deductive propositions derived from formal models can be tested statistically, experimentally, and/or illustrated using case studies. Case studies can lead to explanations that could be easily missed by quantitative measures. Statistical analysis can generate findings that add to insights brought to light by case studies (King et al. 1994, 43–46).

Combining two or three methods of inquiry to tackle IR questions as one form of sensitivity analysis will enable the researcher to:

1. cross validate results based on different methodologies. This is essential in order to isolate the method effect and instrument effects on the results. This should result in greater confidence in our results and help generalize results independent of the method used. The goal is to generate more consistent and conclusive findings and to understand the reasons for divergent findings for the same research question.
2. contribute to theory development, as different methods (e.g., case studies, formal models, experiments, statistical tests) may uncover unexpected findings that may be reincorporated into the theory and reanalyzed. The theory can then be refined, enriched, and re-tested. The multimethod approach can lead to standardized results that are consistent and conclusive. This would hopefully lead to the scientific advancement of international relations.

Comparative Assessment of Findings

We excel in testing hypotheses and theories, some new, some old. It is important that scholars add to the results section of their paper a paragraph or two discussing results generated by other scholars using other methods and/or specifications. In most cases, this is not difficult to do, and can add to the robustness of findings.

Until the 1960s there was very little quantitative research published on international relations. Hundreds of IR books and articles were published in the 1960s using scientific methods. Since then, tens of thousands of articles and books have been written in the area of foreign policy analysis, international security, international political economy, conflict studies, and other areas of international relations. Different methods typically lead us down different paths and produce different results. It is important to identify similarities and explain differences in findings of the same research question across studies that have utilized different designs and/or different methods of inquiry. Even if our findings are only applicable to a highly selective sample of cases and in an extremely limited context, we should state this and identify such contexts (Singer 1969).

The search for commonalities and differences in results across different methods of inquiry will greatly enrich our understanding of international politics. Comparing findings across methodologies, research designs, samples, datasets, geographical regions, and time periods is essential. It will contribute to our understanding of *why* we get divergent rather than convergent results using different methodologies and help generate probabalistic *if . . . then* predictions based on such findings and conditions. Visualization of results from statistical or experimental analysis may also "help improve the interplay between theory and empirical research" (Gleditsch and Ward 2004, this volume).

HOW DOES A MULTIPLE METHOD APPROACH ENHANCE SCIENTIFIC PROGRESS?: AN EXAMPLE

One area of research in international relations that has utilized a considerable amount of multimethod analysis is decision making. The central questions raised by scholars working in this area are: how do leaders make decisions? Do they "maximize" or "satisfice" utility? Do they take cognitive shortcuts *en route* to a decision? Are domestic or international factors more important in explaining foreign policy? These questions can shed light on the understanding of how foreign and domestic elites make decisions, a topic of great interest to the policy and academic communities.

The intellectual roots of the research programs and debates on foreign policy decision making can be traced back to two very different intellectual disciplines: the rational choice (economic) approach to decision making and the cognitive psychology school of thought.

Scholars such as Bueno de Mesquita (1981) have argued that nations are led by leaders who maximize utility. This research program has utilized multiple methods of inquiry, including formal and statistical analysis and case studies (Bueno de Mesquita and Lalman 1992). In contrast, advocates of the cognitive psychology school of decision making (e.g., Stein and Welch 1997; Larson 2003) highlight the importance of schemata, biases, and heuristics (cognitive shortcuts) in decision making. The "cognitive" research program in IR has largely used comparative contemporary and historical case studies to illustrate theory.

Michael Brecher (1997) claimed that no school of decision making should have a monopoly over results as elements of both schools and approaches are valid and relevant (for a critique of rational choice theory in political science, see Green and Shapiro 1994). Brecher did not go on to detail, however, *how* the rational choice and cognitive psychology schools can supplement each other. Important research in economics (e.g., Thaler 1991) does focus on quasi-rational behavior, and the subfields of behavioral finance and behavioral marketing are flourishing.

Recently, experiments with actual decision makers (mainly high ranking military officers) using a computerized decision process tracing techniques revealed that both the rational choice *and* the cognitive psychology schools have a lot to offer: Rational choice focuses on outcome validity (predictions) while cognitive psychology focuses on process validity (the description of the process). Experimental studies showed that elements of both schools can be combined and integrated in a two-stage decision process consisting of the use of heuristics in the first stage of the decision process based on the logic of the cognitive psychology school, followed by an analysis of remaining, acceptable alternatives in the second stage of the decision process, using rational, analytic methods, such as expected utility or lexicographic decision rules (Mintz et al. 1997; Mintz 2004b). Without the use of a multimethod approach to this research question, consisting of formal models, statistical analysis, case studies, and experimental research, it is doubtful that we would have been able to identify the decision rules that leaders use in making foreign policy and national security decisions.

The use of MMA has clearly enriched our understanding of how foreign and U.S. leaders make decisions. IR scholars should be encouraged to test their theories with more than one method of inquiry (formal models and experiments, statistical tests and case studies or any combination thereof). Although scholars have utilized formal models, statistical analysis, and case studies on the diversionary theory of the use of force (see table 1.3), and formal, statistical and case studies of deterrence, most studies have not tackled yet *the same research question* from a multimethod perspective.

WEAKNESSES OF THE MULTIMETHOD APPROACH (MMA)

The use of a multimethod approach is naturally time consuming and labor intensive. It can also be perceived as too focused compared to the study of multiple phenomena using one method.

At times, it is impossible to use a multimethod approach to study a particular phenomenon because certain topics are just not applicable to the use of a multimethod approach. Some methods of inquiry are also superior for constructing theory, while others are more useful for testing theory (see Stoll 2004). This is not the issue, however. The issue is that with greater use of robustness tests and multiple tests using multiple methods of inquiry, we could minimize, although not eliminate, the method-of-analysis problem.

Table 1.3.   The Use of Multiple Methods of Inquiry in International Relations

	Method			
Topic	*Statistical*	*Formal*	*Experimental*	*Case Study*
Alliances	X	X		X
Arms Races	X	X	X	X
Arms Races & Escalation	X	X		X
Balance of Power	X	X		X
Civil War	X	X		X
Decision Making	X	X	X	X
Defense-Growth/Guns-Butter Tradeoffs	X	X	X	X
Democratic Peace	X	X	X	X
Diversionary Theory	X	X		X
Deterrence	X	X	X	X
Enduring Rivalries	X	X		X
Long Cycles	X	X		X
Power Transition	X	X		X
Trading Relations	X	X		X

However, in cases in which a multimethod approach is not applicable, the researcher should not "force" it by using multiple methodologies, just for the sake of demonstrating methodological competence or diversity. There are strains of theories and hypotheses that are difficult, if not impossible, to test using multiple methods. For example, it is often possible to research, using the case study method, a single historical case, but because of lack of data, there is no way of doing a cross-national analysis of the same research question. Similarly, it is possible to run an experiment on a hypothetical case, such as under what conditions will democracies fight each other, but it is virtually impossible to run a large-N empirical test to answer this particular question, in the absence of (futuristic) cases involving democracies fighting each other. Furthermore, different people are experts in different methodologies.

A multimethod approach may at times also compound and multiply problems with research designs and datasets, and may confuse more than enrich research if it produces a wealth of information that is not analyzed and summarized. More importantly, studies that utilize a multimethod approach to international relations may be so focused and specific that, if not done properly, we may not see the forest (big picture) for the trees (individual findings) and may not lead to meta (or broad) theories. So we need a balance of "just right" combinations of multimethods, "not too hot, not too cold."

With regard to robustness tests that use different model specifications and designs, there are typically significant limitations on the number of variables that can be fully explored in a rational choice or game theoretic model or, because of the degrees of freedom problem, in statistical analyses. There are also practical limitations on the number of actors that can be incorporated into a formal model and on the number of manipulations that can be tested in an experiment.

Practitioners in the IR field should pay more attention (beyond the actual production of findings), to setting, as a standard, the reporting of robust, solid research findings. If such results cannot be obtained, it is the researcher's duty to explain the reasons for divergent findings and to point to the conditions (e.g., sample size, time frame, data source) under which the theory holds and the conditions under which it does not hold.

PRACTICAL RECOMMENDATIONS

To move the scientific enterprise in IR forward and produce a more credible knowledge base for our students, the academic community, and the policy community, it is necessary for researchers, graduate students, conference organizers, editors of journals, and reviewers to address the method-of-analysis problem in international relations. Below are a few practical recommendations.

Education

Most Ph.D. dissertations in IR address multiple research questions. This should be commended. However, dissertations should also tackle the same research question from different methodological perspectives. The fact that most dissertations do not offer a multiple-method treatment of the topic or do not test for robust findings using some form of sensitivity analysis, might be attributed to the methodological and conceptual inadequacies of the graduate training which IR specialists traditionally receive. More courses that tackle the same topic (e.g., deterrence, decision making, arms races, enduring rivalry, conflict initiation, escalation and termination, balance of power, long cycles) from different methodological perspectives (formal, statistical, experimental, case study) should be offered.

In many areas of research in IR it is possible to combine the formal deductive process with experiments, an inductive statistical analysis with a case study, i.e., in a greater use of robustness tests of theory. Yet, this requires considerable more work than is typically required from our graduate students. It could be a rewarding experience, however, that may uncover robust findings across methods of inquiry. Research on deterrence, for example, can benefit from greater use of multiple methods of inquiry (e.g., by adding an experimental component) to the analysis of deterrence decisions. Some work on war termination has already benefited from greater use of a combination of such methods.

While some would argue that a multiple-method analysis is too "narrow," as it applies different methodological perspectives to fewer research questions we should be as careful about the robustness and validity of our findings as about the breadth of our study. Students and scholars in IR could benefit from conducting more comprehensive tests prior to reporting results.

Journals

Editors and reviewers should demand greater use of robustness checks and a discussion of results generated (by the author or others) using multiple methods. Currently, our emphasis is on producing significant results, while paying little attention to the robustness of these findings across specifications and methods. However, if editors and reviewers will place premium on the reporting of results based on robustness tests and will devote more journal space to replications, and to multiple tests of the same research question with multiple methods, it may reduce the method-of-analysis problem in international relations. The *Journal of Conflict Resolution* published (in February 2004) a special issue featuring multiple tests using multiple methods of a theory of foreign policy decision making. But this is rare.

Results need to hold up across different research designs. When they do not, editors need to devote more journal space to explanations of *why* results differ across methods and research designs. Greater use of review articles that report and analyze such results can contribute to scientific progress.

Workshop and Conferences

Most panels in scientific conferences in international relations (e.g., the annual meeting of the International Studies Association (ISA), regional conferences at ISA, and the annual meeting of the Peace Science Society International) are organized around specific topics and themes. This is very good. However, considerably less attention is given to the search for commonalities and differences across designs and methodologies that address the same research question. We need more workshops and panels that uncover such commonalities and differences. Such panels can be devoted to the discovery of commonalities and discussion of differences in results stemming from the use of different methodologies, different designs of the same phenomenon, or based on different geographical areas in order to try to reach some consensus. This issue is applicable also to differences in results obtained within methodologies (based on different specifications of statistical models, the use of different groups of subjects in an experimental analysis, and so on). The evidence that IR scholars produce is often less than convincing. Political science and international relations are not "exact" sciences. We therefore need to devote time and effort to the reporting of divergent results and to the understanding of why results addressing the same research question differ across studies. Rigorous scientific analysis is difficult in IR but not impossible. Many high-quality studies do include checks for the robustness of findings.

CONCLUSION

The method-of-analysis problem in international relations is: inconsistent, even conflicting, results of the same research question are often obtained as a function of the method that the researcher uses. This makes method selection critical. When a broader consensus has emerged in IR research (as on the democratic peace result), the policy community has often adopted the finding. However, conflicting results across studies of the same research question make our findings less credible in the eyes of policy makers, business executives, analysts, and academicians from other fields. Moreover, they hinder progress in IR. They lead policy makers and others to refer to our field and our findings as "not serious." Put simply: policy makers and other "outsiders" cannot count on results of IR scholars or use them in strategic planning, decision making, and policy evaluation because they are too often unstable and often not competently done. Students are often also skeptical about our research products when they see that a change in one measure leads to completely different findings. This should not surprise us when IR research produces divergent, even contradictory, results depending on the method we select and the design we use. This keeps international relations from developing into a serious cumulative discipline. Too often we do not make conclusive empirical generalizations and in the absence of such generalizations, we generate a great deal of speculation and confusion.

This chapter has documented contradictory results in IR. Unfortunately, quantitative IR has an extended track record of inconsistent results on some issues (arms races, armament and growth, risk aversion, etc.). The chapter has also offered two potential solutions to the MoA problem and presented an example of how one area of research in IR (decision making) has benefited from the use of multiple methods of inquiry. The solutions offered in this chapter are (1) greater use of sensitivity analysis through the use of multiple methods of inquiry to tackle the same research question, and (2) sensitivity analysis through the increased use of robustness tests using, e.g., different data sources, different time frames, and different samples. More journal space and conference time should be devoted to understanding the reasons for divergent findings of the same research question, for replications of research, and for identifying commonalities in findings.

To move the scientific enterprise in IR forward and to make results in IR useful for policy makers, we need greater convergence of some of our primary findings. When convergence is not achieved we need to understand why differences in results are obtained across studies and report them. We cannot ignore the method-of-analysis problem in our field.

NOTE

This chapter is part of the War Mapping Database Project directed by the author. I thank Bruce Russett and Philip Schrodt for helpful comments and David Brule for research assistance.

2

Four Methods and Five Revolutions

Bruce Russett

Much of the preceding commentary concerning the use of inappropriate theoretical models and methods is on target, and requires changes in our research programs. Nonetheless, some recent developments have allowed the scientific understanding of international relations to progress immensely in recent years. I identify five interacting "revolutions": 1) in the structural conditions of international relations itself, 2) the advance of formal theory, 3) the massive availability of data, 4) the pressure for replicability, and 5) the rapid sophistication of statistical methods. Together with a more active dialogue between methods, they offer the opportunity for more convergence and reliability in producing accepted generalizations. I then introduce the chapters of this book with some reference to methods and the revolutions in research.

Driven by his belief in the potential applicability of our social science to real-world international relations problems, Alex Mintz's opening commentary traces many of the difficulties of translating our findings into effective policy to the way in which our own field carries on social science. The common element of his remarks concerns the failure of international relations scholars to produce sufficient consensus in their research, with robust and replicable findings, to persuade policy makers to take the work seriously and to move our scientific enterprise forward. That failure is rooted more deeply in the use of inappropriate theoretical models and methods. He is correct—we should be very distressed about this. His other principal line of argument attributes this failure largely to the excessive reliance of different segments of the research community on one or two methods of analysis, to the exclusion of others. He thus makes an impassioned plea for major questions to be addressed using a wide range of potentially applicable methods;

namely, formal, statistical, experimental, and case study work in an attempt to identify robust findings. His prescription, however, is not limited to failures to replicate results across methods, but also applies to robustness and replication failures (or even the failure to attempt replication) within methodological approaches. Readers should take his discussion and proposed remedies seriously.

Nevertheless, some major developments and mitigating circumstances should be mentioned. In my view the scientific understanding of international relations, with all its continuing limitations, has progressed immensely in recent years (see Chernoff 2005). It is becoming a proper science (with all the obscurities that technical terms and complex analyses may bring to the outsider trying to make sense of it) because of several related and complementary "revolutions." I list these developments not in order of importance, because all were necessary conditions for the degree of advance that has been achieved. And they should not be considered only in isolation. The five revolutions interact, greatly complementing and strengthening each other.

1. *Revolutions in international relations in the real world*, requiring us— in a field that demands policy advice even before we may be ready to give it competently—to revise our theories drastically. Examples certainly include the end of the cold war (one of the driving forces in our field's new attention to domestic politics), the rise of international terrorism and other aspects of globalization (compelling conflict analysts to take nonstate actors more seriously), and the rise of United States hegemony in the world (demanding change in many realist arguments about various kinds of polarity in the international system, and greater attention to rational choice arguments about the limits of collective action against such hegemony). Being forced to reexamine the assumptions and deductions of our theories is a constructive development.

2. *The formal theory revolution.* Formal theory by definition requires a clear deductive argument expressed in mathematical notation. Intuition provides the inspiration for such theory, but then the logic takes over. Unclear or inappropriate premises and sloppy deduction are immediately exposed to the competent reader. Formal methods are not used just for producing clear theory. Whenever possible, the predictions of theory should be put to the test of sophisticated empirical analysis. Formal methods help insure that a carefully articulated theory will make evident whether the data and testing methods are actually matched to it. Furthermore, the formal methods of greatest interest to scholars of international relations—strategic analysis; namely, game theory—are especially appropriate to our substantive concerns for an anarchic world

of incomplete information and great difficulty in making credible commitments. Additionally, they have sensitized us to inferential problems in sequential games, and the dangers of selection bias that previously led to errors in, for one very consequential example, interpreting the reasons for success and failure in deterrence.

3. *The revolution of massively available data*, in many though hardly all of our research programs. This has been made possible by the effort of thousands of scholars to produce coded information and make it available to the community. Some of this happened spontaneously, led by the commitment of scholars like Karl Deutsch and David Singer more than forty years ago to widen and therefore democratize and internationalize the scientific study of international relations (and some similar efforts in comparative politics which have supplied reliable data on characteristics of national political regimes that IR scholars too long neglected). We are also indebted to scholars in many other disciplines: data provided by scholars (and public agencies) working in other disciplines, notably economics, anthropology (through the comparative data bases of the Human Relations Area Files), historians with their rich case study material, and even comparative public health (e.g., the WHO data which are indispensable for the analysis by Ghobarah et al. in this volume). Facilitating this data revolution are big advances in computerized processing and analysis, from automated coding of events, computerized process tracing, and Geographic Information Systems (GIS), allowing the ability to access and analyze data from anywhere in the world over the Internet.

4. *The revolution of replication,* made imaginable by the data revolution. Although the norm itself is hardly new, it has quite suddenly and overwhelmingly become powerful. To be taken seriously, published empirical analyses must be accompanied by web-posting of all relevant data and computational routines. Such provision is now required by our major journals (see the special feature in the February 2003 issue of *International Studies Perspectives*), and is repeated here for contributors to this book, as noted on the page of acknowledgments at the front. These materials then become public information, and it is no longer possible to publish material with serious errors without the corresponding serious risk of being exposed, at least within research programs that are large and vigorous. Despite the risk of personal pain, this is an altogether salutary development for a science. It plays directly to Mintz's vigorous and appropriate plea for replication and robustness checks. Later studies build on and improve other ones. And it has led to some convergence even in some of the research programs he identifies. (On trade for example, see the latest

statements by a partisan (Oneal 2003) and two neutrals (Gartzke and Li 2003.)

5. *The continuing revolution of statistical method*. Different methods may well give different answers, and within a large class of methods, such as statistical ones, different analyses may give different answers. But that is unavoidable, not necessarily a fault, since if some applications are inappropriate or incompetent they will give different results than appropriate/competent ones. That's how we eventually work toward consensus. Certainly it may not be a quick or easy process, and of course it confuses the policy community. Formal theory helps in this process, of course—statistical diagnostics will not suffice if the models are badly specified. But we must recognize that some dispute about what statistical routines are appropriate is unavoidable given the rapid evolution of statistical methods. Statistical analyses that a few years ago neglected proper controls for such problems as the dependence of conflict in a dyad on the history of conflict in that dyad, or on the presence of conflict in allied or neighboring dyads, may have been unavoidable or at least excusable at the time they were published. They no longer are, and continuing improvement of methods is to be welcomed if our policy prescriptions are to be not only comprehensible but, even more important, valid.

None of the above suggests that Mintz's arguments are mistaken or irrelevant. He identifies a real problem. There is plenty of room for improvement in our procedures within methodological traditions, and for demanding replication across methods. But perhaps it does put them in a perspective that throws less unflattering light on our efforts.

His table 3 shows that of the fourteen major research questions he identifies five of them indeed used all four major methodological approaches—though not necessarily addressing the same research problem. Indeed, the rest used all but experimental methods. Controlled experiments have some clear advantages over post-hoc statistical analysis, and have been relatively and unfortunately neglected. Nonetheless, for our field they have some inherent limitations. Experimental gaming or other experimental tests with human subjects (at the individual level of analysis) are particularly valuable for testing cognitive or other psychological theories as alternatives to rational choice models. Yet they may also pose problems of external validity (reduced by the use of high-level military officers in Mintz's chapter below). When countries are the unit of analysis, experiments in the form of computer simulations (e.g., Cederman 1997) are valuable. But it is simply impossible, for example, for the United Nations to perform a live, real-world experiment by giving a particular form of economic or political assistance to five randomly or systematically selected states while denying it to five others. Imagine the human subjects committee from which that project might seek approval! All of these major approaches suffer from inherent methodological limitations that provide upper limits to our predictive and explanatory power (Bennett and Stam 2004, chaps. 1, 7).

Mintz is also correct to point out the contribution of detailed case study analysis, particularly those using primary material from the archives, to suggest complex causal patterns that evade our other methods. Case studies are valuable for stimulating the production of hypotheses about possible regularities, testing causal inferences derived from correlational regularities, and probing the limits of generalizations to understand cases that do not fit them. An iterative process, with a dialogue back and forth between ideographic and nomothetic analyses, can be highly productive (Russett 1970). Major elements of potential rigor and productive exchange have been introduced, for example, by George's (1980) prescriptions for focused comparison and process-tracing in case studies, King, Keohane, and Verba's (1994) emphasis on the underlying scientific unity of quantity of qualitative and quantitative analyses, and Fearon's (1991) demonstration that both statistical and case study research depend on careful application of counterfactual analyses. These and similar intellectual contributions have helped, but are far from general adoption. Even the massive volume of case studies carried out, for example, in the deterrence research program has had limited utility because too often they have been done without being embedded in a wider framework that includes rigorous formal, experimental, and statistical research. It is not necessarily a result of this volume's editors' preferences that we did not find a suitable case study chapter for this book. Had this book been addressed to a major research program, applying a rigorous framework to a particular topic (as Sambanis, forthcoming on civil wars), it would have been easier to find or commission appropriate case studies.

The need for division of labor between different and complementary experts is inherent in contemporary science. Mintz does not imply that all research methods must be employed in every research program, nor that any one person should be adept at all four methods. (If he had implied that he could be forgiven, because he is one of the very few people in our field who demonstrably is so adept.)

Overall, we should not understate either the accomplishments of our field in producing accepted generalizations or the difficulties in doing so. It took decades for researchers to move from epidemiological studies to successful microlevel work at the level of human genetics to establish the causal mechanism between smoking and cancer. In addition to time to do the multimethod research properly, it takes time to make a constructive policy impact;

to get policy makers' attention requires not just a reasonable degree of consensus among our peers, but a massive effort to understand policy makers' needs and perspectives, and to persuade them in various media (in person as well as in print) to take us seriously. And though he alludes to vested interests in the example of smoking and lung cancer, the implications of having to overcome such interests need to be spelled out. They include—for international relations scholars as well as biologists—enormous economic, cultural, ideological, and political interests in our national decision-making systems, and in our own professions where scholars can be made obsolete (recall Kuhn 1962). Vested interests are about retaining power, and power is a phenomenon that political scientists above all should recognize. It is not easy to do science well; neither is it easy, even when we have done so, to persuade those who might translate it into policy.

The editors of this volume chose nine chapters to illustrate new developments in theory and methods for the analysis of international relations. Our purpose was to look at a range of questions, some already well researched by social scientists of international relations and others much less so, to identify points of achieved or likely progress. Our conference brought together some of the most original researchers in our field, and tried to represent different methods and levels of analysis. We selected some of the most interesting papers from that conference, supplementing them with other papers that were written by participants and informally discussed though not formally presented. The result, we believe, does illustrate new developments and directions.

In terms of the four methods of analysis, statistical analysis and formal modeling are represented most substantially, with one experimental study but no case study as that term is customarily used. Part of the reason for this distribution was simply the luck of the draw, in who attended, what kinds of papers they presented, and what they were prepared to contribute to the book. Case studies are most useful in the context of a multimethod scientific enterprise focused on a particular substantive or theoretical issue—and this volume intentionally lacks such a focus. Yet one or two case studies, carefully taking a key proposition or two from some major statistical or formal analysis to evaluate at the micro level of perceptions and actions by decision makers, could have been valuable. Doing so would nicely bridge both levels of analysis and methods of analysis.

VARIATION IN SPACE AND TIME

I now offer thoughts on some commonalities among the substantive chapters. Four chapters explore, in quite different ways, how spatial and temporal variation combine to affect politics. And all of them benefit enormously from three of the above-mentioned revolutions—of data, replication, and statistics. The first two chapters work on aspects of the international system, but not in the traditional sense of addressing hegemony, balance of power, or the polarity of the global system. Rather, they identify regional networks and other subsystems of interactions—a level of analysis more inclusive than the now-common dyadic (pairs of states) focus and a "new direction" for research that may have as much potential for explanation of international phenomena.

The first, by Zeev Maoz, Lesley Terris, Ranan Kuperman, and Ilan Talmud, derives in part from Maoz's (1996) work on politically relevant environments, which found that states' political stability and war proneness depended markedly on the types of political regimes predominant among contiguous and other nearby states and regional powers. Here that perspective is joined with theory and methods of network analysis, frequently used in sociology to identify networks of status, prestige, and influence (see Willer 1999). Such analysis is somewhat rare in international relations research, but Maoz and his colleagues employ it here to examine characteristics like the density and polarization of international networks of ethnic similarity, alliances, and democratic states. Though applied here in a predominantly descriptive mode, their effort is informed by several implicit theoretical perspectives and tests several hypotheses. For example, they find that alliance density in the system is associated with more militarized disputes and wars, and that democratic networks are associated with fewer disputes and wars. Further systematic hypothesis testing will require more sophisticated methods to compare networks over time with varying numbers of actors, given the increasing attention in our field to differentiating variation over time and space in a single dataset, but these authors lay much of the intellectual groundwork.

In their chapter, Kristian Gleditsch and Michael Ward extend their earlier work to illustrate various characteristics of regional systems with visual representations (maps) that reflect regional systems based on distance and neighborhood. Their interest in spatial connectivity and local clustering of peace and democracy incorporates major elements of network analysis, and explicitly extends explanatory models beyond the single state or dyadic level. Their work, too, is theoretically informed but in large part descriptive—successfully so, as their maps visualize dramatically, for example, how transitions from autocracy to democracy are far more likely in regions where democracy is common than where the predominant form of government is autocracy. Furthermore, peace is also much more common in democratic regions, not necessarily because democracies may be intrinsically peaceful (national or monadic level of analysis) or even that pairs of democracies are particularly peaceful. Rather, in regions where most states are democratic, individual democracies are more stable and security threats from all sides are reduced. Their maps show vividly how these clusters develop, and they confirm their point with a "traditional" regression analysis showing that the number of years a state is at peace depends as much or more on the average level of democracy in its region as on its own level of democracy. The behavior and regime characteristics of individual states cannot be adequately understood by treating states as independent observations, in space or time. More hypothesis testing of this sort will come with the further development of statistical methods for addressing these multiple dependencies. Meanwhile, we have some striking illustrations of how regions of peace and democracy do evolve over time.

Another analysis, by Hazem Ghobarah, Paul Huth, and Bruce Russett, addresses the neglected problem of identifying long-term and indirect casualties of civil wars. Immediate deaths in wartime are relatively easy (though certainly not unproblematic) to measure, but the deaths that may later follow from the consequences of war—e.g., malnutrition, disease, bad health care, and the dissolution of social bonds—are very hard to estimate. They in effect require a counterfactual perspective, to compare deaths from those conditions following a war to the level of death from such conditions that would be observed if there had been no war. The method they use is a standard application of multiple regression analysis. First they hypothesize a number of conditions, like level of education, health spending, urbanization, inequality, and geography, generally believed to affect health and life expectancy to provide an "as if" baseline, but also include the number of direct and immediate deaths suffered in civil war in a country or in one or more of its neighbors. They then can measure the number of "excess" deaths from such a baseline actually observed, by population age group, gender, and type of disease. Their analysis of the temporal effects is limited in part by the absence of long-term health data; what they have is essentially a single cross section. But their somewhat primitive measurement of how long such conditions may linger after the war is over links to the first two papers concerned with regional effects. The human cost from a civil war is not only to the country undergoing a war, but also to its neighbors, depending in part on the permeability of its borders with those neighbors. Such analysis could in principle be linked to new work on the diffusion of civil wars, again using spatial illustrations of whether an insurgency arises on the border, with what effect for support or spillover.

Ashley Leeds's chapter studies the effect of alliances on the spatial expansion and escalation of militarized interstate disputes (MIDs). This chapter is informed by previous formal work, including that of Leeds herself, on how an institutionalized alliance can signal a commitment to fight on behalf of one's ally, in a situation in which states' information is incomplete and credible commitment is difficult. Bargaining is more complex and difficult in a multilateral context. Furthermore, alliance as a signal of intention may serve as a deterrent to initiating violent conflict but, if deterrence fails, in further stages may lead to the expansion of conflict beyond the two initial disputants and raise the level of dispute from low-level military/diplomatic on up to war. Her analysis is primarily statistical, using a new dataset on the content of alliance agreements, and distinguishing among offensive alliances, defensive ones, and pacts promising only neutrality in case the "ally" goes to war. She finds that if one or both states in a dyad have alliances, especially defensive ones, the apparent commitment of their allies has a strong effect in diminishing the risk that a militarized dispute will break out within the dyad. But when militarized disputes do occur, the alliances are more likely to bring in the allies to produce a multilateral expansion of the conflict, and an escalation of the level of violence to full-scale war. Overall, the effect of alliances is to reduce the number of MIDs, but at the cost of greater expansion and escalation of many of those that do occur.

THE INTERACTION OF DOMESTIC AND INTERNATIONAL POLITICS

The interdependence of domestic and international politics has been increasingly recognized by social scientists, especially in the domain of national security. Many analysts, for example, have considered how leaders' use of force internationally boosts or damages their popularity in democratic political systems, and whether leaders may time their use of force to help them at the polls or in their bargaining with a legislature. Analysis of the "diversionary" use of force abroad to strengthen oneself at home has become common, but somewhat inconclusive. William Howell and Jon Pevehouse bring the examination of this question to a higher level, addressing work on the U.S. government and bringing together the perspectives of the subfields of American politics and international relations. Specifically, they ask about the president's ability to get his agenda adopted in Congress and his ability to obtain congressional support to pursue his international agenda. The diversionary hypothesis suggests that a president will be more likely to use military force abroad when his party is weak and his position is endangered by inflation or unemployment at home. In a very sophisticated statistical analysis they do find that unemployment and inflation are correlated with uses of force internationally. But, controlling for that, they conclude just the opposite about political weakness. Just as the president is better able to pursue his domestic political agenda when his party is in firm control of the Congress, he also has more discretion to use military force abroad. Fewer effective veto players can inhibit his action. They supplement their statistical analysis with a brief discussion of the conditions affecting the use of force by President Bush in 2003 against Iraq, testing some of the limits of their analysis. Overall, they give a powerful illustration of why scholars of domestic political institutions and scholars of international relations should collaborate in the examination of security policy in the United States and other countries.

Karl DeRouen and Shaun Goldfinch address the interaction of domestic and foreign policy partially in the context of the democratic peace program, and extend that program. They begin with a "new institutional" perspective that treats norms and institutions as distinctive explanations of policy, and specifically of democratic peace. They hold, rather, that democratic institutions socially construct individuals who prefer to use non-violent means of dispute resolution. In this they revive the normative perspective that has recently been upstaged by developments on the institutional side (e.g., Bueno de Mesquita, Smith, Siverson, and Morrow 2003), and treat normative and institutional perspectives as mutually reinforcing. They also take a firm stand on the monadic vs. dyadic understanding of the democratic peace as recently elaborated by Rosato (2003), Zinnes (2003), and Kinsella (forthcoming). DeRouen and Goldfinch hold that democratic publics are, from their experience of political life, more peaceful vis-à-vis other democracies but also, in lesser degree, toward other countries in general. In other words, diversionary theories of war in democracies have been looking in the wrong place: democracy provides a structure for managing and accommodating social unrest that provides less incentive for diversionary acts than exists in dictatorships. Moreover, a preference for non-violent dispute resolution should show up in democracies' relative use of a spectrum of resolution techniques ranging from negotiation through coercion to actual violence. For this they look at the order of behavior in international crises. Their results largely support their hypotheses, including at the dyadic and, less strongly, the monadic level. While theirs will certainly not be the last word, it is a significant step forward.

BARGAINING AND NEGOTIATING IN WARS

Bargaining and negotiation are not just for peacetime. Parties to wars in effect bargain during the war as part of an explicit or implicit negotiating process to achieve wartime goals and the military and political conditions for post-war peace. Some recent work (for example, Slantchev 2003a, 2003b) regards war as a process of narrowing uncertainty about the costs each party is willing to incur as well as the costs it can inflict on each other, ending when sufficient information is revealed by the fighting. They may also fight wars for the purpose of being able to bargain better at the peace table afterward. Formal models of rational behavior are well suited to exploring such questions, and this book has two good examples.

In their chapter, Alastair Smith and Allan Stam ask why a state's leaders may sometimes choose to fight a war even though they believe they are likely or even near-certain to lose the war. In doing so, they may not just be taking a long-odds gamble on doing better in the war than they expect, but they may be expecting to lose yet still be able to turn their action into an asset at the postwar negotiating table. They may gain negotiating advantage by demonstrating capability, resolve, and even restraint, which can subsequently help in the postwar political bargaining process. The wartime exchanges may delay peacetime negotiation, but ultimately make it more productive, especially in instances where control of territory is at issue. Their analysis is purely formal, with no systematic empirical tests, but well illustrated with a nice case study of the 1973 war initiated by Egypt against Israel despite Egypt's known military inferiority, with the ultimate result that Egypt recovered control of the Sinai Peninsula in subsequent negotiation.

Suzanne Werner and Amy Yuen address the problem of third-party mediation of peace negotiations and enforcement of agreements reached. It also is primarily a formal analysis, with some brief references to experience in the Bosnian and Rwandan wars. As so often in international relations, the key problem is the difficulty each party may have in committing credibly to keep an agreement. They distinguish among four actors: an opposition (treated here as a unitary actor), in conflict with another side that is in fact divided between a group of moderates and a smaller group of extremist "spoilers," and a third-party enforcer of the agreement. Each actor has imperfect information about the intentions of all the others. The extremists can succeed in destroying the agreement even if they cannot disrupt it unilaterally—their actions can suffice to feed the moderates' fears of exploitation by the opposition as supported by the enforcer. Particularly if the third party should have strong enforcement capabilities, it must decide whether to be even-handed in enforcement in order to keep the moderates aboard. If it comes down too hard on the extremists, the moderates on their side will abandon the agreement. Werner and Yuen thus distinguish between the third party's goals as treaty-keeper and peace-keeper. Should it seek primarily to ensure that all the terms of the peace agreement are kept even at the risk that the whole agreement will break down and conflict be renewed? United Nations enforcement efforts do indeed face this dilemma, as expressed in its peacekeeping doctrine about the need not to be partisan toward either side as such, but neither to maintain neutrality when one side violates key elements of the agreement.

These two formal chapters follow the common analytical choice of assuming actors who rationally maximize their expected utility. The rational-actor model has many critics, and one form of criticism is that political actors may seek not to maximize expected utility but, as in Alex Mintz's chapter on "poliheuristic" actors, may first act to avoid a policy that could cause severe losses in some key dimension of their multiple goals. Explicit consideration of this model might productively enhance either of the two chapters exploring the interactions of domestic and international politics; for example, a leader may first simply exclude any option that might lead to electoral defeat, and then move to consider her expected utilities under the remaining options. But it may be more useful to consider it here in a context following the explicit formal models. After giving a list of provocative historical examples, Mintz investigates this in an experimental design, using senior U.S. Air Force officers as subjects. They must make decisions under varying conditions of ambiguity of information and familiarity with similar situations. He finds that even air force officers working with a computerized "decision board" frequently reject otherwise attractive alternatives that fail the "avoid political loss" test. They are more likely to do so under familiar conditions with unambiguous information.

NOTE

I thank Alex for productive discussion and ideas reflected in this chapter.

II

NEW DIRECTIONS

3

International Relations: A Network Approach[1]

Zeev Maoz, Lesley G. Terris,
Ranan D. Kuperman, and Ilan Talmud

We offer a demonstration of the potential of social networks analysis for international relations research. We argue that social networks analysis is eminently suitable for the study of a wide variety of issues that have plagued research in international relations for a long time. A social network is a set of units (people, organizations, states) that are bound together by some kind of tie (friendship, kinship, exchange relations, alliances, trade), or by affiliation with some institution or attribute (international organizations, ethnic groups). Social networks analysis is a comprehensive framework that allows the systematic analysis of patterns of ties and affiliations across a wide variety of networks. As such it is eminently suitable for the study of international relations. We discuss the promise of the application of the social networks approach by examining alliance and ethnic networks over the period of 1816–2000, and explore the implications of this method.

Over the last two decades, the study of international relations has made revolutionary leaps in a number of fields. We have learned more about the causes of war and the conditions for peace in the past twenty years than we learned in the preceding eighty years of the twentieth century. Despite continuing debates in the field, the scientific study of international relations can tell us—in as precise terms as possible in the social sciences—that joint democracy, participation in international organizations, alliances, and—to a lesser extent—economic interdependence reduce significantly the probability of dyadic conflict and war. It can also tell us that geographic contiguity, a history of past conflict, and parity in military capabilities increase significantly the probability of international conflict between states (Russett and Oneal 2001).

We know, for example, that national and dyadic conflict involvement patterns exhibit a fundamental inequality: a vast majority of the states have been involved in a small number of disputes and wars, while few states have been involved in the vast majority of disputes and wars. The same applies for dyadic conflict patterns: a small fraction of politically relevant dyads are responsible for the vast majority of militarized interstate disputes (MIDs) and wars in the past two centuries. These dyads are composed mostly of enduring rivals; dyads the members of which repeatedly fight each other. The characteristics of these dispute-prone states and dyads are also clearly discernible. The high-risk population in terms of exposure to conflict consists of powerful, economically developed states that have many neighbors, as well as politically unstable states. Jointly democratic dyads tend to be pacific (Maoz 2005).

Despite these dramatic strides in knowledge accumulation, the empirical study of international politics is still riddled with significant puzzles. Much of the knowledge gained over the past few years is due to the abandonment of the systemic level of analysis in favor of an almost exclusive focus on the dyadic level. National-level studies of international relations using quantitative data have also become quite rare recently. Attempts to combine levels of analysis in the study of important questions such as the relationship between democracies and war reveal important puzzles (Maoz 2001; Ray 2001). The same applies for the relationship between alliances and international conflict (Maoz 2000).

The decline in popularity of systemic studies of world politics, however, does not diminish the importance of this level in our ability to reach a comprehensive understanding of international processes over time. Nor does the focus on the dyadic level detract from the fact that certain trends in international relations over the last two centuries have assumed regional patterns. For example, Ward and Gleditsch (2000) argue persuasively for a spatial effect on the relationship between democratization and war.

These points pose an old/new challenge. How do we develop a better understanding of international relations that is (a) general, i.e., focuses on the entire set of units that we wish to study (i.e., states, dyads, regions, global systems), (b) dynamic, i.e., allows us to trace changes over time in the phenomena under study, (c) multilevel, i.e., allows us meaningfully to connect processes at one level of aggregation to processes at other levels of aggregation, and (d) logically coherent, i.e., embedded in a unifying logical framework rather than based on distinct and loosely related theoretical frameworks.

This paper seeks to provide the general outlines of an approach that may well meet these challenges. We offer a conceptual and methodological scheme that identifies international relations as a set of networks, networks that are interrelated at a given point in time, and over time. We suggest that this framework can provide us with new and more general insights into the evolution of international relations, in the sense that it has the potential to meet all of the elements of the challenge listed above. After identifying the basic characteristics of the network approach to international politics, we discuss some of the directions in which this approach may be taken and some ways of better fitting the network approach to the study of international politics. We illustrate some of the advantages of the network approach with examples using alliance and ethnic composition data. The chapter concludes with a brief discussion of the theoretical and empirical implications of this approach. We start with a very brief overview of the network literature.

NETWORK LITERATURE: GENERAL APPROACH AND IR APPLICATIONS[2]

Wasserman and Faust (1994, 10–11) note that the development of social network analysis has evolved independently in several social science disciplines. Pioneering studies in this genre originated in sociology, social psychology, and anthropology. From there, social network approaches have proliferated into all of the social science disciplines. The social network approach can be likened to the rational choice approach: both contain a set of fundamental assumptions and analytical tools that can be applied to a wide variety of problems across substantive disciplines.

Network analysis consists of a series of analytical measures that allow for systematic description of a system of relationships between and among units. Some measures describe the entire system of relationships. Other measures allow for description of subsystems. Still others allow for comparison of subgroups of the system. Finally, a host of measures allows for comparison between and among units. Because it offers a unified framework for describing social relations at various levels, network analysis allows a wide variety of applications. In this respect, as we will argue, we can adapt it easily to the analysis of international relations.

Whereas the rational choice approach has received significant attention in international relations research, the social network approach has rarely been used in international relations. In its infancy, this approach was used to study transaction flows in the international system (Brams 1966, 1969). Since then, there have been few cases wherein IR scholars have used network approaches to examine international problems. On the other hand, a number of sociologists attempted to study aspects of the "world system" through network approaches (e.g., Snyder and Kick 1979; Steiber 1979; Nemeth and Smith 1985; Van

Rossem 1996). Knoke (1990), who reviews the literature on political networks, hardly mentions international relations applications by political scientists.[3]

One of the few recent attempts to examine international political problems using a network analytic approach is Maoz (2001) who applied a rather rudimentary network conception in an attempt to resolve the level of analysis problem in the democratic peace phenomenon. This effort seemed quite promising in that it suggested that the democratic peace puzzle can be resolved through a better understanding of the interaction of democratic states within their politically relevant international environment (PRIE).

This attempt led us to develop a more systematic and general network conceptualization of international politics (Maoz, Terris, and Kuperman, 2002; Maoz, Terris, Kuperman, and Talmud 2002). In these papers we argue that it is possible to develop a multilayered and evolutionary perspective of international politics using a network approach. Some of these international networks are relational; they describe how actors are linked with other actors in terms of certain ties, such as formal alliances. Some of these networks are affiliational: they describe how actors are organized in terms of their affiliation with certain attributes—such as their ethnic composition and their regime structure. We show that several characteristics of alliance, ethnic, and regime networks tend to affect the extent of international conflict in the system.

These findings suggest that a general understanding of systemic structure has a significant potential for the study of war and peace in international politics. This understanding, however, must be couched in a suitable network-related framework. This is what we turn to next.

INTERNATIONAL RELATIONS ARE ABOUT NETWORKS

Social interactions in general, and international interactions in particular, can be conceived of as a set of networks. A network *is a group of units bound together by a certain rule, link, or other type of connection.* We can describe these interactions from the point of view of a specific unit (individual or state); for example, the relations of the United States with its allies. We can describe these interactions from the point of view of a subset of the units, for example, the politics of NATO. We can describe these interactions from the perspective of the entire system, for example, the polarity of the alliance configuration in the international system prior to World War I. The problem is, however, that our selection of units of analysis and of a given substantive problem determines in many respects our general choice of theoretical models, methods, and the substantive results. As these examples indicate, it would be difficult to use a unified theory and an identical set of methods to study the

U.S. behavior toward its allies, the politics of NATO, and the effect of the polarity of the system on the outbreak of World War I. J. David Singer's classical essay on the level of analysis problem (1961) makes this point very clear.

Moreover, when we wish to study the relationship among types of relations—for example, between IGO membership, alliances, regime type, and conflict—we run into complex theoretical and methodological problems that typically require us to reduce the problem by focusing on a specific level of analysis and by reducing its complexity through some choices of units, or subsets of data (e.g., political relevance), and by methodological devices that provide for controls. But these reductions carry a price: they reduce our ability to generalize. If we could preserve all our analyses within a unifying framework that contains an integrated set of concepts, theories, and methods, we could achieve a better sense of cumulation. In most cases, however, we use different concepts for different problems, rely on different theoretical frameworks and different methodologies, and our substantive findings differ so much that cumulation is rendered difficult, if not impossible.

Consider for example Russett and Oneal's (2001) triangle of factors—democracy, economic interdependence, and IGO participation—that is hypothesized to contribute to peace among nations. This conception hinges almost exclusively on the dyadic level of analysis at which it was tested. We cannot reliably say that if a state is a democracy, a significant proportion of its GDP is based on trade with other states, and it participates in many international organizations, then it will be less likely to engage in conflict overall. In fact, democracies are not less war prone than nondemocracies. We also know that there is no relationship between the number of IGO memberships in the system and the extent of conflict within it. So, generalizing across levels of aggregation—even if we accept the dyadic-level set of findings—is difficult, if not dangerous (Maoz 2001).

If we can approach these problems from a unified analytic framework that allows an examination of the three levels of aggregation within one logical set, then perhaps we can develop better explanations for the level of analysis problem. More important, perhaps we can be in a better position to understand the logical transitions of certain international processes across different levels of aggregation.

INTRODUCING NETWORK ANALYSIS IN INTERNATIONAL RELATIONS RESEARCH

In this section we focus on two issues. First, we employ existing network concepts and measures to demonstrate how network analysis can be used to create a multilevel framework of international relations. Second, we explore new avenues for the application of network approaches to the unique demands of international relations research. We use alliance data to illustrate our points. Before we begin, it is useful to say a few words about the data.

The alliance data are annual level data on formal alliances between members of the international system. The Correlates of War (COW) conception of formal alliances is based on a threefold typology (Gibler and Sarkees 2004; Singer and Small 1968): (1) defense pacts stipulate that the attack on one member of the alliance is equivalent to an attack on all other members; (2) nonaggression pacts stipulate that members of the alliance undertake not to attack each other; and (3) *entente* pacts stipulate that members of the alliance undertake to consult and inform each other in the event of a crisis within the alliance or between a member of the alliance and an actor outside the alliance.[4]

SYSTEM/NETWORK CHARACTERISTICS AND CROSS NETWORK COMPARISONS

We start our tour of the network approach at the systemic level with the year 1840 as an example. The first part of figure 3.1 shows the alliance ties between states making up the interstate system that year.[5] This figure can also be represented as a matrix form. Let A_{1840} be a 30 × 30 matrix where each row and each column represents a state. Entry a_{ij} in this matrix represents the presence (1) or absence (0) of an alliance of any type between states. We call this the *adjacency matrix* of alliances in 1840. For the time being, we look at alliance relations in binary terms only. The matrix shows only direct links between states. Note that this matrix is a square $n \times n$ symmetric matrix (such that each entry $a_{ij} = a_{ji}$).[6] One way of examining the attributes of this particular matrix is by measuring its density, by

$$D = \frac{\sum\limits_{i=1}^{n} \sum\limits_{j=1}^{n} a_{ij}}{n(n-1)} \qquad (0.1)$$

where D is the density of the matrix. This simply measures the proportion of alliance ties of all possible alliance ties in the system. As noted, the matrix given in figure 3.1 provides only first-order alliance ties. What it does not show is indirect, that is, second-, third-, ...$n-1$ degree alliance ties between states. To get this information, we calculate a *reachability matrix, R*, defined as

$$R=\sum_{i=1}^{n-1}A^i \qquad (0.2)$$

Specifically, the first-order adjacency matrix can be denoted as A^1. When squared, the product matrix A^2 contains all the second-order alliance relations (the allies of my ally). For example, in the first-order adjacency matrix, Sardinia (state #325) is connected with Austria-Hungary (state #300) which is connected with Hanover (state #240). However, Sardinia does not have a direct alliance with Hanover. When the first-order adjacency matrix, A, is squared (A^2), the indirect alliance between Sardinia and Hanover shows up. When the squared adjacency matrix A^2 is multiplied again by the initial adjacency matrix, we get third-order alliance ties, and so forth. The sum of all adjacency matrices (normalized to a binary matrix) tells us if two states are reachable, that is, if there is any kind of alliance tie—direct or indirect—between them.[7]

The second part of Figure 3.1 shows the alliance system of 1840 now defined in terms of reachability. Any line between two states implies that these states are *reachable*. This means that there exists a—direct or indirect—alliance relationship between them. We can compare the densities of the first-order adjacency matrix (0.104) with the density of the reachability matrix (0.283) and see that the density of the latter is almost three times that of the

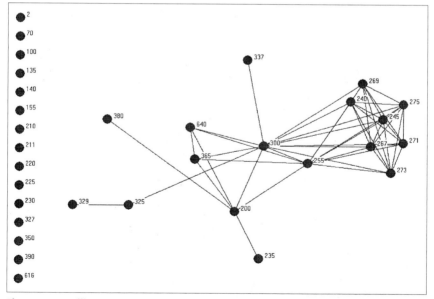

Figure 3.1.   Alliance Network, 1840
a.   First-order adjacency
Note: Numbers are COW state numbers

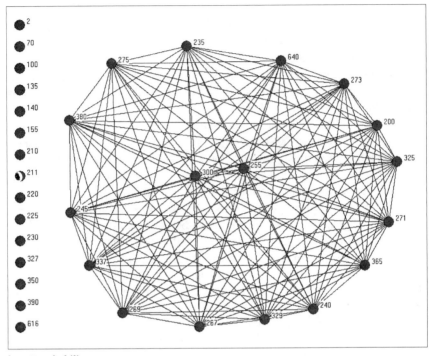

b.   Reachability

former. This implies that looking only at direct alliance ties between states causes considerable omission.

There are additional ways of examining this system of alliances. One is to examine the *clique* structure of this system. Briefly, a clique is a set of three or more actors who are directly connected with each other. In this system, there are two cliques, shown in table 3.1. (This can also be inferred from figure 3.1, but it is more difficult.)

The clique structure allows us to calculate a new measure of network polarization (Maoz, 2003), as follows:

$$NPI = POL \times CO = \frac{\sum_{j=1}^{k} \sum_{i=1}^{N-1} \sum_{r=i+1}^{N} (a_{ij} - a_{rj})^2}{max(POl \mid N)} \times \left(1 - \frac{\sum_{i=1}^{k-1} \sum_{j=i+1}^{k} CO_{ij}}{Max(CO \mid N, k)}\right) \quad (0.3)$$

where *NPI* is the network polarization index. Network polarization is a product of two elements. First, the column polarization (*POL*) index stipulates the extent to which a given clique is polarized with respect to all other members in the system. This index is a ratio of the sum of squared differences between any two rows within a given column, divided by a theoretical maximum

Table 3.1.   Clique Affiliation Matrix[8]

State	Clique 1	Clique 2
200	0	1
240	1	0
245	1	0
255	1	1
267	1	0
269	1	0
271	1	0
273	1	0
275	1	0
300	1	1
365	0	1
640	0	1
Total	9	5

squared rank differences given the row-dimension of the clique affiliation matrix. Second the Clique Overlap (*CO*) index stipulates the degree of membership overlap across cliques. The degree of clique overlap is the ratio of the number of members that any two cliques have in common, divided by the maximum possible overlap in a clique affiliation matrix of size $N \times k$. The NPI varies from zero (no polarization) to one (maximum polarization). In our case, $NPI = 0.334$, indicating a fairly low level of polarization.

Because these indices control for the size of the system, they can provide a way in which to describe changes in the alliance structure of the international system over time. For example, if we look at the alliance system of 1940 as another point in time, we find that the density of the system then went up to 0.278, and the network polarization index went down to 0.201.

Quite a few other measures describe properties of this system, but the above provides a fairly good sense of the ability to characterize an international system at a given point in time as an alliance network, as well as to examine change in a given system over time.

We can also compare different attributes of the system by comparing two or more networks at a given point in time. In order to demonstrate this, let us employ the second type of network, *affiliation network*. An affiliation network is represented by an $N \times k$ matrix that has the members of the system as rows, and a certain set of groups at its columns. For example, we can examine the ethnic composition of states by generating an ethnic affiliation matrix of states at a given point in time. This matrix has N states at its row (listed lexicographically), and k ethnic groups (also listed lexicographically) as its columns. Each entry in the matrix tells us the proportion of the population of state i that belongs to the ethnic group j. (In our case, the entries in this matrix tell us only whether at least 5 percent of a state i's population belonged to ethnic group j.) In order to transform the affiliation matrix into an adjacency matrix, we simply multiply the affiliation matrix by its transpose, so that

$$A_{n \times n} = X_{n \times k} X'_{k \times n} \qquad (0.4)$$

The derived adjacency matrix has a special structure. Its main diagonal consists of the number of affiliations of each of its elements, that is, of the number of distinct ethnic groups that make up 5 percent or more of a state's population. Each nondiagonal entry a_{ij} represents the number of distinct ethnic groups that states i and j share in common. For convenience, we transform this matrix to a binary matrix where entry a_{ij} receives a score of one if two states share at least one ethnic group that accounts for 10 percent or more of their respective populations, and zero otherwise.

Let us examine the ethnic composition of the system as a reference for cross-network comparison. We use the ethnic dataset compiled by Phil Schafer at the University of Michigan for this purpose (Singer 1995; Henderson and Singer 2000). In contrast to the other datasets that are coded on a yearly basis, this dataset is coded once every decade, and includes all ethnic, religious, and linguistic groups that exist in a given state. We employ only the ethnic division and include groups that accounted for 5 percent of the population or more. Ethnic composition is also an affiliation network of size $N \times 203$, where N represents all independent states for a given decade. The breakdown of the ethnic dataset into groups that accounted for 10 percent or more of a given state's population, gives us a subset of 203 groups out of a maximum of 675 ethnic groups listed in the Schaffer dataset. The graphic representation of the adjacency matrix that is derived from the ethnic affiliation data for 1840 is given in figure 3.2.

We can now compare the alliance and ethnic network in terms of their statistical attributes, such as density and network polarization. But we can also compare these two networks by examining the overlap in the matrices. One way of doing this is to overlay the alliance and ethnic networks on each other. We recode the ethnic network such that each entry that is off-diagonal receives an arbitrary score of 5. We then subtract the alliance matrix for 1840 from the ethnic matrix, and then by interpreting the numbers in the resulting matrix we can examine the degree of overlap. Table 3.2 shows this comparison.

This comparison reveals that the density of the two networks is roughly similar, but the alliance network is more polarized than the ethnic network. We can see that from the graphs representing the two networks (figures 3.1 and 3.2). The alliance network is composed of two cliques that share two

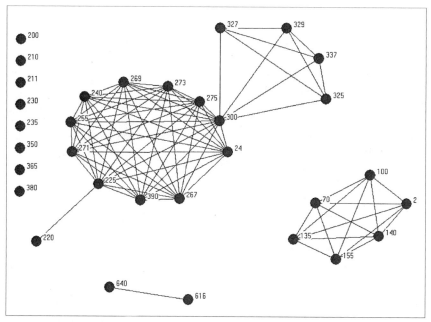

Figure 3.2.   Ethnicity Networks, 1840

members in common. The ethnic network is composed of three cliques, two of which have one member in common and one (the Western Hemisphere clique) shares no member in common with the other cliques.

As noted, beyond the conventional measures of network attributes, we can examine how much *overlap* there exists between or among different networks in systems that have exactly the same members (Maoz, Terris, and Kuperman 2002). If we look at the two networks, we can see that—taking the alliance network as a baseline—its overlap with the ethnic network is nearly 80 percent. This implies that about 80 percent of the states that shared alliance ties with each other also shared considerable ethnic overlap with their allies. On the other hand, if we take the ethnic network as a baseline, its overlap with the alliance network is only slightly less than 50 percent. That means that about half of the members of the network who share ethnic affinities also share security alliances.

The network approach allows us systematically to compare a set of networks in systems that have exactly the same nodes. However, we still need to develop methodologies that allow comparison of networks over time, when membership in the system changes. Current network approaches offer an approach to such a comparison through log-linear estimation procedures that are based on network characteristics (Faust and Skvoretz 2002). While these efforts are promising in that they have the potential of developing systematic

Table 3.2.   A Comparison of Alliance and Ethnic Networks, 1840

Measure	Alliance Network	Ethnic Network	Overlap
Density	0.283	0.274	
Network Polarization Index	0.334	0.201	
Alliances with ethnic affiliation[9]			0.790
Nonaligned ethnic affiliations[10]			0.525

measures of similarity and differences across different types of networks and over time, they are unsatisfactory because they entail far too many measurement and estimation-related assumptions that may be violated in reality. Thus, new methodologies for comparing networks are needed. We now turn to subsystem characteristics.

Subsystem/Subnetwork Characteristics

There are several ways of treating subsystems in network analysis. One is to identify subsystems in terms that are extraneous to the network. For example, dividing the international system into regional subsystems, or into major/minor power subsystems, represents such a partitioning. Another way to do so is to derive subsystems endogenously. For example, deriving cliques or *n*-cliques allows examining relations within the system in terms of existing ties among members.

Let us illustrate the first approach. For that purpose, we take the alliance network of 1953 and examine three regional subsystems: the Western Hemisphere, Europe, and the Middle East. Consider figure 3.3 below.[11]

We can compare the three subsystems through their attributes as we have done above. This is done in table 3.3.

All of the states in the Western Hemisphere, through the OAS, make for a complete bloc that is totally nonpolarized internally. Likewise, the Middle East is highly dense, with Israel the only actor in the region that is excluded from the alliance system. Since there were three discernible cliques in the region, with considerable overlap across the blocs, the NPI is fairly low, but it is significantly higher than in the other two regional systems. In Europe, the system density is low, because the number of states that are excluded from the alliance systems in the region is comparatively high. However, the degree of polarization is extremely low because there is a bridge between NATO and the Eastern bloc states through the UK-France-Soviet Union alliance (that ended in 1955). Since all three states are central members of the respective alliance systems in the region, the overlap across cliques is fairly large, thus reducing the NPI.

Another way of examining subsystems is by focusing on endogenous groups. One approach to the problem that is suitable for some networks but not

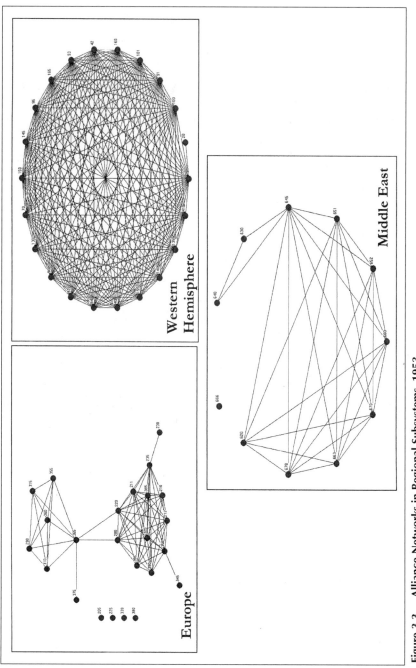

Western
Hemisphere

Europe

Middle East

Figure 3.3.   Alliance Networks in Regional Subsystems, 1953

Table 3.3.   Comparative Alliance Structure of Three Subsystems in 1953

Attribute	Western Hemisphere	Europe	Middle East
Density	1.000	0.688	0.818
Network Polarization Index	0.000	0.031	0.178

for others, is to compare cliques with n-cliques. For example, in the case of alliances, the relationship between the cliques that are formed from first-order, that is, direct alliance ties, may be a (smaller or larger) subset of the cliques that are formed from first- and second-order alliance ties. This issue may have important implications for the analysis of such issues as wars between allies. Specifically, while wars between allies may occur with some frequency (Bueno de Mesquita 1981), the probability of war between second-, third-, and fourth-order allies may be even more common, thus defeating the notion of the "friend of my friend is my friend."

Consider the clique structure of the system in terms of alliances in 1840 and 1953 in terms of the relationship between first-order cliques and second-order cliques. This is given in table 3.4.

The results of this table show an interesting difference in the alliance networks in the two periods. Whereas the initial clique polarizations of the two years are fairly close, the system polarization based on 2- and 3-clique levels declines dramatically in 1840 but less so in 1953. What this implies is that the connectedness of the alliance structures in 1840 is much higher than it is in 1953. In fact, this analysis suggests that we reach an alliance structure that is a completely closed system (that is, all states that are in alliance with each other become indirect allies of all other states that are aligned) when we get to the third-order alliance relationship between states. This is not the case in 1953. The alliance structure of the third-order clique structure is more cohesive than the first order set, but not completely cohesive.

Thus, the sub-systemic analysis may provide useful insights into the regional or substantive structure of different subsystems and to the interrelationship between a systemic structure and sub-systemic structure.

Dyadic Analysis

It seems that in recent years almost all the innovations that could be introduced in dyadic analysis were indeed introduced. We examined all possible

Table 3.4.   Clique and n-Clique Polarization of Alliances, 1840 and 1953

Year	Clique Polarization	2-Clique Polarization	3-Clique Polarization
1840	0.317	0.201	0.000
1953	0.249	0.218	0.181

dyads in the system. We examined theoretically meaningful subsets of the dyadic population (e.g., politically relevant dyads, enduring rivalries), and we developed measures that can characterize dyads (e.g., the joint democracy measures, the weak link measures, the joint trade and interdependence measures, the joint IGO membership measures, and so forth).[12]

Several recent studies (e.g., Bennett 1998; Maoz 2000b, 2001) noted that in studying dyadic processes, it is important to identify also—beyond the characteristics of the dyad itself—the relationship between dyad members and their respective environments. For example, Bennett (1998) argued that in order to understand rivalry termination, it is important to examine whether dyad members develop new rivalries that offset the tendency to fight in the focal rivalries. Maoz (1996, 2000b, 2001) argued that in order to understand conflict patterns within dyadic structures it is important to understand the general attributes of the threat perception (defined either in terms of alliances in each state's environment that do not include the focal state, or conflict directed at the focal states from other states in its environment). Likewise, Maoz argued that the level of democratization and the level of political stability in each state's environment may affect their tendency to fight with each other.

Network theory has developed a set of interesting indices to examine how and to what extent members of a dyad are equivalent in terms of their structural role (Wasserman and Faust 1994, 347–375; Van Rossem 1996; Snyder and Kick 1979). Briefly, structural equivalence measures the degree of similarity or dissimilarity in a dyad in terms of the ties between each of the dyad members and third parties. A dyad *ij* is structurally equivalent if the ties between actor *i* and all other members of the network *k (k≠i, j)* are exactly the same as the ties between actor *j* and all *k*'s. There are several measures of structural equivalence but we will focus here on a correlation-based measure (Wasserman and Faust 1994: 368–369). The advantage of this measure is that it can resolve the dispute regarding other measures that have been developed in the IR literature to measure similarities between states on a dyadic level (e.g., Bueno de Mesquita 1981; Signorino and Ritter 1999; Bennett and Stam 2000b). Briefly, the measure of structural equivalence is obtained from the adjacency matrix (it could also be obtained from the reachability matrix) using the Pearson product-moment correlation formula (for multiple networks, the multiple correlation coefficient can be substituted for the bivariate *r* coefficient):

$$r_{ij} = \frac{\sum_{i,j=1}^{n}(x_{ki} - \bar{x}_j)(x_{kj} - \bar{x}_j) + \sum_{i,j=1}^{n}(x_{ik} - \bar{x}_i)(x_{jk} - \bar{x}_j)}{\sqrt{\sum_{i,j,k=1}^{n}(x_{ki} - \bar{x}_i)^2 + \sum_{i,j,k=1}^{n}(x_{jk} - \bar{x}_i)^2} + \sqrt{\sum_{i,j,k=1}^{n}(x_{kj} - \bar{x}_j)^2 + \sum_{i,j,k=1}^{n}(x_{jk} - \bar{x}_j)^2}} \quad (0.5)$$

Table 3.5.   Ethnic and Alliance Structural Equivalence, 1840
Table 3.5.a.   Stuctural Equivalence in the Western Hemisphere

	2	70	100	135	140	155
2	1.00					
70	0.78	1.00				
100	0.91	0.92	1.00			
135	0.84	0.95	0.90	1.00		
140	0.89	0.75	0.81	0.63	1.00	
155	0.77	0.86	0.94	0.91	0.57	1.00

The measure of structural equivalence has a number of important advantages over the more traditional measures of affinity. First, it considers how similar or dissimilar members of a dyad are in terms of their relations to all third parties. Second, this similarity can be based both on primary relations and on second-, third-, ... $n-1$-order relations. Third, and perhaps most importantly, this measure of structural equivalence can be performed on a single network or on several networks with the same actors. For structural equivalence measured on several types of networks, we use the multiple correlation coefficient, instead of the bivariate correlation coefficient (Wasserman and Faust 1994: 369).

Table 3.5.b.   Structural Equivalence in Europe

	200	210	211	220	225	230	235	240	245	255	267
200	1.00										
210	0.63	1.00									
211	0.63	1.00	1.00								
220	0.63	1.00	1.00	1.00							
225	0.00	0.00	0.00	0.00	1.00						
230	0.63	1.00	1.00	1.00	0.00	1.00					
235	0.66	0.70	0.70	0.70	0.00	0.70	1.00				
240	0.13	−0.05	−0.05	−0.05	0.00	−0.05	−0.07	1.00			
245	0.29	0.28	0.28	0.28	0.00	0.28	0.16	0.83	1.00		
255	0.56	0.48	0.48	0.48	0.00	0.48	0.50	0.63	0.85	1.00	
267	0.13	−0.05	−0.05	−0.05	0.00	−0.05	−0.07	1.00	0.83	0.63	1.00
269	0.13	−0.05	−0.05	−0.05	0.00	−0.05	−0.07	1.00	0.83	0.63	1.00
271	0.13	−0.05	−0.05	−0.05	0.00	−0.05	−0.07	1.00	0.83	0.63	1.00
273	0.13	−0.05	−0.05	−0.05	0.00	−0.05	−0.07	1.00	0.83	0.63	1.00
275	0.13	−0.05	−0.05	−0.05	0.00	−0.05	−0.07	1.00	0.83	0.63	1.00
300	0.59	0.71	0.71	0.71	0.00	0.71	0.59	0.37	0.64	0.82	0.37
325	0.28	0.36	0.36	0.36	0.00	0.36	0.22	0.02	0.24	0.26	0.02
327	0.21	0.43	0.43	0.43	0.00	0.43	0.28	−0.11	0.18	0.23	−0.11
329	0.18	0.39	0.39	0.39	0.00	0.39	0.25	−0.12	0.14	0.19	−0.12
337	0.32	0.39	0.39	0.39	0.00	0.39	0.25	0.04	0.28	0.30	0.04
350	0.63	1.00	1.00	1.00	0.00	1.00	0.70	−0.05	0.28	0.48	−0.05
365	0.89	0.70	0.70	0.70	0.00	0.70	0.74	0.17	0.36	0.66	0.17
380	0.70	0.89	0.89	0.89	0.00	0.89	0.95	−0.06	0.22	0.53	−0.06
390	0.63	1.00	1.00	1.00	0.00	1.00	0.70	−0.05	0.28	0.48	−0.05

To illustrate this measure consider table 3.5 that provides a combined, alliance-ethnic structural equivalence matrix of 1840. The top part of the table shows structural equivalence for all dyads in the Western Hemisphere. The second part shows structural equivalence measures for all European dyads. The third part of the matrix shows structural equivalence data for European-Western Hemisphere dyads. This table suggests that the structural equivalence measures of states within the Western Hemisphere are generally positive and high, and so are the structural equivalence measures of the German states. The structural equivalence measures of the Italian states are generally lower. Again, this demonstration suggests a powerful new approach to dyadic analysis.[13]

Monadic (Nation-Level) Characteristics

In the mid-1970s, several studies attempted to examine prestige-related issues of states (e.g., Gochman 1975; Ray 1974; Midlarsky 1975). These authors attempted to develop a number of measures of national prestige based on such attributes as diplomatic missions, IGO memberships, and alliances. These measures were then related to the conflict behavior of states.

Table 3.5.b. **Structural Equivalence in Europe (*continued*)**

269	271	273	275	300	325	327	329	337	350	365	380	390
1.00												
1.00	1.00											
1.00	1.00	1.00										
1.00	1.00	1.00	1.00									
0.37	0.37	0.37	0.37	1.00								
0.02	0.02	0.02	0.02	0.50	1.00							
−0.11	−0.11	−0.11	−0.11	0.56	0.83	1.00						
−0.12	−0.12	−0.12	−0.12	0.57	0.92	0.91	1.00					
0.04	0.04	0.04	0.04	0.57	0.92	0.91	0.82	1.00				
−0.05	−0.05	−0.05	−0.05	0.71	0.36	0.43	0.39	0.39	1.00			
0.17	0.17	0.17	0.17	0.70	0.34	0.26	0.23	0.38	0.70	1.00		
−0.06	−0.06	−0.06	−0.06	0.70	0.30	0.37	0.33	0.33	0.89	0.78	1.00	
−0.05	−0.05	−0.05	−0.05	0.71	0.36	0.43	0.39	0.39	1.00	0.70	0.89	1.00

Table 3.5.c.   Structural Equivalence between Western Hemisphere and European States

	2	70	100	135	140	155
200	0.55	0.43	0.49	0.35	0.63	0.32
210	0.89	0.75	0.81	0.63	1.00	0.57
211	0.89	0.75	0.81	0.63	1.00	0.57
220	0.89	0.75	0.81	0.63	1.00	0.57
225	0.00	0.00	0.00	0.00	0.00	0.00
230	0.89	0.75	0.81	0.63	1.00	0.57
235	0.62	0.51	0.56	0.42	0.70	0.39
240	−0.06	−0.10	−0.08	−0.09	−0.05	−0.08
245	0.22	0.14	0.18	0.10	0.28	0.09
255	0.41	0.29	0.35	0.23	0.48	0.21
267	−0.06	−0.10	−0.08	−0.09	−0.05	−0.08
269	−0.06	−0.10	−0.08	−0.09	−0.05	−0.08
271	−0.06	−0.10	−0.08	−0.09	−0.05	−0.08
273	−0.06	−0.10	−0.08	−0.09	−0.05	−0.08
275	−0.06	−0.10	−0.08	−0.09	−0.05	−0.08
300	0.61	0.46	0.53	0.37	0.71	0.33
325	0.30	0.00	0.26	0.18	0.36	0.16
327	0.37	0.29	0.33	0.23	0.43	0.21
329	0.33	0.25	0.29	0.20	0.39	0.18
337	0.33	0.25	0.29	0.20	0.39	0.18
350	0.89	0.75	0.81	0.63	1.00	0.57
365	0.62	0.50	0.55	0.41	0.70	0.37
380	0.79	0.66	0.72	0.55	0.89	0.50
390	0.89	0.75	0.81	0.63	1.00	0.57

Network approaches have a diverse number of prestige and centrality-related measures based on the relationship of a state with other members of the network (Wasserman and Faust 1994: 169–219). Briefly, the *Degree Centrality* of a state is the number of nodes to which this state is directly connected. (We can do this on both first-order adjacency matrices as well as on reachability matrices.) The *Closeness Centrality* of the state takes into account the length of the paths (geodesics) from each state to all other states. The *Betweenness Centrality* measures the extent to which a state serves as a bridge between any two other states. Finally, the *Eigenvector Centrality* measures the eigenvector of the principal eigenvalue of a distances matrix between states. Wasserman and Faust (1994) discuss at length the functions of these and other measures, so we will not elaborate here. However, in order to demonstrate these measures, table 3.6 provides a sense of several measures of centrality of the various states based both on alliance networks and on ethnic networks for the year 1840. The bottom row for each two sets of columns provides the correlation between the centrality measures based on alliances and the same centrality measure based on ethnicity. All measures are standardized

Table 3.6. Standardized Centrality Measures Based on Alliances and Ethnicity Networks: All States, 1840

Centrality State	Degree		Closeness		Between		Egnvector	
	Alliances	Ethnicity	Alliances	Ethnicity	Alliances	Ethnicity	Alliances	Ethnicity
2	0.00	0.03	0.02	0.03	0.00	0.00	0.00	0.00
70	0.00	0.03	0.02	0.03	0.00	0.00	0.00	0.00
100	0.00	0.03	0.02	0.03	0.00	0.00	0.00	0.00
135	0.00	0.03	0.02	0.03	0.00	0.00	0.00	0.00
140	0.00	0.03	0.02	0.03	0.00	0.00	0.00	0.00
155	0.00	0.03	0.02	0.03	0.00	0.00	0.00	0.00
200	0.06	0.00	0.04	0.02	0.24	0.00	0.03	0.00
210	0.00	0.00	0.02	0.02	0.00	0.00	0.00	0.00
211	0.00	0.00	0.02	0.02	0.00	0.00	0.00	0.00
220	0.00	0.01	0.02	0.04	0.00	0.00	0.00	0.01
225	0.00	0.07	0.02	0.04	0.00	0.24	0.00	0.09
230	0.00	0.00	0.02	0.02	0.00	0.00	0.00	0.00
235	0.01	0.00	0.04	0.04	0.00	0.00	0.00	0.00
240	0.08	0.06	0.04	0.04	0.00	0.00	0.09	0.09
245	0.08	0.06	0.04	0.04	0.00	0.00	0.09	0.09
255	0.11	0.06	0.04	0.04	0.15	0.00	0.10	0.09
267	0.08	0.06	0.04	0.04	0.00	0.00	0.09	0.09
269	0.08	0.06	0.04	0.04	0.00	0.00	0.09	0.09

(continued)

Table 3.6. Standardized Centrality Measures Based on Alliances and Ethnicity Networks: All States, 1840 (continued)

Centrality	Degree		Closeness		Between		Egnvector	
State	Alliances	Ethnicity	Alliances	Ethnicity	Alliances	Ethnicity	Alliances	Ethnicity
271	0.08	0.06	0.04	0.04	0.00	0.00	0.09	0.09
273	0.08	0.06	0.04	0.04	0.00	0.00	0.09	0.09
275	0.08	0.06	0.04	0.04	0.00	0.00	0.09	0.09
300	0.13	0.09	0.04	0.04	0.49	0.76	0.11	0.09
325	0.02	0.02	0.04	0.04	0.13	0.00	0.01	0.01
327	0.00	0.02	0.02	0.04	0.00	0.00	0.00	0.01
329	0.01	0.02	0.04	0.04	0.00	0.00	0.01	0.01
337	0.01	0.02	0.04	0.04	0.00	0.00	0.01	0.01
350	0.00	0.00	0.02	0.02	0.00	0.00	0.00	0.00
365	0.04	0.00	0.04	0.02	0.00	0.00	0.03	0.00
380	0.01	0.00	0.04	0.02	0.00	0.00	0.00	0.00
390	0.00	0.06	0.02	0.04	0.00	0.00	0.00	0.09
616	0.00	0.01	0.02	0.02	0.00	0.00	0.00	0.00
640	0.04	0.01	0.04	0.02	0.00	0.00	0.03	0.00
Correlation	0.66		0.40		0.79		0.82	

to be proportions of a total in order to give a comparative sense of these measures.

As we noted for the system-level measures, the centrality of states based on alliance ties is generally correlated at a medium or fairly high level with its centrality score based on ethnicity-related affinities. States ranked high on alliance-related centrality tend to rank highly on ethnicity-related centrality and vice versa. These measures demonstrate, then, how network analysis can be used to derive status and prestige properties of states on multiple indices. The traditional measures of status inconsistency that were applied to international politics can now be expanded considerably in order to obtain a more diverse sense of states' structural position and prestige, and to relate these measures to states' behavior.

This section demonstrated how network approaches can be used to develop cross-level-of-analysis characteristics of both the system and subsets of actors making up this system. It also demonstrated how international relations can be treated as a set of networks among states, and how network approaches can serve as an overarching framework for a multitude of descriptive and analytic studies of international politics. In order to highlight this issue, the next section provides a systematic description of changes in international politics over time in terms of alliances and ethnic networks.

The Evolution of the International System, 1816–2000: Alliances and Ethnic Patterns

The alliance and ethnic datasets allow us to characterize patterns of change in the international system over the 1816–2000 period in terms of alliance patterns and in terms of the ethnic structure of its members. Using the measures of density and network polarization indices, we first present the evolution of the international system over the 1816–2000 period in terms of these two networks. Figure 3.4 presents this evolution in terms of the density of these two networks. Figure 3.5 presents the network polarization indices on these two networks.

Before discussing these figures, two methodological notes are in order. First, as noted, the ethnic dataset is arranged by decade. In order to create equivalence with the annual-level alliance dataset, we extrapolated the ethnic dataset within decades. As can be seen from the two figures, this does not create major distortions because the ethnic network measures show distinct monotonically declining patterns. Second, we add for purpose of comparison two additional variables in these figures. In Figure 3.4, we present the density of democratic networks as defined by Maoz (2001).[14] In Figure 3.5, we present the power concentration index (Singer, Bremer, and Stuckey 1972) that reflects the centralization or diffusion of power scores of states.

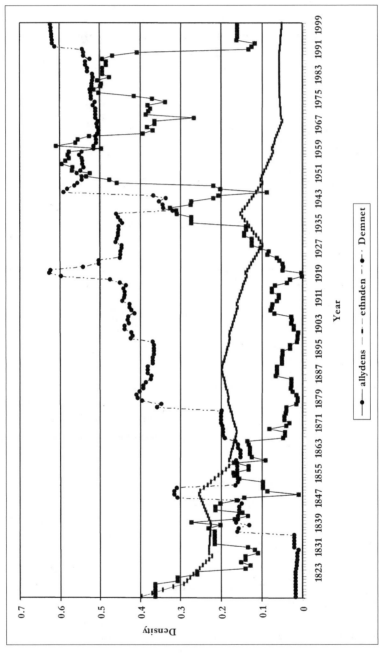

Figure 3.4.   Alliance and Ethnic Density and the Proportion of Democratic Networks in the Interstate System, 1816–2000

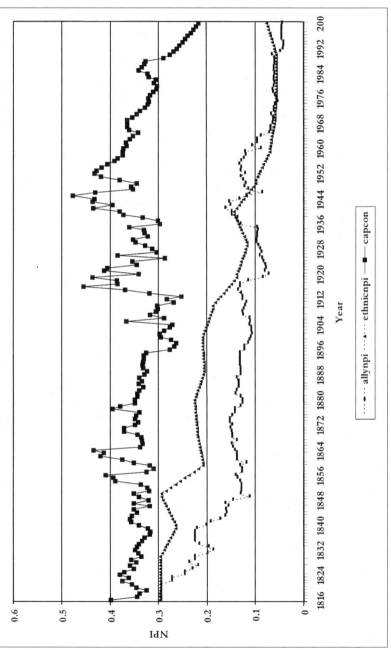

Figure 3.5. Alliance, Ethnic Polarization, and Capability Concentration in the International System, 1816–2000

The alliance network shows both a general trend and cyclical patterns in terms of density. The trend suggests a decline in density during the nineteenth century, and a general increase in density in the twentieth century, with a marked decline in the last decade of the century. There are also local cycles of rise and decline in density: each cycle ranges about twenty to twenty-five years.

In contrast, the density of ethnic networks displays a persistent decline over time, suggesting that the international system is becoming increasingly diverse in terms of its ethnic structure. Recall, that we define an ethnic network as one composed of states that share at least one ethnic group that makes up 10 percent or more of their respective populations. The reason that the density of the system in the nineteenth century was fairly high is that most independent states in the system were fairly homogenous and shared strong ethnic ties. In the twentieth century, the system becomes more diverse, and the newly established states show more ethnic diversity, hence the system becomes less ethnically dense over time. Note that the density of democratic networks shows a significant secular trend with significantly higher density in the twentieth century, and gradual increase in the latter part of the century.

The NPI indices in figure 3.5 tell us a similar story with respect to the ethnic polarization of the international system. The ethnic polarization of the system is declining. This suggests that more states share ethnic affinities and that fewer states belong to distinct ethnic blocs that do not overlap with other ethnic blocs. Alliance polarization suggests significant decline over time. The trend largely parallels that of the ethnic polarization index. Indeed the correlation between the NPI measures based on alliance and ethnic cliques, is very high ($r = 0.820$, $p < .001$, $N = 185$ years). On the other hand, the more traditional measure of capability concentration shows significant fluctuations over time, with a declining trend only in the second half of the twentieth century (largely as a result of the significant growth in the number of states in the system). It does not correlate highly with any of the other two polarization indices.

These data provide us with a sense of the changes in the characteristics of the system over time in terms of standard measures of density and network polarization. We can also examine the changes on the national, dyadic, and subsystemic levels.

We conclude the empirical demonstration by examining the effect of the characteristics of the ethnic structure and the alliance structure of the interstate system on the level of conflict in it over time. We examine two sets of principal hypotheses. The first concerns the effects of network density on conflict levels at the system level, and the second concerns the effects of network polarization on systemic conflict.

The conventional wisdom on alliances and systemic conflict (e.g., Singer and Small 1968; Oren 1990), tells us that as the system becomes increasingly dense in terms of alliance ties between states, the extent of conflict in the system is likely to rise. This is so because more alliances indicate greater security threats by more states (given that alliances represent a strategy to respond to security challenges—e.g., Maoz 2000b). Moreover, the risk of expanded conflict due to chain ganging increases as well (Christensen and Snyder 1990).

On the other hand, the density of ethnic networks implies greater degree of ethnic homogeneity in the system. This may suggest that there is less of a reason for clash of civilizations (Huntington 1996). As density declines, though, interethnic conflicts may become more frequent. Thus, ethnic density is expected to have a negative impact on the extent of systemic conflict.

With respect to democratization-related density, the basic contention of the democratic peace school—a contention that has received only mixed empirical support (e.g., Maoz and Abdolali 1989; Maoz 2001; Gleditsch and Hegre 1997)—is that increased democratization (beyond a certain point) reduces the extent of systemic conflict. This implies a negative relationship between the density of democratic networks and systemic conflict.

There are conflicting views on the effect of alliance polarity on conflict.[15] The neorealist school contends that polarization (defined as increased bipolarity) increases stability, thus reducing the extent of conflict in the system. The multipolarity school contends that as polarization increases so does the extent of conflict. We tend to side with the latter school because findings from dyadic research (e.g., Maoz and Russett 1993; Bremer 1992; Russett and Oneal 2001; Bennett and Stam 2000b) suggest that equal capability balances increase the probability of dyadic conflict. Greater alliance polarization would suggest a balancing process. If this is the case, then greater alliance polarization creates higher conflict tendencies. Likewise, power concentration was hypothesized to increase the risk of war (Singer, Bremer, and Stuckey 1972).

The polarization of the system in terms of ethnic configuration of its members is also expected to be positively related to conflict, because it indicates a clash of civilizations. On the other hand, reduced ethnic polarization suggests greater diversity and a greater degree of cross-cultural cooperation.

The dependent variables are the number of MID dyads and the number of war dyads per year. MID and war data are derived from the Dyadic MID dataset (Maoz 1999).[16] The alliance and ethnic density and NPI measures are described above.

In addition to these measures, we used two additional independent variables. First, we employed a measure of democratic networks initially developed by Maoz (2001) and further developed in the context of a network analysis of the international system (Maoz, Terris, Kuperman, and Talmud 2002). This measure is the average proportion of democratic states in politically relevant networks (Maoz 2001). Second, we employed the Singer, Bremer, and

Stuckey (1972) measure of capability concentration (calculated for the entire system, rather than for the major power system only).[17] The results of these analyses are given in table 3.7 below.

The results of table 3.7 lend support to some of our hypotheses but offer surprising findings for other hypotheses. Alliance density increases the frequency of MIDs during the entire period and in the twentieth century. Alliance density also increases the frequency of war in the twentieth century. Ethnic density, again in support of our hypothesis, has an inverse impact on the frequency of MIDs in the entire period and in the twentieth century. It also has a negative impact on war for the entire period. Yet ethnic density has a marginally significant positive effect on war in the twentieth century, in contrast to the expected relationship. Democratic networks have a negative impact on MIDs and wars, especially in the twentieth century, thus lending support to the systemic version of the democratic peace proposition.

Alliance polarization has a significantly positive and fairly robust impact on MID and war frequency, thus lending greater credence to the argument that as the system approaches bipolarity it is more likely to be conflict-ridden than when it is multipolar in nature. However, in contrast to our expectation that ethnic polarization increases conflict propensities in the system, we find that as ethnic polarization increases, conflict levels tend to go down. On the contrary, as the system becomes more ethnically diverse, the level of conflict tends to go up. This requires some theoretical exploration. This is, however, beyond the scope of the present chapter. Finally, capability concentration levels are not related to conflict in the system. Again, this is in contrast to the findings on the effect of capability concentration on war found in previous studies.

These results suggest a number of interesting theoretical propositions. We do not wish to delve into them right now as this analysis was only a demonstration of the potential theoretical and methodological contribution of network approaches and network-based measures to the study of traditional international relations issues. But they certainly warrant additional attention. This will be the focus of future studies.

CONCLUSION

In this study the networks approach was shown to offer a comprehensive framework that offers considerable potential for dealing with a wide variety of issues in international politics. In particular:

1. It offers us strategies for systematic mapping of change and stability in international politics in terms of a wide variety of relational and affiliational attributes.

Table 3.7. The Effects of Alliance and Ethnic Network Indicators on the Frequency of MIDs and Wars, 1816–2000: Autoregressive Poisson Regression

Independent Variable	Entire Period	19th Century	20th Century
Number of MID Dyads per year (Autoregressive Poisson Model)			
Density Measures			
Constant	4.496**	5.705**	3.072**
	(0.208)	(1.306)	(0.276)
Alliance Density	1.066**	−1.609	1.902**
	0.257)	(1.570)	(0.267)
Ethnic Density	−8.140**	−13.651**	1.876
	(0.718)	(4.249)	(1.232)
Democratic Networks	−0.885*	−2.297	−0.543
Density	(0.460)	(1.539)	(0.570)
Rho 1	0.801**	0.307**	0.775**
	(0.043)	(0.110)	(0.064)
N	184	82	102
Pseudo R^2	0.800	0.236	0.698
Polarization Indices			
Constant	4.775**	3.199**	4.587**
	(0.179)	(0.802)	(0.203)
Alliance NPI	16.600**	−2.379	16.528**
	(1.530)	(4.348)	(1.618)
Ethnic NPI	−11.057**	−2.637*	−9.690**
	(0.585)	(1.362)	(0.827)
Capability Concentration	−0.078	1.197	−0.254
	(0.433)	(2.223)	(0.457)
Rho 1	0.669**	0.096	0.726**
	(0.057)	(0.115)	(0.074)
N	179	82	97
Pseudo R^2	0.766	0.266	0.717
Number of War Dyads per Year			
Density Measures			
Constant	2.911**	5.209**	3.917**
	(0.650)	(1.328)	(1.474)
Alliance Density	−0.231	6.631	2.251*
	(0.756)	(4.159)	(0.917)
Ethnic Density	−5.254**	−27.600	8.389+
	(1.845)	(7.795)	(5.030)
Democratic Network	−2.160+	−0.332	−7.315**
Density	(1.297)	(2.230)	(2.019)
Rho 1	0.763**	0.382**	0.659**
	(0.049)	(0.108)	(0.089)
N	184	82	102
Adjusted R^2	0.581	0.238	0.474

(*continued*)

Table 3.7.   The Effects of Alliance and Ethnic Network Indicators on the Frequency of MIDs and Wars, 1816–2000: Autoregressive Poisson Regression (*continued*)

Independent Variable	Entire Period	19th Century	20th Century
Polarization Indices			
Constant	1.271**	0.757	0.898
	(0.437)	(2.132)	(0.676)
Alliance NPI	33.111**	8.613	31.107**
	(3.179)	(13.825)	(3.606)
Ethnic NPI	−13.301**	−8.110[+]	3.621[+]
	(1.226)	(4.245)	(1.994)
Capability Concentration	1.352	5.928	−1.202
	(0.998)	(5.577)	(1.154)
Rho 1	0.649**	0.204	0.660**
	(0.058)	(0.117)	(0.080)
N	179	82	102
Adjusted R^2	0.607	0.123	0.647

2. It offers us a meaningful way to compare a large number of relationships and attributes of members of the system across space and over time.

3. It allows a comprehensive framework for dealing with the level of analysis problem in international politics.

4. It offers new insights into the relationship between structural features of the international system and the behaviors of its members.

As noted, this is a feasibility study. It offers a mere demonstration of the power of the social networks approach to international politics. It is important to note that this approach would probably require significant modifications to fit into the modes of analysis that are required in order meaningfully to analyze international politics. We have to develop methodologies that allow comparisons of networks over time with varying numbers of actors. We need to develop new measures that are better suited to tap the complexities of the international system and its subsystems. However, as some sociologists who examined the world system using a network approach have demonstrated, the potential of this approach is extremely promising. Subsequent studies will demonstrate more clearly to what extent this approach can sharpen our methodological tools and empirical knowledge of the evolution of world politics.

NOTES

1. A previous version of this paper was presented at a conference on new directions in international relations, February 21–23, 2003, Yale University. We wish to

thank the participants of the conference for their comments. We thank in particular Bruce Russett and Alex Mintz for their comments and suggestions. Lior Elazar has been our research assistant. His work on the data management for this study is appreciated.

2. This is a brief review of the network literature. Wasserman and Faust (1994) offer a comprehensive review of social network studies. Knoke (1990) offers a comprehensive review of the use of network approaches in political science.

3. There are a number of examples of studies in international politics that address network analytic problems, albeit in different terms. Schrodt and Mintz (1988) examined conditional probability models of interdependence based on sets of dyadic interactions. Lee, Muncaster, and Zinnes (1994) modeled triadic hostility-friendship relationships among states in a manner that examines ties between direct and indirect relations. However, these examples do not use network analytic approaches or measures.

4. The updated alliance data covering the 1816–2000 period is available from the COW2 website at: http://cow2.la.psu.edu/.

5. Each number next to a circle represents a state number, using the COW national units index. A line between two states represents an alliance of any type between them. States that have no ties are nonaligned.

6. Diagonal entries are set to zero, because nonzero entries on the main diagonal have a special meaning in network analysis.

7. We discuss below problems of interpreting reachability matrices in the context of such links as alliances, and ways of dealing with these problems.

8. This is a reduced matrix for the purpose of illustration. The full matrix is a $N \times k$ matrix with N the total number of actors in the system and k the number of cliques. In our formulation, the clique affiliation matrix is organized such that the columns are ordered by declining sizes of cliques.

9. Proportion of all alliance ties in the alliance network the members of which share one or more ethnic group that accounts for at least 10 percent of their respective populations.

10. Proportion of all network members that share one or more ethnic group that accounts for at least 10 percent of their population that also share an alliance tie.

11. We examine only alliances endogenous to the subsystem. We do not examine, although this could be done quite easily, alliance ties between subsystem members and external actors.

12. See, for example, Bremer 1992, 1993; Maoz and Russett 1992, 1993; Russett and Oneal 2001; Bennett and Stam 2000b; Diehl and Goertz 2000; Maoz and Mor 2002.

13. It must be noted that there are ways of developing triadic, quadradic, and other types of analyses. But we genrally refer to these as subsystemic analyses.

14. Briefly, Maoz (2001) defines a democratic network as a subset of a politically relevant clique (in which all members are either contiguous or include major and regional powers) that is made up of democratic states. The density of democratic cliques is the average proportion of democratic cliques over the political relevant cliques.

15. See e.g., the articles in Vasquez and Elman (2002). The classical debate is that between Waltz (1964) and Deutsch and Singer (1964).

16. These have been updated with the MID 3.02 dataset. See http://cow2.la .psu.edu/.

17. Capability data are also derived from the updated COW national military capabilities dataset at the COW2 website.

4

Visualization in International Relations

Kristian Skrede Gleditsch and Michael D. Ward

Geographical features exert a strong influence on the ways in which actors in international politics interact with one another, yet our empirical analyses often ignore such aspects. We demonstrate how visualization can help reveal spatial patterns in political processes, which in turn can help researchers discover new features of these processes that are not apparent from aggregate analysis and standard representations of the data. We review how maps can help display, identify, and highlight trends in political data, and illustrate exploratory and descriptive spatial statistical techniques. Our example is based on the relationship between democracy and violent conflict. We demonstrate that although conflict and democracy may not be related at the level of individual states, once we look at the regional level and take into account where conflict is located, we find considerable overlap between areas where democracies cluster and regions where stable peace prevails.

International relations take place within geographical space, and geographical features shape the ways in which actors in international politics interact with one another. Empirical data, however, are rarely arranged in ways that reflect their spatial characteristics, and empirical analyses all too often tend to ignore the geographical features of the substantive phenomena in which we are interested. In this chapter, we demonstrate how geographical visualization of political data can allow researchers both to represent key aspects of the phenomena of interest and discover new features that are neither apparent from the data in numerical form nor from the results from aggregate analyses. We provide a review of how to use maps to display, identify, and highlight trends in political data, and illustrate some techniques of exploratory and descriptive analysis of spatial statistical approaches. Our overview is idiosyncratic, and our examples are based on our work on democracy and violent conflict. We demonstrate how zones of peace and zones of democratic rule tend to overlap, once researchers look at the geographic features of where conflict is located. Despite the questionable value of much that has purported to be a "geographical" approach to politics, we suggest that a return to a focus on the role of space and geography may help advance the scientific study of world politics.

MAPS AS MODELS OF THE WORLD

Maps can be seen as models representing geographic information about the world. Such devices have been used since the dawn of time, and maps may have been one of the earliest forms of shared information. From early cave paintings and navigation devices, to modern Geographical Information Systems, information about where things are located in relation to other things has been an essential part of daily life. The fifteenth-century development of the printing press made it possible to share this kind information even more widely than before, helping to bring about more systematic navigation and discovery. The twentieth-century development of visually displayed computer environments made it possible further to develop and disseminate geographic information.[1]

Like all models, maps highlight particular features, and simplify the representation of a complex world. Although models are theoretical abstractions that leave out many features of the system they represent, good models have invaluable practical applications. The father of geology, William Smith, for example, expressed his theory of the geological strata or the order of layers of rock through the first geological map, "A Delineation of the Strata of England and Wales" (1815), which had major consequences for the development of the early industries in the nineteenth century.[2] The practical value of good and accurate maps in international politics is illustrated by the reliance on geographic information in the precision bombing employed so extensively in the recent U.S.-led military campaigns, as well as the spectacular failure of the accidental NATO bombing of the Chinese embassy in Belgrade on 7 May 1999.[3]

Like all models, maps can also be helpful analytical devices for understanding the world. *The State of the World Atlas* (Smith and Kidron 2003) and *The State of War and Peace Atlas/Penguin Atlas of War and Peace* (Smith 2003) present maps as a way of describing political data. Such topical atlases have frequently been used in classrooms around the world. Many scholars and writers tend to use maps primarily as a method of displaying data that is putatively less boring to readers than frequency tables. Beyond mere description, however, maps can often serve to alert us to the ways in which many aspects of politics have clear spatial patterns. Often, patterns in data may not be obvious from the raw data alone without geographical visualization. Maps and geographical statistics can often help us see spatial relationships that would not be immediately obvious from the raw data. Perhaps the most famous early use of a map to display data in nonobvious ways was British physician John Snow's map of deaths from cholera in an epidemic in London in the mid-nineteenth century. By mapping the location of each death in an affected neighborhood, "Snow observed that cholera occurred almost entirely among those who lived near (and drank from) the Broad Street water pump. He had the handle of the contaminated pump removed, ending the neighborhood epidemic which had taken more than 500 lives" (Tufte 1983, 24).

Our experiences from our own research convince us that there are many similar examples in the study of international relations. In a previous research project on the diffusion of democracy (O'Loughlin et al. 1998), we created a movie of annual slides that displayed trends in transitions to democracy and autocracy over time.[4] A colleague (George Modelski) who viewed an early version of the movie (Ward et al. 1996) thought "something" did not look right with values for Russia in 1991. Upon reexamining the original data we found that the values of two indices for Russia had been transposed in the original Polity III data, as well as a host of other errors, leading to an improvement in the data source.

Likewise, geographical mapping can help alert us to conceptual flaws in the research design or the way that an issue is studied. A wealth of studies, for example, have examined the potential diffusion of conflict from the initial set of combatants to other states, using borders as a proxy for interaction opportunities. However, in most countries, the area where the conflict actually occurs rarely encompasses the whole state. In the case of large countries such as Russia, where violent conflicts may be concentrated on a small share of its territory such as Chechnya, it is clearly unreasonable to expect that all contiguous neighboring states should be exposed to spill-over effects from the conflict. While Finland, Norway, and Mongolia are all contiguous neighbors, their boundaries with Russia are thousands of kilometers away from the location of the conflict in Chechnya. Testing theories about the diffusion of conflict in this sense requires location-specific conflict data (see Buhaug and Gates 2002, Gleditsch 2002, Gleditsch and Ward 2001). Maps can also reveal how the practice of taking nation-states as the only units of interest can be seriously flawed. Mapping conventional data of African states prior to 1974 will invariably show the Portuguese colonies of Angola and Mozambique as blank nonentities. If we are interested in how externalities from neighbors in conflict, such as refugee flows, influence the risk of civil war, however, we should not restrict ourselves only to flows from independent states (see Sale-hyan and Gleditsch 2003). For both of these countries, conflict and refugee flows to neighboring states preceded national independence.

Despite the centrality of geographical factors, the study of geography as a component of world politics was to a large extent discredited by the use and abuse of geopolitics prior to World War II. The term *geopolitics* was introduced by Kjellén (1916), who applied evolutionary notions to the putative organic nature of states. Kjellén was influenced by Ratzel's concept of *Lebensraum*, or the presumption that states had an innate propensity to seek growth and territorial expansion. Such thoughts gained considerable influence in scholarly and political circles around the turn of the twentieth century. Kjellén's ideas were especially salient with a retired German general and university professor, Haushofer who founded the *Zeitschrift für Geopolitik*. Geopolitics as introduced by Ratzel, Kjellén, and especially Haushofer was used to rationalize and provide a putatively scientific basis for Hitler's expansionist foreign policy (e.g., Østerud 1988).[5] The German geopolitical tradition had an Anglo-Saxon counterpart in Mackinder's (1904) theory that the pivotal area in the closed "Heartland of Euro-Asia" was the key to world power, Mahan's (1890) works on the role of sea power, and Spykman's (1944) work on the Rimland, emphasized the importance of control over the Eurasian coastal regions. Although an emphasis on the geographical bases of military strategy has survived in the field of strategic studies (see Gray 1999), the legacy of World War II left theories relating geography and politics rather out of favor in both policy and academic circles.

Much of the work on geopolitics is indeed of questionable analytical value. Political misuses, however, should not blind us to the idea that geography plays an important role in world politics. A more interesting antecedent is the work by Lewis Fry Richardson (1960)—a physicist turned meteorologist who later developed an interest in psychology and conflict. Richardson was the first to undertake empirical analysis of the spatial aspects of *deadly quarrels* or violent conflicts. Richardson noted a strong relationship between a state's conflict proneness and its number of borders. He later expanded on the relationship between configuration and opportunities for conflict in an insightful theoretical essay on spatial topology and conflict (Richardson 1942).[6] Scholars have recently begun to reexplore international conflict using a standpoint that encourages understanding the context of world politics from a spatial perspective (see Buhaug and Gates 2002, Cederman 1997, Diehl 1992, 1999, Gleditsch 2002, Gleditsch and Ward 2000, Hensel 2000, Maoz 1996, Siverson and Starr 1991, Starr 1997, Ward and Gleditsch 2002). In the remainder of this chapter, we review how visualization and insights about spatial processes can help improve our understanding about the linkages between democracy and conflict. We start with an overview of basic geographic visualization.

MAPS AS GRAPHICAL REPRESENTATIONS OF THE WORLD

A first step to look for spatial patterns in political variables is simply to map the data. This may be seen in broad analogy to using a scatterplot. In a scatterplot, we use visual patterns to examine heuristically the relationship *between variables*, which may suggest more formal relationships as well as the degree of variation. Similarly, a map examines the distribution *among units* for the variable and allows us to see whether there appears to be a geographical pattern to the distribution over the spatial units.

Map 4.1 presents a map of data for the number of consecutive years of peace that a country has experienced without involvement in war in 1996. War is here defined as conflict involving more than 1,000 casualties in a calendar year. The data displayed are based on a modified compilation of conflict data from the Correlates of War project and the Department of Peace and Conflict resolutions at Uppsala University, as explained in Gleditsch (2002, 2004).

The world map of consecutive years in 1996 is clearly not homogeneous, nor does the length of time at peace vary randomly across space. There appear to be zones of stable peace as well as zones of conflict or a more tenuous "absence of war." As can be seen, we find high levels of years at peace among countries in Europe and to a lesser extent in the Western Hemisphere. At the same time, we find many countries with few years of consecutive peace—reflecting fairly recent conflict involvements—across a band of countries in Africa, the Middle East, and Asia. What emerges from this visual display of peace and conflict over time is that the distribution of peace and conflict shows clear spatial patterns. Although most research tends to look for relationships between attributes of countries and violent conflict, the distribution of conflict itself across countries seems strongly associated with regional context. Most wars tend to be fought between neighboring states, and the prospects of conflict are changed by processes in neighboring states. Civil wars in India, for example, may not stem from problems with its political institutions, but the fact that it is next to an antagonistic neighbor (Pakistan) which is willing to supply insurgents with resources. As such, it seems downright misleading to treat countries as isolated from their broader regional context, or independent observations irrespective of location, as most statistical analyses of conflict tend to do (see Beck and Tucker 1996, Gleditsch and Ward 2000, Ward and Gleditsch 2002).

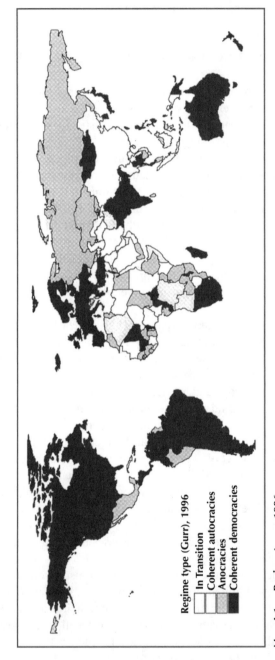

Regime type (Gurr), 1996

☐ In Transition
☐ Coherent autocracies
▨ Anocracies
■ Coherent democracies

Map 4.1. Regime types, 1996

Are these zones of conflict and peace associated with other variables that appear to cluster geographically? Map 4.2 displays the distribution of political institutions as indicated by the tripartite typology suggested by Jaggers and Gurr (1995) of coherent democracies, coherent autocracies, and incoherent "anocracies," combining features of both democratic and autocratic polities, based on the Polity data. Operationally, these categories are defined based on a 21-point scale of institutionalized democracy ranging from −10 to 10, where coherent democracies have scores above 6 and coherent autocracies have scores below −6.[7] As can be seen, political institutions do not appear to be randomly distributed in space. Rather, we find clear regions of coherent democracies and regions of autocracies.

Whereas Eastern Europe and Latin America look relatively democratic in 1996, a map of the prior 10 years would have shown a dramatically different picture. Map 4.2, indicating changes in the 21-point institutionalized democracy scale from 1986 to 1996, suggests a clear spatial pattern to changes over the period. This raises doubts as to whether the individual transitions really are independent events, or whether transitions or changes in one state may have influenced the likelihood of transitions among another states (see Gleditsch 2002, Gleditsch and Ward 2003, O'Loughlin et al. 1998).

In what ways do these visual displays of data on democracy and conflict change the conclusions we would reach about their relationship from traditional ways of looking at the data? A large amount of ink has been spilled over whether the democratic peace is a dyadic phenomenon (pertaining to pairs of states) or a monadic phenomenon (applicable to individual countries). Many analysts have argued that democracy only matters for the conflict behavior of states toward other democracies, or at the so-called dyadic level (e.g., Ray 2000, Rousseau et al. 1996). However, democratic institutions are attributes of nation-states and not dyadic characteristics. Efforts to measure democracy at the dyadic level have led to some convoluted measures of "joint democracy" of questionable validity. Although researchers have tried to come up with theoretical arguments for why the least democratic state determines the character of interactions between states (this is sometimes referred to as the weak-link argument, see Oneal and Russett 1997), ideally one would like to have clearer theoretical accounts of when democracies are more or less likely to experience conflict.

The spatial approach helps one to understand when a relationship should be expected to hold between democracy and conflict. It turns out that even though there is not a particularly strong association between conflict and democracy at the level of individual countries in the data, we find a clear relationship between institutions and conflict at the regional level. Zones of democracy—where democratic states are consistently surrounded by other

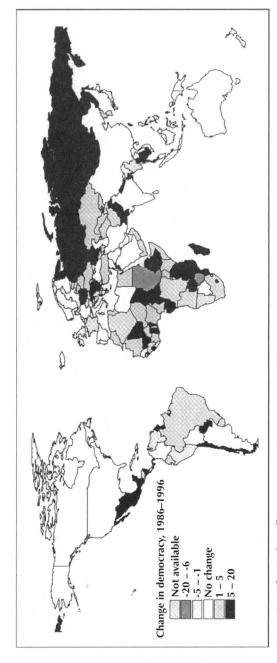

Change in democracy, 1986–1996

Not available
-20 – -6
-5 – -1
No change
1 – 5
5 – 20

Map 4.2. Change in Polity Democracy Score, 1986 to 1996

democratic states—go together with zones of peace, or regions with states that all have a high number of consecutive years of peace. Stated differently, democracies that are located among other democracies face few security concerns, while democracies in mixed zones are much more likely to find themselves involved in conflict. A large body of work in international relations has set forward such hypotheses about attributes of regions and their prospects for conflict and peace (see Kacowicz 1998, Lake and Morgan 1997, Solingen 1998), but it is hard to discern these relationships from the raw data or a scatterplot of the individual observations, taken out of their spatial context. Taking the information about the geographical location into account through displaying data on a map, however, makes it easier both to see spatial patterns for single variables as well as to explore whether these may be related to spatial patterns on other variables.

The relationships gleaned from the spatial associations can also serve as a point of departure for further theoretical research. Cederman and Gleditsch (2004) use the insights from empirical estimates of spatial relationship to calibrate a computational model of the emergence of democracy in the international system. The last two centuries have witnessed a remarkable growth in the number of states governed by democratic institutions within the international system. Whereas only about 5 percent of the world's states could be characterized as democratic at the outset of the nineteenth century, about half of the states in the contemporary world qualify as democracies by common definitions of the term. What mechanisms are required to allow a small set of initial democracies to survive, when faced with the threat of conquest from other states?

Cederman and Gleditsch (2004) show that it is almost impossible to "grow" democracies in a hostile international system unless one introduces locally dependent transition probabilities, where the likelihood of transitions from autocracy to democracy are not fixed, but increase when autocracies are located in more democratic zones. The main feature driving their results is that a locally dependent regime change mechanism brings about more democracies in proximity to other democratic states. This increasing geographical clustering in turn allows initial clusters of democracies to capitalize on the separate peace between democracies and to rely on collective defense against other states and reduce their threat of conquest from autocracies. The geographical clustering that emerges in the computational model is critical for replicating the observed changes in democracy in the international system, but the role of spatial configuration would not have been clear without the prior empirical work on the spatial relationship of democracy and conflict.

We conclude this section by a brief review of some practical considerations in using maps to summarize information. Simple descriptions by color maps such as maps 4.1–3 are sometimes called *choropleth* maps (from Greek *choros*/χόρος meaning area and *plethos*/πλέθος, which is quantity).[8] Despite the wide availability of tools for generating maps, these tools by themselves carry few guidelines for the production of quality maps. Merely going with default options is rarely desirable, and never optimal. Bertin (1983), Cleveland (1993, 1994), and Tufte (1983, 1990, 1997) provide good references for some general principles of visualization that apply to maps as well.[9] One of the biggest challenges is the choice of suitable color and shading. Brewer (1994a, 1994b)[10] has done research on the visual and analytic information necessary for the production of both screen and print quality color maps. Geography and regional science journals typically use special referees to review the quality of graphics, especially maps submitted for publication. Publishing maps can also present problems. In our experience, editors often like visual color displays, but are reluctant to include color representations in scholarly publications simply because of cost constraints. Such displays require the actual production process to move from a single printing pass that lays down black ink, to several that lay down the different colors to be produced.[11] Grayscale maps are possible for many applications, but will not allow the same number of gradations as color maps, a point visible in the graphics in this chapter, as well.

SPATIAL STATISTICS AND VISUALIZATION

Whereas numbers in a table usually require additional analysis to convey meaningful information, maps can be informative and allow quick, intuitive transmission of information with little need for additional processing. In some cases, displaying the raw data on a map itself might suffice to convey important aspects of the spatial properties of relationships. In other cases, spatial relationships in the data may be summarized more clearly by assessing clustering more formally. Methods for spatial statistical analysis of data on geographical units have been developed in several fields, ranging from regional science applications, ecology, to applied statistical work on the restoration of partial images (see Cressie 1991 for a comprehensive review).[12] Spatial relationships may be described at two levels. We may first ask whether there is a nonrandom spatial pattern that emerges at the global level. In this case, we are interested in whether the distribution, or the values for countries over the entire map of observations, appears to be distributed in a nonrandom geographical pattern. Global clustering indicates that we are dealing with features that cluster in the aggregate, but do not indicate where features cluster geographically. Local measures of geographical association help discern cases where states with "high" or "low" values are surrounded by states with similar values. These can help indicate specific regions that exhibit different forms of clustering.

Representing Space

Before we can turn to describing these two aspects of spatial clustering from empirical data, we first need a more formal representation of space and the relationship between entities. In international relations, it is usually substantively meaningful to assume that closer entities are more connected than far away units. Since distance is such a powerful modifier of the opportunities for positive and negative interaction, we can identify the most important relationships between states by examining dependence determined by geographical proximity. More formally, we can assume a local Markov random field, where observations are dependent if they are geographic neighbors (see Isham 1981). In the case of conflict, for example, this would imply that the likelihood of war in Guinea would change depending on whether neighboring states such as Sierra Leone are at war, but not be affected by conflict in remote countries such as Colombia.

Geographical proximity between states can be identified in many possible ways, including direct contiguity or measures of distance between particular points. We have previously developed a data set on measuring distance systematically based on the shortest distance between the two closest physical locations for every pair of independent polities between 1875 and 1996 (see Gleditsch and Ward 2001). The database records the shortest distance in statute kilometers between points on the outer boundaries for two polities, regardless of whether the states are separated by land or sea, given the borders in place in a particular time period. Actual shared borders are coded as having distances of zero. The minimum distance framework has advantages both over measures of contiguity that ignore any distances between states that do not share a direct border (e.g., Luxembourg and the Netherlands) and over continuous distance data based on some form of mid-points for each state such as capital cities, which in some cases may be quite far from the outer boundaries and understate the proximity between states (e.g., the distance between Washington, D.C., and La Havana clearly understates that Cuba is less than 100 miles off the coast of Florida).[13] The minimum distance database can be used both to derive continuous data on distances as well as to generate binary or categorized contiguity data, and the analyst can vary the cut-off points for what is to be considered contiguous and weigh entries in proportion to their degree of closeness.

For an applied example, consider the connectives for polities in the Middle East identified in table 4.1. For simplicity, we will in this example consider these fifteen states as a separate subsystem, ignoring for the time being linkages that these actors have to other states.[14] Viewing the columns of this table, from left to right, for each row or state indicates the additional entities that would be considered connected, as the strict definition of land borders in the second column is expanded to increasingly more inclusive criteria for proximity or closeness. As can be seen, there are many pairs of states that are not connected by a strict criterion of direct contiguity that would be considered connected with a slightly more inclusive threshold. Israel, for example, does not have a land border with Iraq and Saudi Arabia, but expanding the threshold to a higher cut-off value (e.g., 50 km or 475 km) makes these pairs connected. Unlike other fixed alternatives, the minimum distance data allow researchers to set the threshold for relevance and test the sensitivity to differences in operationalization. The relevant distance or metric for a given problem is typically not known with certainty in advance, and may differ considerably between research questions and over time.

Data on distance can be converted to a graph or matrix representation. The information in the minimum distance data as displayed table 4.1 can be represented numerically in the form of a spatial connectivity matrix to study relations between the actors.[15] Generally stated, for a set $S = \{1, \ldots, n\}$ of N spatial units, a connectivity matrix is a $n \times n$ matrix $\mathbf{W}$ which entries w_{ij} acquires nonzero values if units i and j are somehow considered to be connected, adjacent, or associated. The binary connectivity matrix $\mathbf{W}$ is similar to the idea of an "adjacency matrix" in graph theory (e.g., Harary, Norman, and Cartright 1965). Bavaud (1998) stresses the resemblance of connectivity matrixes and Markov chains, and sets forward some important proofs on their properties.[16] Equation 2 displays a binary spatial connectivity matrix for the Middle East based on land borders or a threshold for relevance of 0 km.[17] The binary spatial connectivity matrix $\mathbf{W}$ in (2) provides a network representation of the linkages among all the fifteen polities in the Middle Eastern subsystem. It describes not only the first order contiguities but also permits derivation of nth order contiguities or the "neighbors of neighbors" by powering the matrix.[18] Connectivity matrixes may also be defined by metrics other than Euclidean distances, for example alliances, international trade, cultural similarity, or media networks. In the next section, we outline how such a connectivity matrix can be used in visualization and statistical analyses.

Assessing Clustering at the Global Level

Given a connectivity matrix for relations between states, it is possible to calculate a variety of spatial statistics. To assess the extent of global clustering

Table 4.1. Connectivities for Middle Eastern States

Reference Country	Land Border	States Connected to Reference Country, Cumulative		
		50 km	475 km	950 km
Bahrain	Saudi Arabia	Qatar	Iran, Iraq, Kuwait, Oman, United Arab Emirates	Yemen
Egypt	Israel, Libya, Sudan	Saudi Arabia, Jordan	Lebanon, Syria, Cyprus, Greece, Chad	Iraq, Turkey, Eritrea, Ethiopia
Iran	Afghanistan, Armenia, Azerbaijan, Iraq, Pakistan, Turkmenistan, Turkey	Kuwait	Bahrain, Georgia, Kazakhstan, Kuwait, Oman, Qatar, Russia, Syria, Saudi Arabia, United Arab Emirates, Uzbekistan	Cyprus, India, Jordan, Lebanon, Ukraine, Tajikistan
Iraq	Iran, Jordan, Kuwait, Saudi-Arabia, Syria, Turkey		Armenia, Azerbaijan, Bahrain, Georgia, Israel, Lebanon	Cyprus, Egypt, Iraq, Kazakhstan, Oman, Qatar, Russia, Turkmenistan, United Arab Emirates
Israel	Egypt, Jordan, Lebanon, Syria	Saudi Arabia	Cyprus, Iraq, Turkey	Greece, Sudan, Libya
Jordan	Iraq, Israel, Lebanon, Saudi Arabia	Egypt	Cyprus, Turkey	Armenia, Greece, Iran, Kuwait, Sudan
Kuwait	Iraq, Saudi Arabia	Iran	Bahrain, Qatar	Jordan, Oman, Syria, Turkey, United Arab Emirates

(continued)

Table 4.1. Connectivities for Middle Eastern States (continued)

Reference Country	Land Border	States Connected to Reference Country, Cumulative		
		50 km	475 km	950 km
Lebanon	Israel, Jordan, Syria		Cyprus, Egypt, Iraq, Saudi Arabia, Turkey	Greece, Iran
Oman	Saudi Arabia, United Arab Emirates, Yemen		Pakistan, Iran, Qatar	Afghanistan, Bahrain, India, Iraq, Kuwait, Somalia
Qatar	Saudi Arabia	Bahrain	Iran, Kuwait, Oman, United Arab Emirates	Iraq
Saudi Arabia	Bahrain, Iraq, Kuwait, Jordan, Oman, Qatar, United Arab Emirates, Yemen	Egypt, Israel	Djibouti, Ethiopia, Eritrea, Iran, Lebanon, Sudan, Syria	Armenia, Azerbaijan, Cyprus, Pakistan, Somalia, Turkey
Syria	Iraq, Israel, Jordan, Lebanon, Turkey		Armenia, Cyprus, Egypt, Iran, Saudi Arabia	Azerbaijan, Georgia, Kuwait, Russia, Ukraine
Turkey	Armenia, Azerbaijan, Bulgaria, Greece, Georgia, Iran, Iraq, Syria		Albania, Cyprus, Israel, Lebanon, Jordan, Macedonia, Moldova, Romania, Russia, Saudi Arabia, Yugoslavia	Bosnia, Czech Republic, Croatia, Hungary, Egypt, Italy, Kazakhstan, Kuwait, Libya, Poland, Slovenia, Turkmenistan.
United Arab Emirates	Oman, Saudi Arabia		Iran, Bahrain, Yemen, Qatar	Afghanistan, Iraq, Kuwait, Pakistan
Yemen	Oman, Saudi Arabia		Ethiopia, Qatar, United Arab Emirates	Bahrain, Sudan

	Bahrain	Egypt	Iran	Iraq	Israel	Jordan	Kuwait	Lebanon	Qatar	Oman	Saudi Arabia	Syria	Turkey	United Arab Emirates	Yemen	
	0	0	0	0	0	0	0	0	0	0	1	0	0	0	0	Bahrain
	0	0	0	0	1	0	0	0	0	0	1	0	0	0	0	Egypt
	0	0	0	1	0	0	0	0	0	0	0	0	1	0	0	Iran
	0	0	1	0	0	1	1	0	0	0	1	1	1	0	0	Iraq
	0	1	0	0	0	1	0	1	0	0	0	1	0	0	0	Israel
	0	0	0	1	1	0	0	1	0	0	1	1	0	0	0	Jordan
	0	0	0	1	0	0	0	0	0	0	1	0	0	0	0	Kuwait
$\mathbf{W} =$	0	0	0	0	1	1	0	0	0	0	0	1	0	0	0	Lebanon
	0	0	0	0	0	0	0	0	0	0	1	0	0	1	1	Qatar
	0	0	0	0	0	0	0	0	0	0	1	0	0	0	0	Oman
	1	1	0	1	0	1	1	0	1	1	0	0	0	1	1	Saudi Arabia
	0	0	0	1	1	1	0	1	0	0	0	0	1	0	0	Syria
	0	0	0	1	0	1	0	0	0	0	0	1	0	0	0	Turkey
	0	0	0	0	0	0	0	0	1	0	1	0	0	0	0	United Arab Emirates
	0	0	0	0	0	0	0	0	1	0	1	0	0	0	0	Yemen

among geographical units for some input variable x, the most common descriptive statistic is the so-called Moran's (1950) I coefficient defined as

$$I = \frac{n}{\sum_i \sum_j \tilde{w}_{ij}} \sum_i \sum_j \tilde{w}_{ij} \frac{(x_i - \bar{x})(x_j - \bar{x})}{\sum_i (x_i - \bar{x})^2} \quad (5)$$

where $\tilde{w}_{ij}$ denotes an element $[i, j]$ of a row-standardized matrix $\tilde{\mathbf{W}}$ that acquires a nonzero value if units i and j are contiguous. The value of the Moran's I statistic can be seen as a correlation coefficient of the value x_i for each unit i with its J neighboring entities x_j. However, the coefficient is not bounded by ± 1, and the expected value $E(I)$ is $\frac{-1}{N-1}$ rather than 0. The expected value of the variance $E\sigma_I^2$ turns out to be somewhat cumbersome to express, and depends upon sampling assumptions,[19] but the estimated standard error of the Moran's I statistic $\sqrt{VI} = E\sigma_I^2 - EI^2$ allows significance tests of the extent to which the observed levels of global clustering in a given sample as measured by Moran's I differ from the null hypothesis of no spatial clustering.

For level of democracy in 1996, Moran's I is 0.333 ($Z = 10.777$). For consecutive years of peace in 1996, Moran's I is 0.214 ($Z = 7.02$). The high values of the Moran's I and the corresponding Z scores indicate significant global clustering in both the time of peace and the levels of democracy. In other words, the likelihood of observing whether a given country will be democratic or not differs according to the properties of neighboring countries in the observed data.[20] The pattern seems generally consistent and robust between different contiguity specifications as well as over time (see Gleditsch 2002, Gleditsch and Ward 2000).

Assessing Clustering at a Local Level

The Moran's I statistics indicate that democracy and time at peace are clustered geographically in the aggregate, but these measures do not by themselves indicate where these aspects cluster geographically in different "zones" or regions. The Moran's I is composed by aggregating the similarity of each observation with its neighbors, but it is possible to examine the local components of the overall clustering separately.

One common indicator of local clustering of the values of some variable around some location is the so-called G_i^* statistic (Ord and Getis 1995), defined as

$$G_i^* = \frac{\sum_j w_{ij} x_j - \sum_i (w_{ij} + w_{ii}) \bar{x}}{\hat{\sigma}_x \sqrt{n \sum_j w_{ij}^2 - \sum_i w_{ij}^2 / (n-1)}} \qquad (4)$$

where w_{ij} denotes element $[i, j]$ in a binary connectivity matrix $\mathbf{W}$ and x_j denotes an observation at location j. The G_i^* statistic indicates the extent to which similarly valued observations are clustered for a set of J entities around a particular observation i.[21] A positive value for the G_i^* statistic at a particular location implies spatial clustering of high values around that location, while a negative value indicates a spatial grouping of low values. The values of the G_i^* statistic can be interpreted as a standardized Z-score, where large values indicate significant local clustering around observation i.

Looking at the local clustering in the time at peace that countries have experienced since either the last case of conflict involvement or the emergence of statehood, local clustering helps illuminate enduring patterns of conflict and peace over time. In map 4.3, countries that display values of G_i^* indicating significant clustering of low values around particular locations are shown in black, whereas grey indicates countries surrounded by significant concentrations of high numbers of states with consecutive years of peace. Since the G_i^* statistic is distributed as a standard normal variable, we consider values to be

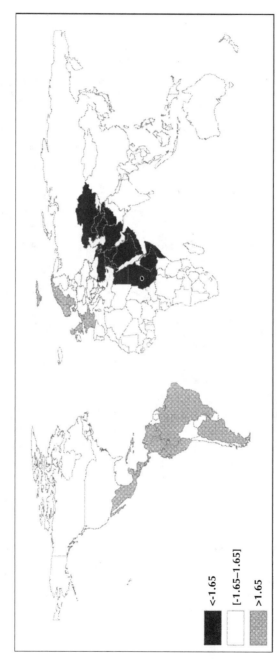

Map 4.3. Values of G_i^* for consecutive years at peace, 1992

<-1.65

[-1.65–1.65]

>1.65

significantly different from 0 if they exceed an absolute value of 1.65, that is, are significant at the 0.1 level. Map 4.4 indicates clustering of low values in the Caucasus, the Middle East, the Horn of Africa, and Eastern Africa, reflecting recent regional conflict involvement. Most notably, however, there is clear evidence of a converse clustering of high values of time at peace or longer spells without conflict involvement, or two seemingly peaceful zones, in parts of Europe and Latin America.

Map 4.4 displays the values of the G_i^* statistic indicating the localized clustering in the 21-point institutionalized democracy scale in the Polity data in 1992. In this map, gray shades are used to denote observations with values of G_i^* indicating significant positive spatial clustering, or clustering of high levels of democracy around the particular location. By contrast, black indicates observations with significant negative spatial clustering, or high concentrations of autocracy or low levels of democracy. As can be seen, there is significant positive clustering of democracy throughout most of Europe in 1992, and a similar, though less strong, tendency for positive geographical clustering of democracy in the Western Hemisphere. Conversely, these zones of democracy are matched by a belt of strong clustering of authoritarianism, stretching from Central and East Africa through the Middle East. As such, Map 4.4 yields additional evidence that the distribution of authoritarian and democratic states in the international system displays discernible zones of clusters of states with similar institutions.

Such statistics for local clustering combined with maps can be useful in alerting one to regional connections between variables. However, these are exploratory statistics, and certainly not foolproof. One of the main problems with the statistic for local clustering for units on an irregular lattice is that these are sensitive not only to the values of the variable itself but also to the total number of adjacent states, since the denominator of Equation (4) depends on the number of connectivities. France and Canada may both be quite similar to their neighboring countries. However, the fact that Canada has a much more limited number of neighboring states implies that we are less likely to see clustering around Canada as measured by G_i^*. Regional scientists appear to have ignored these problems with measures of local clustering altogether, presumably because they work with units more uniform and regularly shaped than countries. There is no such thing as a free lunch, and caution must be used when applying these tools.

Spatial Variables

Are such zones of democracy and peace associated? The Pearson correlation of the values of the local clustering of democracy and consecutive years of

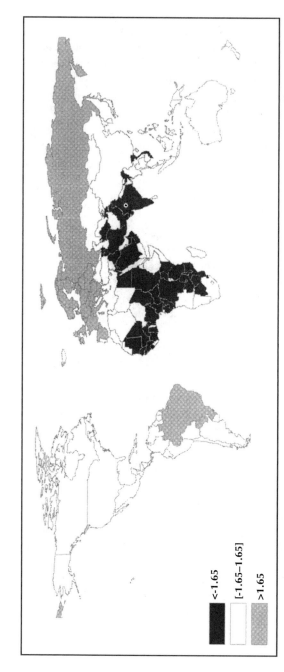

Map 4.4. Values of G_i^* for levels of democracy, 1992

<-1.65

[-1.65–1.65]

>1.65

peace in 1996 is 0.812. Such descriptive statistics are interesting as a first cut. In light of the more problematic aspects of these standardized values, however, we would rather make inferences with simpler and more transparent variables that are less sensitive to the number of adjacent units. A more general approach is to render clustering and regional differences variables that can be used in further statistical analysis.

The most common type of spatially constructed variable for a unit i is the local mean or the average of some input variable x for all units J deemed to be connected with i.[22] The resulting variable can be interpreted as a summary measure of the regional context of the variable x for each unit i. To create such a regional weighted average, the binary spatial connectivity matrix is first *row-standardized* by dividing each row by the sum of the entries in the row. This yields a so-called row-standardized connectivity matrix $\widetilde{W}$ where all the entries of each row sum to 1 (i.e., $\sum \tilde{w}_j = 1 \ \forall j \in \{1, \ldots, n\}$). The mean or average over the regional context of the variable x, denoted x^R, can then be found as the product of $\widetilde{W}$ and the vector of the values of x over the set $S = \{1, \ldots, n\}$ of the N spatial units.

Standardization of the binary connectivity matrix W has the advantage that the values of spatial variable x^R will have the same metric as the original variable, and that each individual observation x_i^R can be interpreted as a spatial mean or weighted average of all entities within the given unit i's regional context. Unlike the measures of local clustering of levels of democracy, Canada will have a score of 10 whenever all its adjacent countries have a level of democracy of 10.

Although this is by far the most common form to derive spatially based variables, merely reverting to average values based on standardized matrixes with zeros on the diagonal entries may not be warranted as a standard solution for all purposes. Other approaches can make more sense theoretically in particular settings. In many applications, the aspect of interest is not so much the *average* of the values of a variable over other entities in the region, but rather the spill-in of the *total amount* of the activities reflected by the variable in the region. In such cases, a spatial variable with the sum of values for all entities connected to i (i.e., Wx^T) might be a more appropriate measure. Enterline and Gleditsch (2000), for example, use a variable indicating the sum or total spill-in of regional conflict for each state as a measure of threat. Murdoch, Sandler, and Sargent (1997) examine how differences in the total sum of emissions from geographic neighboring countries vary the extent of collective action problems in achieving emission reductions among European states.[23]

One way to assess the importance of regional- versus country-level factors is to consider how a country's number of consecutive years of peace is affected by internal attributes and attributes of the region. A simple linear regression of national democracy and the average level of democracy among adjacent states on a state's number of years of peace yields the results in table 4.2. As can be seen, these results indicate that while both a state itself being a democracy and the extent of democracy prevailing in neighboring states increases the number of peace years, the coefficient estimate for regional democracy is greater than the coefficient for a country's own level of democracy.[24]

Visualizing geographically the results of statistical analyses can in many cases reveal additional information. In this case, we could, for example, display the predicted values from the regression in table 4.2, and examine the plot of the predicted values to assess whether taking into account the distribution of democracy among countries and its geographical distribution appears to account for regional differences in conflict and peace. As can be seen in map 4.5, this simplistic model—looking only at the political institutions of states and their neighbors, disregarding differences in time since independence and countries' history of conflict involvement—actually does a reasonable job at recovering regional patterns of the more and less conflict-prone regions reflected in map 4.6.

In other cases, we may gain better understanding of empirical relations by plotting the values of regression diagnostics such as DFFIT (indicating the change in fitted values from the regression when observation *i* is omitted) for the geographical units in our data (see, e.g., Belsley, Kuh, and Welsch 1980). In some cases, we may find clear geographical patterns to influential or deviant observations that lead to a refinement of existing theories. It is well known in comparative research on economic growth, for example, that there are regional differences. East Asia has grown more rapidly than other regions and Africa has tended to lag behind other areas of the world. Such stylized facts have often been modeled by a set of regional dummy variables (see, e.g., Barro 1991). Such regional dummies are merely proper names, and provide no explanation for such divergences. However, Easterly and Levine (1998), show that in a model taking into account effects of policies in neighboring outcomes such regional dummies are no longer significant.

Table 4.2.　Regression of Regional and National Democracy on Years of Peace, 1996

Variable	Coefficient Estimate	Standard Error
Constant	24.9134	3.534
Democracy	1.493	0.486
Regional democracy	2.310	0.792

N=151, F(2,146)=19.01

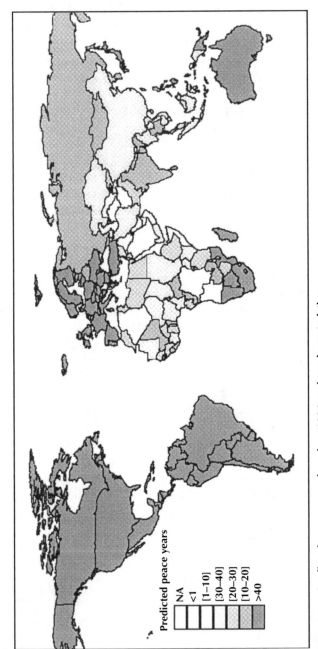

Map 4.5. Predicted peace years, based on 1996 regime characteristics

Predicted peace years

NA
<1
[1–10]
[30–40]
[20–30]
[10–20]
>40

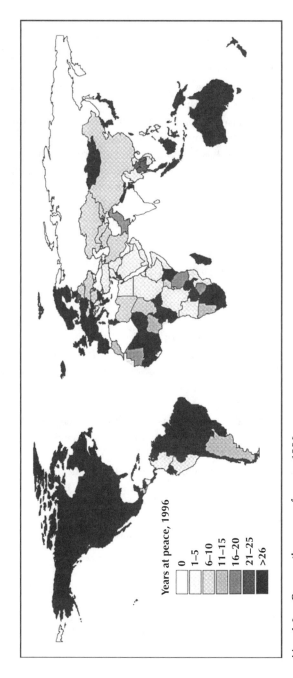

Map 4.6. Consecutive years of peace, 1996

Years at peace, 1996

0
1–5
6–10
11–15
16–20
21–25
>26

CONCLUSIONS

Maps are useful and important, but widely overlooked as a descriptive tool for the analysis of politics. Visualization of results from statistical analysis may help improve the interplay between theory and empirical research. The same may be said for spatial statistics. We have shown how careful attention to the spatial attributes of political phenomena has helped improve our understanding of the relationship between conflict and democracy and how this should be modeled. Even though we do not observe strong linkages between democracy and conflict at the country level, taking regional attributes into account indicates when we would expect democracies to be relatively secure and when the risks of conflict are larger. The zones of democracy or regions of war and peace indicated by the simple analyses here suggest that states are not independent observations, but that the interplay between states shape each nation's prospects for peace, conflict, and democracy. In the case of world politics more generally, a geographical focus suggests fundamentally different ways to study relationships between states and actors in world politics. International relations is after all the study of relationships between actors. Although theories of international relations suggesting dependence between observations at a universal system level may be flawed (see Cederman 1997, Waltz 1979), the simple steps here corroborate that world politics may be meaningfully studied as patterns of interaction and interdependence within regional systems (e.g., Gleditsch 2002, Lake and Morgan 1997, Solingen 1998). Our argument *is not* that the simple linear regression model with the regional average of democracy is the optimal way of analyzing the substantive linkages between democracy and peace, but rather that simple visualization and data exploration have helped yield quantum leaps toward new substantive insights into the democracy and peace nexus. We have used these types of spatial findings to inform more comprehensive statistical analyses as well as formal computational models (see, Cederman and Gleditsch 2004, Gleditsch 2002). It takes a map, however, to start orienting ourselves in a complex world. We firmly believe that greater attention to the spatial characteristics will help produce better roadmaps for understanding international relations.

NOTES

We thank Alex Mintz and Bruce Russett as well as Nils Petter Gleditsch and Jan Ketil Rød for informed and helpful comments on our research into visualization of political processes. We would also like to thank Dennis L. Ward, University Corporation for Atmospheric Research, Boulder, Colorado, USA, for his help with preparing the final graphics.

1. For overviews of the development and early uses of maps, see the volumes of the *History of Cartography* series, published by the University of Chicago (Burnett et al. forthcoming, Harley and Woodward 1992, Harley and Woodward 1994, Monmonier and Woodward forthcoming, Woodward forthcoming-a, Woodward forthcoming-b, Woodward and Lewis 1998).

2. See Winchester (2001) for a highly readable account of a map that literally changed the world.

3. Leaving conspiracy theories about the "real" motive aside, U.S. officials attributed the unfortunate bombing to an outdated map of Belgrade. The intended target was a Yugoslav federal directorate for supply and procurement. Although the procurement directorate was near the building they had targeted, the maps used located the Chinese embassy in a different part of the city. If the map had correctly depicted the location of the Chinese embassy, NATO would have rejected the original target as embassies are on a list of "no strike" targets (cf. statements by William Cohen, *Newshour* 10 May 1999).

4. The most recent, corrected version of this movie is available at http://www .colorado.edu/IBS/GAD/diffmov.exe (December 2003).

5. One of Haushofer's most impressionable students was Rudolf Hess. Hess introduced Haushofer to Hitler, and his influence is evident in *Mein Kampf*. However, Haushofer was highly critical of Germany's actual conduct of the war, which he claimed was inconsistent with the strategic principles of geopolitics.

6. Written in the 1930s and 1940s, Richardson's work in international relations was not widely available, and remained virtually invisible to scholars of conflict at the time. Despite some resurgence of interest and appreciation of Richardson's work in the 1960s, Richardson remains largely unknown in international relations or political geography outside more statistically and formally oriented scholars (see Ashford 1985, Hess 1995, Nicholson 1999 for overviews of Richardson's work on war and peace).

7. We refer to Gleditsch and Ward (1997) for further details on the construction of the institutionalized democracy scale in the Polity data.

8. The technical and practical details of actually putting maps on a screen or on paper via publication can be quite encompassing and complicated. Such maps can be made in a variety of different software packages, ranging from specialized GIS packages (ArcInfo, ArcView, GRASS, or Mapmaker) as well as mapping options in other software packages such Microsoft Office. All of these packages have their strengths and weaknesses. Of the commercial packages developed by ESRI, the mapping program ArcView is relatively easy to learn but offers only limited programming features, whereas their full GIS package ArcInfo is prohibitively expensive (about $6,000 for an annual license). GRASS is a powerful, free open source GIS package (see Bivand 2000, Neteler and Mitasova 2002), but this package is relatively difficult to learn and based on a UNIX platform. For users who primarily wish to display data as maps and do not need to display historical boundaries, the mapping options in Excel will probably suffice.

9. Tufte (1983) actually recommended against the use of computer-generated graphics, suggesting instead that one work with and rely on cartographers and graphic

artists. Such resources, however, are expensive, and not readily available for most social scientists. Moreover, Tufte did not anticipate the improvement in computer-generated graphics following the revolution in digital computing.

10. See also Brewer's website at http://www.personal.psu.edu/faculty/c/a/cab38/, and in particular, the ColorBrewer tool for selecting good color schemes for maps and graphics (December 2003).

11. Based on our limited experience with publishers in the United Kingdom and United States over the period from 1997 to 2003, printing a single four-color map can cost between U.S. $400 and U.S. $1,000, with a mode closer to $1,000. Typically, these costs will have to be carried by the authors.

12. Spatial statistical analysis is becoming more increasingly common in the social sciences. The U.S. National Science Foundation has funded the Center for Spatially Informed Social Sciences to encourage the use of spatial analysis (see http://www.csiss.org). The availability of new tools and routines for spatial statistical analyses implemented in standard statistical packages such as R, S-plus, and Stata have also helped promote more widespread use of spatial statistics.

13. The perhaps best-known data on geographical contiguity, maintained by the Correlates of War project, include a categorical scale of "contiguity by sea," with different brackets of distances. In these data, states that are close across land, but not over sea, such as Israel and Iraq can by construction not be identified as close to one another.

14. This is for purposes of illustration only. In an actual analysis we would obviously want to include linkages of other entities. This example is adapted from Gleditsch (2002).

15. This is sometimes referred to as a "contiguity" or "spatial weight" matrix (e.g., Anselin 1988). Since the entries need not refer to contiguities, space, or weights, we prefer the more general term "connectivity matrix."

16. Note that the diagonal of the connectivity matrix $\mathbf{W}$ by convention is set to zero so that countries are not considered contiguous with themselves.

17. From the measures of the distance between units in the minimum distance data, we can generate a series of different sets of connectivity matrices at different distance thresholds. Though the choice of any single distance threshold may seem arbitrary, the minimum distance data allow the researcher to vary the definition of context and conduct specification tests.

18. More specifically, the entries in a $\mathbf{W}^n$ matrix indicate the number of n-order linkages between i and j (see., e.g., Harary et al. 1965).

19. Cliff and Ord (1973,15) develop the expected value of the variance of Moran's I under a normality assumption and a randomization assumption.

20. Since the Moran statistic is based on a prespecified $\mathbf{W}$ of dependence relations, a nonsignificant value strictly speaking only means that the observations do not appear to cluster according to structure specific in $\mathbf{W}$. Researchers should therefore consider different plausible specifications before concluding that the data do not display spatial dependence.

21. Since we are interested in to what extent observations are similar to the values of their neighbors, the diagonal entries $w_{i,j} \; \forall \; i = j$ in the binary matrix $\mathbf{W}$ are all set

to one. An alternative statistic G_i does not include the values of i itself, and indicates to what extent values *surrounding* location i have similar values on the input variables. See Ord and Getis (1995) for further details.

22. Borrowing from the terminology of proximity for time-series analysis, this is commonly referred to as "the spatial lag" of a variable x.

23. Although no research or applications to our knowledge have explored such alternatives as of yet, it might in many settings also make sense to devise spatial variables constructions based on moments other than the mean and the total sum. More generally, the appropriate spatial variable type depends upon the causal mechanism that we believe operates across space. The public goods literature has explored various alternative supply technologies for public goods or externalities that may be helpful for thinking systematically about choices for construction of spatial influence or spill-in variables (see, e.g., Mueller 1989, 22–25). If the amount of an externality is determined by the individual units' total consumption within some geographical bounds as in the "tragedy of the commons," an additive form would be appropriate (see Cornes and Sandler (1996, 492–94) for a more general discussion). In the case of a "weakest-link"/"best-shot" technology where the externality is determined by the smallest/largest contribution of any of the individual units' provision, useful spatial variables could be constructed from the minimum or maximum of the values among contiguous entities. If we are interested in the difference or variation among entities within a region, we could use measures based on moments such as the range or variance of the values. Clearly, the range of opportunities for innovative research is wide open.

24. Statistical analysis with spatially dependent data raises a number of estimation problems that we have ignored here. For continuous dependent variables we have established maximum likelihood estimators with good properties (see, for example, Anselin 1988), but the issues are more complicated for categorical dependent variables (see Cressie 1991, Ripley 1988, Ward and Gleditsch 2002).

5

The Postwar Public Health Effects of Civil Conflict

Hazem Adam Ghobarah, Paul Huth, and Bruce Russett

Civilian suffering from civil war extends well beyond the period of active warfare. We examine longer-term effects in a cross-national analysis of World Health Organization data from 1999 on death and disability broken down by age, gender, and type of disease or condition. We find substantial long-term effects of civil war both within a war-torn country and on neighboring countries, even after controlling for several other factors. We estimate that the additional burden of death and disability incurred in 1999 alone, from the indirect and lingering effects of civil wars in the years 1991–1997, was nearly double the number incurred directly and immediately from all wars in 1999. This impact works its way through specific diseases and conditions, and disproportionately affects women and children.

Civil wars kill people directly and immediately. They also destroy property, disrupt economic activity, and divert resources from health care. Huge refugee flows put people into crowded conditions without access to clean water and food; refugees become transborder vectors of infection. Crime and homicide rates rise in wars, and may remain high afterward in a culture accustomed to violence. Many of these effects last for years after the fighting. A recent article reviewed the public health literature on both immediate and long-term effects of civil wars (Pedersen 2002; also see Krug, Dahlberg, Mercy, Zwi, and Lozano 2002, chap. 8). The health effects during specific civil wars are relatively well known,[1] but the general and longer-term impact is not. These new deaths (and disabilities) are overwhelmingly concentrated in the civilian population. For example, Davis and Kuritsky (2002) report that severe military conflict in sub-Saharan Africa cut life expectancy by more than two years and raised infant mortality by 12 per thousand.

Most reports on the consequences of civil wars for civilians are case studies. This is an important limitation, not least because they require a baseline of reliable prewar conditions and long-term postwar reporting. Moreover, the severity of war for civilians both in the immediate and longer-term varies considerably across wars, as do the specific diseases and conditions by which the impact occurs. Here we offer a comprehensive worldwide analysis of the post-conflict consequences for healthy life expectancy. We modify a previously developed statistical model (Ghobarah, Huth, and Russett 2003) to explain World Health Organization data which take into account both years of life lost to disease and injury and years of healthy life lost to long-term disability. They allow us to assess the effect of civil wars on the subsequent impact of twenty-three major diseases and conditions, on segments of the population distinguished by gender and five age groups.

The model here improves on our previous analyses in several important respects discussed below: (1) deletion of two independent variables—ethnic heterogeneity and type of government—that have a strong impact on health spending but little further direct impact on health outcomes; (2) improved data on civil war casualties; (3) a more sensitive term for the effect of civil wars in neighboring countries, measuring the interaction of the severity of such wars with the permeability of the borders; (4) substituting the rate of female educational achievement for that of both sexes combined. These improvements produce much clearer and stronger effects.

Overall, WHO (2000, 168, 174) estimates that 269,000 people died and 8.44 million years of healthy life were lost to death and disabilities in 1999 as direct and immediate effects of all wars, civil and interstate. Based on the results we report here, perhaps another 15 million were lost in 1999 to death and disability indirectly, from various diseases in war-torn countries and their neighbors, from the lingering effects of civil wars during the years 1991–1997. Those outcomes in return increase poverty, quality of life, income inequality, and personal security—and hence affect politics (e.g., Price-Smith 2002, chap. 2).

THEORETICAL FRAMEWORK

In developing hypotheses about the longer-term effects of civil war on public health we draw on a general theoretical framework for studying the factors affecting public health. We identify four major influences on public health in societies, and contend that political conditions and processes are important causes of each of these major influences on health.

1. *The extent to which populations are exposed to conditions that increase the risk of death, disease, and disability.* At the most basic level, populations

across and within countries are exposed in varying degrees to the risk of disease, injury, and death. Geography and levels of economic development are basic factors. People in tropical climates are at greater risk of many infectious diseases. In poor countries much of the population lives in rural areas where access to good health care is generally lower than in urban areas. As a result, preventive care is less available and the treatment of disease and injury is less extensive and effective. At the same time, health care systems can suffer in large urban areas experiencing rapid population growth, with the result that some urban populations are at great risk to a variety of health problems and exposure to new environmental and occupational hazards.

2. *The financial and human resources available for addressing the health needs of populations.* Higher levels of income and wealth provide a larger pool of financial and human resources to draw upon. Public and private actors can afford to spend more on health care and to support the purchase of more advanced medical technologies. A larger pool of available financial resources will enable greater investments in developing human resources for medical care by training more doctors and health care specialists. Political unrest and irregular transfers of power reduce growth rates (Przeworski, Alvarez, Cheibub, and Limongi 2000, chap. 4), and hence the pool of financial resources for health services.

3. *The level of resources actually allocated to health needs by the private and public sectors.* Public health analysts (e.g., Evans, Tandon et al. 2000) consistently argue that a more educated population will be more knowledgeable about health risk factors, support greater investment and expenditures, and better utilize health care services. Yet claims to resources for public health compete with other demands, and politics can prove crucial in deciding how resources are allocated. Political leaders wish to retain power. They must form a winning coalition among those who are politically active. To do so they distribute private goods to their supporters, and provide collective goods widely for the population. All leaders provide both private and collective goods in some degree. But since democratic leaders must satisfy a wide range of supporters, not just their cronies and the military, they are less able than authoritarian ones to extract rents for the private benefit of small groups, and must respond more to broad demands for public well-being (Olson 1993; Bueno de Mesquita et al. 1999b; Lake and Baum 2001). They are more likely to invest in public goods such as health programs because populations will hold them accountable for failing to address pressing health care problems. For example, famines are far more common in authoritarian states (Sen 1981), which spend less to prevent them or to relieve

the consequences. Przeworski et al. (2000, 239) report that the strong effect of democracy in lowering infant mortality operates largely through health expenditures, and other research found a strong impact of democracy in increasing public health spending (Ghobarah, Huth and Russett 2004; Dasgupta 1993; Moon 1991, ch.6).

4. *The degree to which resources allocated to health are efficiently utilized.* Politics can influence efficiency in two ways. Public health services may not be directed to groups with the greatest need. Lower income groups are often at greater risk of health problems and therefore in need of public health services, yet such groups are likely to be less effectively represented in the political competition for scarce resources. Consequently, health care services are skewed in favor of wealthy segments of the population who on average are healthier and less at risk.

NEW MEASURES OF PUBLIC HEALTH

Our dependent variable derives from WHO's measure of overall health achievement, Health Adjusted Life Expectancy (HALE). That measure discounts the total life expectancy at birth in each country by the number of years the average individual spends with a major disability as the burden of disease or injury—the gap between total life expectation and expected years without disability. It is estimated from three kinds of information: the fraction of the population surviving to each age level (calculated from birth and death rates), individual-level data on the prevalence of various diseases and disabilities at each age, and a weight assigned to debilitation from each type of condition. The result is a measure expressed in intuitively meaningful units: the average number of years of healthy life that a newborn member of the population could expect to live.

It varies substantially by region of the world and income level. In rich countries, more disabilities are associated with chronic conditions of old age—and, at that point, relatively short life expectancies. By contrast, in poor tropical countries infant mortality is much higher, and more health problems derive from the burden of infectious diseases, like malaria and schistosomiasis, which are carried by children and young adults who may live a long time with seriously impaired health and quality of life. Empirically, the share of simple life expectancy lost to disability varies from under 9 percent in the healthiest regions of the world to over 14 percent in the least healthy ones (WHO 2000, p. 28).

This information-intensive measure requires not just vital registration data for births and deaths but expensive health surveys of death, disease, and disability by age and gender. These data only began to be collected on a global basis by WHO for the year 1990 (Murray and Lopez 1996), with the most comprehensive report being its 1999 and 2000 surveys (WHO 2000). Life tables for all 191 WHO members were developed from surveys supplemented by censuses, sample registration systems, and epidemiological analyses of specific conditions. WHO experts provided estimates of uncertainty about the data's accuracy, subjected it to statistical tests for bias, and adjusted it accordingly. Then they estimated disease-specific disability rates for all countries in each of fourteen regions of the world defined geographically and epidemiologically, and used these to adjust available data on death rates at different age levels and life expectancy for each country (Mathers et al. 2000). The index ranges from 74.5 (Japan) to 29.5 (Sierra Leone).

While the limitations must be kept in mind (Anand and Hanson 1996), these data are the best that have ever been available, and do permit us to make some plausible systematic inferences about the influences on health conditions across countries (Williams 1999; Murray and Lopez 2000; Murray et al. 2002; Filmer and Pritchett 1999, 1312). Here we use a more disaggregated measure, from data that produce the summary HALE estimates. This metric for Disability Adjusted Life Years (DALY) measures the effect of death and disability on population groupings comprised of each gender in five age groups (0–4, 5–14, 15–44, 45–59, and 60 and older). These are initially compiled from data on the number of deaths in a year from each of more than 100 categories of disease or health condition. To the deaths are added estimates of the years of healthy life typically lost due to disability from the incidence of the condition and the estimated number of new cases in the period. The number of years of healthy life lost is obtained by multiplying the average duration of the condition (to remission or death) by a severity weight for the disability. Thus the DALYs for 1999—combined into twenty-three major disease categories for analysis—reflect the life years lost due to deaths from a particular condition contracted during the year plus the expected disability to be incurred by other people who suffered from the same condition in that same year.[2] In other words, these are not disabilities incurred from conditions contracted in earlier years when a civil war was active.

HYPOTHESES ON POST–CIVIL WAR HEALTH CONSEQUENCES

The introductory framework of important general causal connections between politics and public health allows us to focus specifically on the linkages between civil war and long-term health. Civil wars directly affect all the major contributors to health: exposure to disease, medical care, public health interventions, and overall socioeconomic conditions. We posit two related hypotheses for how civil wars produce health consequences that extend well into the postwar period:

H1: More DALYs are lost with the occurrence and increasing severity of civil wars within a country.

H2: More DALYs are lost if a geographically contiguous state has had a civil war.

Our reasoning addresses the four major influences on public health:

1) *Civil wars substantially increase the exposure of the civilian populations to conditions that increase the risk of disease, injury, and death.* Prolonged and bloody civil wars are likely to displace large populations, either internally or as refugees. The Rwandan civil war generated 1.4 million internally displaced persons and another 1.5 million refugees into neighboring Zaire, Tanzania, and Burundi. Often these people do not return to their homes after the war ends, but stay in crowded makeshift camps for years. Bad food, water, sanitation, and housing make these camps into new vectors for infectious disease—measles, acute respiratory disease, and acute diarrheal disease—while malnutrition and stress compromise people's immune systems. As a result, in many countries ravaged by civil wars the crude mortality rates among newly arrived refugees were five to twelve times above the normal rate (Toole 2000). Children may be especially vulnerable to infection.

Non-displaced populations may also be at greater risk. Diseases that become rampant in refugee camps may easily spread to other regions. Prevention and treatment programs already weakened by the destruction of health care infrastructure during wars become overwhelmed, especially if new strains of infectious disease bloom. For example, efforts to eradicate Guinea worm, river blindness, and polio—successful in most countries—have been severely disrupted in states experiencing the most intense civil wars. Drug resistant strains of tuberculosis develop and in turn weaken resistance to other diseases. War-induced refugee movements and soldiers, both in the war zone and on their return home, are heavily implicated in the spread of AIDS in Africa (World Bank 2003; U.S. Institute of Peace 2001).

Finally, violence is likely to increase in the aftermath of long and severe civil wars (Pedersen 2002; Bracken and Petty 1998). Homicide and other crime rates rise within countries during international wars, tending to peak in the first year after the war (Stein 1980; Archer and Gartner 1976). Gerosi and King (2002) report a rise in homicides and suicides, transportation deaths, and other unintentional injuries (both the latter are likely to include misclassified suicides) in the U.S. population immediately following the Korean and Vietnam wars. If international war has this effect, surely the direct and immediate experience of civil war will do the same. These psychosocial changes are magnified by the widespread availability of small arms after many civil wars. Young men may be disproportionately both victims and perpetrators.

2) *Civil wars reduce the pool of available resources for expenditures on the health care system.* Civil wars are an extreme form of political instability which reduces rates of economic growth. Poor economic performance cuts the pool of tax revenues that governments can use to finance health care. One study concludes that, after ending, civil wars typically have a severe short-term (approximately five years) negative impact on economic growth (Murdoch and Sandler 2002). A weak economy and lower profit margins also decrease the resources that the private sector can devote to employee health, and reduce the private resources individuals can draw on to compensate for reduced state or employer contributions.

In addition to reducing financial resources, civil wars deplete the human and fixed capital of the health care system. For example, heavy fighting in urban areas is likely to damage or destroy clinics, hospitals, laboratories, and health care centers, as well as water treatment and electrical systems. Rebuilding this infrastructure is unlikely to be completed quickly in the postwar period. Finally, severe civil wars may induce a substantial flight of highly trained medical professionals, and this loss of human capital may not be reversed by their return or replacement until long after the war's end.

3) *Civil wars constrain the level of resources allocated to the public health care system in their aftermath.* Postwar governments face multiple competing demands for public expenditure. Long and destructive civil wars lead to such fundamental problems as: (*a*) a broad range of needs for reconstruction and environmental repair, (*b*) the need to reform and rebuild army and police forces, judicial systems, and administrative capacity, and (*c*) military and security spending needs that are a response to continuing military threats. Pressure for military capability raises the classic question about trade-offs between military spending and nondefense needs such as public health (e.g., Adeola 1996; Ball 1988; DeRouen 2000a; Mintz 1989). Security threats may derive from internal insurgent groups, or from a powerful military force built up by a neighboring state to fight its own civil war. (See Braveman et al. 2000 on Nicaragua; Grobar and Gnanaselvam 1993 on Sri Lanka; also Collier and Hoeffler 2001; Murdoch and Sandler 2002) Despite needs for better health care, the demands of postwar peace building and recovery make resource trade-offs involving health care spending hard to avoid (Collier 1999; Stewart 1993).

4) *Civil wars reduce the efficient use of resources that are allocated to public health, and those reductions in efficiency extend into the post–civil war period.* Destruction of health infrastructure that supported surveillance and control programs for diseases like tuberculosis and malaria sows the seeds of

short- and long-term health problems. Civil wars reduce the productivity of the entire economy, especially of facilities needed to maintain previous levels of health care. Wartime destruction of transportation infrastructure (roads, bridges, railroad systems, communications, and electricity) weakens the distribution of clean water, food, medicine, and relief supplies, to both refugees and those who stay in place. Military forces often deliberately target hospitals, health care facilities, and medical personnel so as to weaken the opposition. Much of this takes years to restore.

These theoretical underpinnings for the causal impact of war on health lead to our key independent variable: civil wars. For *H1* we use deaths from civil war in the years 1991 to 1997. When expressed as the number of deaths per 100 people in the country it becomes a measure of both the existence and the intensity of civil war. Civil wars are armed conflicts that challenge the sovereignty of an internationally recognized state and occur within that state's boundary, resulting in 1,000 or more fatalities in at least one year.[3] For most countries the value is 0; for those that experienced civil war during the period it ranges from .001 to 9.421 (Rwanda). A total of 51 countries experienced civil wars in this period. Table 5.1 arrays the twenty-four countries having the most intense civil wars, in descending order of direct fatality rates. Three countries with civil wars—Bosnia, Liberia, and Somalia—are not in our analysis due to missing data on other variables, but we take their wars into account in estimating the effects on their neighbors and total world DALYs lost.

Using civil war deaths in the years 1991–1997 gives us a lag to the DALY rates for 1999. Theory does not give us a single correct lag.[4] For most infectious diseases—which we hypothesize as the principal cause of indirect civil war deaths—the lag time would seem short (less than five years) while the effects of damage to infrastructure and the health care system would probably last longer (between five and ten years). The lag for some cancers could be so long that we cannot reasonably test for many of them.

For *H2* our measure is an interactive variable: contiguous civil war deaths × border permeability. The first term is the number of deaths per 100 in each contiguous state that experienced a civil war during 1991–1997, and the second is a 1.0 to 4.0 scale for the permeability of that border; that is, the ease of interaction across it as determined by Starr and Thomas (2002) from geographical information systems. Borders readily open to interaction encourage forays of troops across them and the outflow of refugees to burden health systems in the receiving country. For a state with no land border, or if no contiguous state experienced a civil war, the value is of course zero. If more than one contiguous state experienced civil wars their measures are summed. The maximum value for the interactive indicator is 38.26 for Zaire, with seven adjacent civil wars, including big ones in Rwanda, Angola, Sudan, and Burundi.

Table 5.1.   Direct Deaths from Civil
Wars per 100 Population, 1991–1997

Rwanda	9.421
Liberia	3.068
Somalia	2.447
Bosnia	2.176
Angola	2.117
Sudan	1.522
Burundi	1.212
Cambodia	1.131
Tajikistan	.755
Sierra Leone	.678
Afghanistan	.608
Lebanon	.317
Azerbaijan	.312
Guatemala	.196
Morocco	.196
Mozambique	.196
Algeria	.189
Papua New Guinea	.188
Georgia	.166
Congo-Brazzaville	.143
Djibouti	.137
Sri Lanka	.122
Chad	.116
Zaire	.113

Plus 27 countries below .100 each

CONTROLLING FOR OTHER CAUSES OF PUBLIC HEALTH

While our primary focus is on the impact of civil wars on public health, we must control for other factors that public health scholars and health economists argue are important causes of cross-national variation.

H3: The higher the level of total health expenditures the fewer DALYs lost.

Higher income improves health *through* public and private decisions to spend money on hospitals, preventive and curative health care, sanitation, and nutrition. Earlier work by economists (e.g., Pritchett and Summers 1996) showed that "wealthier is healthier." Ghobarah et al. (2004) built on their findings with a finer-grained causal argument about *how* higher income leads to better health. Per capita income does not directly determine the production of health outputs. Rather, it permits a high level of expenditure for health purposes, and though highly collinear ($r = 0.90$) with income, health expenditure levels are also influenced by political process and institutions. And expenditures are subsequently distributed in a political process that produces actual health outcomes. Thus that full two-stage model, in the economics tradition of production function analysis, treats income as an uncontrollable variable outside the direct process that produces good public health outputs. Here we follow WHO (Evans, Tandon, et al. 2000, 13) in using total 1998 health expenditures per capita to incorporate prior political processes that affect spending, which in turn makes a direct impact on health outcomes like DALYs. It includes health services and prevention, but not the provision of clean water and sanitation, which are affected by national levels of income and education. Note that 1997 is the end of the time for which civil wars are measured. Since it picks up the indirect effect of civil war in reducing income and health spending it probably understates the full effect of our civil war variable.

We use data on total health expenditure compiled by WHO, from IMF and national sources, supplemented by UN and OECD national accounts data, household surveys, and WHO estimates (Pouillier and Hernandez 2000). Total health spending per capita ranges from $4,055 (United States) to $11 (Afghanistan). WHO authors say it is very hard for countries to provide good health outputs with a total expenditure under $60 per capita, and that it would cost just over $6 billion per year to bring up to this threshold the forty-one countries with lower expenditures (Evans, Tandon et al. 2000, 24). These distributions are skewed, and we use the natural logarithms to reflect the declining marginal product of additional dollars at higher levels of spending. Following WHO's practice, we use total health expenditures as an explanatory variable, rather than public or private spending alone. Public and private health spending complement each other somewhat in achieving health goals, and the measure of total health expenditures has more explanatory power than does either component alone.

H4: The more educated the female population the fewer DALYs lost.

At high levels of education preventive and treatment programs become more widespread and effective, that is, demand for health care rises as does knowledgeable and effective consumption throughout the population. Education is strongly associated with the health of both children and adults in both rich and poor countries. It constitutes the other independent variable, with total health expenditures, in WHO analyses of health attainment (Evans, Tandon et al. 2000, 13).

WHO regards the average level of schooling of adults the most widely available and sensitive measure. Nevertheless, it seems inferior to one that is sensitive to the educational levels achieved by women. Cross-national studies show female empowerment to be associated with lower mortality: countries with high mortality rates for their income levels tend to be those that discourage female education, contact between the sexes, female economic participation outside the household, and equal access for women to health care (Mechanic 2002, 53; Thomas 1997). The most complete data are compiled by UNESCO, reported in UNDP (2002, 222–25).[5] They measure the rate of female enrollment in primary, secondary, and tertiary levels combined, which runs from 100 (Australia and others) to 12 (Niger). The gap between female and male enrollments is negligible in most industrialized countries, but can be as high as 43 percentage points (29 female, 72 male in Yemen) in less developed ones.

H5: The higher the pace of urbanization the more DALYs lost.

New urban residents are exposed to new diseases in crowded environments, and inadequate access to care when the supply of health services to large numbers of new residents lags behind the surge in need (Garrett 2001; Szreter 2001; Shah 1997). Surveillance, immunization, and providing safe water all become more difficult. A high rate of urbanization often reflects the influx of poor and marginalized people from rural areas, who are under-organized in unions and underrepresented in established political parties. They find it hard to create effective pressure for health care either politically or in the workplace, leaving a gap between need and delivery. Marginal utility analysis predicts that individuals receiving less than an equal supply of health care lose more disability-adjusted life expectancy than is gained for those receiving more than an equal share.

Our measure of recent urbanization is the average annual percentage change in the urban portion of the population, 1990–1995 (United Nations 1998, 132–35). It ranges from –0.41 percent (Belize) to 7.35 percent (Botswana).

H6: The more unequal the distribution of income, the more DALYs lost.

The more unequal the income distribution, the fewer public resources will be committed to the health care system and the more unequal will be access to health facilities. Economically advantaged groups will be more able to dominate the political system for their own benefit rather than that of the majority. As a result, state spending is diverted from public to private goods; what is spent is more concentrated on the privileged and politically powerful segments of the population. The large poor segment of the population will have lower incomes, less leverage with employers, and fewer private resources for health. High-quality health care is thus limited to a smaller segment of the general population, producing lower overall levels of health performance. The rich get more access—at low marginal utility, and the poor get less (Foege 2000, 7; Moon 1991; Szreter 2001; Wilkinson 1996; UNDP 2002, 59).

Our measure of inequality is the Gini index of income distribution in 1997. It is derived from a Lorenz curve of the actual distribution of income by households, with the index representing the area between the curve and the 45 degree line representing a totally equal distribution of income. We use World Bank estimates for 111 countries, supplemented by WHO multiple imputation estimates using information on socioeconomic development and life expectancy at birth (Evans, Bendib et al. 2000). In theory the Gini index ranges from zero (complete equality) to 1.00 (one person has all the income); in practice national indices for income distribution range from a very equal .187 (Slovakia) to .609 (Sierra Leone).

H7: Tropical countries will suffer from more DALYs lost.

WHO (2000, 164; also see Sachs 1999) reports that, among infectious disease categories, the major causes of deaths in Africa are, in descending order, HIV/AIDS, respiratory infections, malaria, diarrheal diseases, measles, and tuberculosis. Such diseases are often endemic to tropical countries, where conditions for their spread are more favorable despite public health programs to contain them. If civil wars are more likely to occur in such countries, we risk mistakenly identifying civil wars as the cause of diseases that are already prevalent because of these background conditions. To prevent this error we add a dummy variable, *tropical*, with all countries where the majority of the population resides in tropical regions coded 1 and all other countries coded 0.

We do not include two other possible control variables: democratic versus autocratic political system and ethnic diversity. This is not because either is irrelevant. To the contrary, there is much evidence that they matter substantially. But in research discussed above and confirmed in Ghobarah et al. (2004) that incorporated health spending and the other variables here, democracy makes little direct impact on health conditions—its substantial effect operates earlier in the causal chain, on decisions to allocate available resources. Since health spending is a variable here we do not also include political system type.

Similarly, differences in the racial and ethnic makeup of a country's population can produce various forms of discrimination and unequal access to political power. Political inequality in turn skews the distribution of resources committed to public policy programs, including the health care system. As noted above, expenditures on public health programs are often most beneficial to poor and disadvantaged social groups. Minorities suffering from discrimination are therefore likely to be in greater need of such basic health care services but in a weak position to apply political pressure to procure them. Furthermore, dominant ethnic groups may seek to limit basic health programs that would primarily benefit minorities, and to shift resources into other state programs that are of greater benefit to themselves. Overall, public health spending will reflect the political weakness of groups discriminated against, and thus will be lower than in more homogenous populations. Indeed, some analysts (e.g., Deaton 2002) regard racial composition as more important than income inequality.[6] But again, since other work (Ghobarah et al. 2004) found ethnic diversity impacts primarily on health expenditures and hence only indirectly on health outcomes, we omit it here.

One further reservation about the potential complexity of this causal chain must be acknowledged. It is likely that our measure of the severity of civil wars is in part a proxy for other economic and political variables associated with civil wars. To answer this fully we would also need a model to explain the incidence and severity of civil wars, but some relevant influences on civil war are included, as follows:

For our purposes the intensity of war is more relevant than its mere occurrence. Our measure of deaths over the duration of the war, controlled for size of population, captures duration and especially intensity. It also addresses the likelihood that large states will have more potentially disaffected groups able to mount a war effort.

The initial level of economic development raises the opportunity costs of violence. In richer countries employment opportunities are better, and governments have more resources to satisfy discontented elements of the population. Whereas some analyses find that a low rate of economic growth contributes to the likelihood of civil war, a low level of development seems a more robust influence (Sambanis 2001, 2002; Elbadawi and Sambanis 2002). Although we do not include GDP per capita as a direct influence in this model, it makes a prior contribution through its influence on total health expenditures per capita, and also is closely related to educational attainment. Indeed, Collier and Hoeffler (2000) identify low educational level as a key influence on the risk of war. Thus our model already controls for level of development. Poor health conditions may of course also depress income levels for individuals and nations, in a feedback process we cannot properly analyze here.

Two other influences on civil war also come into our analysis by their effect on health spending. Ethnically polarized societies may be more war prone than either homogenous ones or highly fragmented states whose small minorities may suffer from collective action problems in organizing for violence (Bates 1999; Collier and Hoeffler 2000). Lack of democratic rights can threaten the core of ethnic identity and reduce the chances for redress of grievances (Gurr 2000). Civil wars may be more frequent in countries between the extremes of full democracy and full autocracy (Hegre et al. 2001), but that distinction contributes little to the continuation of wars (Elbadawi and Sambanis 2002).[7]

In sum, we believe our key explanatory variable—deaths from civil wars— is not simply a proxy for the structural conditions that produce civil wars, and that the diseases bringing death and disability after civil wars are not simply a consequence of those conditions. A fuller analysis of the multiple and reciprocal relations among development, democracy, civil wars, and health must await later research.

A MULTIVARIATE ANALYSIS OF ALL DEATHS AND DISABILITIES

We test these hypotheses using cross-sectional least squares regression analysis. Missing data for some countries on some variables reduces the number of observations to 165, with most of the missing being ministates. Table 5.2 shows ten equations for deaths and disabilities from *all causes combined,* with breakdowns by age and gender. The explanatory variables are listed across the top, and each column gives the estimated coefficient and the t-ratio. Coefficients and t-ratios which reach the 0.05 level of significance (one-tailed) are in bold face. (A t-ratio of 1.66 would just reach the 0.05 level.) Because DALY represents years of healthy life *lost* we anticipate positive coefficients for all variables except health expenditures and female education.

Most of our hypotheses are also supported in the disaggregated analyses. In 8 of the 10 equations, total health spending has a strong and statistically significant impact in reducing the loss of healthy life expectancy. Only for men and women aged 15–44 is there no effect. A high level of female educational enrollment strongly reduces DALYs among children, and weakly (p < .07 and .09) among women over 45 and over 60. This is just what one should expect: female empowerment brings measurable health benefits to women and to their offspring. Rapid urban growth and an unequal income distribution, however, consistently increase death and disability in all age groups. But simply being in a tropical country has no discernible impact, suggesting that what is often considered the endemic unhealthfulness of such climates may really be attributable to identifiable economic, social, and political conditions like those in the equations. Most of the equations show high R^2s, indicating a reasonably complete specification of the relevant influences. (The exceptions are those 60 and older, consistent with the view that for people who reach that age genetics and life style are relatively more important to continued health than are some socioeconomic conditions.)

These relationships are not, however, the focus of attention in this article — *civil war is.* For that we see some strong effects. Countries experiencing a civil war earlier in the 1990s subsequently suffered a significantly increased loss of healthy life in seven of the age-gender groups, and more weakly (p < .06 for two groups, p < .12 for females age 0–4). The substantive impact varies, but frequently is very high — at worst, nearly seven years of healthy life lost per 100 people in that age group for every 100 civil war deaths. The

Table 5.2. DALYs Lost to All Disease Categories

Group	Statistic	Intercept	Civil War Deaths 1991-97	Contiguous Civil War Deaths	Total Health Spending	Female Enrollment Rate	Urban Growth Rate	Income Inequality Gini	Tropical Climate	Adjusted R-square
Females 0–4	Coefficient	**198.87**	4.68	0.62	**-19.57**	**-1.00**	**7.44**	60.26	-3.61	.66
	T-ratio	7.54	1.19	0.99	-5.21	-3.95	2.38	1.47	-0.45	
Males 0–4	Coefficient	**217.74**	6.71	0.56	**-21.49**	**-1.07**	**6.59**	68.06	-4.91	.66
	T-ratio	7.87	1.63	0.85	-5.45	-4.04	2.01	1.59	-0.58	
Females 5–14	Coefficient	**17.65**	**1.42**	**0.35**	**-2.56**	-.07	**1.47**	**16.18**	0.35	.67
	T-ratio	4.82	2.60	3.98	-4.92	-1.89	3.38	2.85	0.32	
Males 5–14	Coefficient	**18.16**	**1.39**	**0.31**	**-2.61**	-.07	**1.45**	**18.44**	0.68	.69
	T-ratio	4.92	2.54	3.59	-4.96	-2.08	3.32	3.22	0.60	
Females 15–44	Coefficient	-11.77	**5.86**	**1.70**	-1.49	-0.04	**11.11**	**82.87**	0.67	.51
	T-ratio	-0.78	2.59	4.72	-0.69	-0.29	6.17	3.53	0.15	
Males 15–44	Coefficient	-5.74	**4.29**	**1.19**	-1.52	-.002	**7.64**	**73.70**	2.07	.53
	T-ratio	-0.51	2.58	4.49	-0.96	-0.16	5.77	4.26	0.61	
Females 45–59	Coefficient	**28.38**	**2.98**	**0.52**	**-2.96**	-0.09	**3.60**	**25.40**	1.96	.66
	T-ratio	4.92	3.35	3.64	-3.49	-1.49	5.09	2.75	1.08	
Males 45–59	Coefficient	**27.67**	**3.21**	**0.68**	**-3.68**	-0.02	**5.11**	**43.69**	-0.11	.55
	T-ratio	3.22	2.50	3.34	-3.01	-0.21	5.00	3.28	-0.04	
Females 60+	Coefficient	**43.12**	**3.05**	**0.43**	**-2.90**	-0.12	**2.91**	**36.26**	-2.82	.33
	T-ratio	6.01	2.25	2.01	-2.24	-1.39	2.70	2.57	-1.02	
Males 60+	Coefficient	**46.67**	1.63	0.29	**-3.07**	-0.02	**2.67**	**22.31**	-3.27	.33
	T-ratio	6.01	1.41	1.57	-2.78	-0.22	2.90	1.86	-1.38	
Total Populace	Coefficient	**28.91**	**3.87**	**0.91**	**-4.05**	**-0.14**	**6.22**	**54.03**	-0.13	
	T-ratio	5.92	5.31	7.84	-5.81	-3.74	10.70	7.12	-0.09	

N = 165; bolded cells are significant at <0.05 one-tailed level.

coefficients mean, for instance, that the impact in 1999 of living in a country that had experienced an intense civil war a few years earlier (such as Sudan with 1.5 civil war deaths per 100 people) rather than in a median country with no war at all is a loss of over 13 healthy life years in 1999 per 100 boys under 5 years of age. This is long after the war ended in a settlement, and over and above the impact of all the other sociopolitical and economic variables in our model. In other age groups the coefficient for impact is statistically more significant for females than for males, and usually higher.

Finally, even living in a country adjacent to a state that experienced a civil war imposed big human costs on some of these groups, especially men and women aged 15–44. All these are over and above what they experienced if there also had been a civil war in their own country.[8]

The entries for the total population (all age and gender groups), at the bottom of the table, provide a useful summary. They show the average coefficients over all groups combined, with each group weighted by its proportion of the global population (http://esa.un.org/unpp/p2k0data.asp). If all countries' immediate civil war deaths 1991–1997 are added up, the total comes to just over 3.1 million worldwide. The coefficient[9] for civil war deaths (3.87) at the bottom of the table means that they eventually produced, in 1999, a loss of 12 million disability years of healthy life in the world. Adding the rough estimate of .91 million additional disability years lost per civil war death in contiguous countries, for nearly 3 million more DALYs, gives a total of almost 15 million DALYs ultimately lost, or about 178 percent more than WHO reported for direct and immediate losses from wars in 1999.

THE WHO AND HOW OF CIVIL WAR EFFECTS

We can now look at the impact of civil wars through specific diseases and conditions. The WHO data on impacts of various diseases by age and gender allow us to compute 210 equations.[10] With a threshold of $p < .05$ for a one-tailed test of statistical significance we would expect, purely by chance, to find 10 or 11 equations producing a "significant" relationship for civil war's impact on an individual grouping. In fact, we find many more: 64 equations in which the civil war coefficient is significant at $p < .05$. Furthermore, most of the significant coefficients make sense from our expectations. Table 5.3 shows the effects of preceding civil war deaths (using the same multivariate equation presented in table 5.2, but only listing the civil war deaths column). It gives a row for each such equation, arraying the equations by major disease/condition groups, and within groups by age and gender.

By far the most common impact is by raising the incidence of infectious diseases that are usually already present, consistent with our theoretical

Table 5.3.   The Long-term Impact of Civil Wars: DALYs Lost by Disease Categories

Cause	Gender	Age Group	Civil War Deaths Coefficient	Civil War Deaths T-ratio
AIDS	Female	0–4	1.205	2.03
	Male	0–4	1.144	2.02
	Female	5–14	.0641	2.06
	Male	5–14	.0619	2.01
	Male	15–44	2.0960	1.72
	Female	45–59	.6773	1.94
	Male	45–59	1.1820	1.80
	Female	60+	.0394	2.05
	Male	60+	.0929	2.07
Malaria	Male	0–4	1.7540	1.92
	Female	5–14	.3747	2.28
	Male	5–14	.3679	2.16
	Female	15–44	.0471	2.80
	Male	15–44	.0691	2.39
	Female	45–59	.0129	2.45
	Male	45–59	.0060	1.85
	Male	60+	.0034	1.85
Tuberculosis	Female	5–14	.1081	2.44
	Male	5–14	.0984	2.19
	Female	15–44	.1446	2.22
	Male	15–44	.1761	2.17
	Female	45–59	.1682	2.31
	Male	45–59	.2435	2.05
	Female	60+	.1406	2.14
	Male	60+	.2500	2.23
Respiratory Infections	Female	5–14	.1593	2.09
	Male	5–14	.1523	2.13
	Female	15–44	.1436	2.83
	Male	15–44	.1401	2.12
	Female	45–59	.1717	2.89
	Male	45–59	.1618	2.41
	Female	60+	.1924	1.84
Other Infections	Female	5–14	.4639	2.17
	Male	5–14	.4425	2.24
	Female	15–44	.5267	2.35
	Male	15–44	.5292	2.00
	Female	45–59	.4555	2.81
	Male	45–59	.3561	2.41
	Female	60+	.3916	1.71
	Male	60+	.1657	1.93
Transportation Accidents	Female	15–44	.0307	1.73
	Male	15–44	.1779	2.04
	Female	45–59	.0938	2.08
	Male	45–59	.1618	2.09

(*continued*)

Table 5.3. (*continued*)

Cause	Gender	Age Group	Civil War Deaths Coefficient	Civil War Deaths T-ratio
Homicide	Male	5–14	.0095	1.85
	Female	15–44	.0523	2.32
	Male	15–44	.1770	2.32
	Female	45–59	.0612	2.10
Other Unintentional Injuries	Female	45–59	.1566	1.71
Cervical Cancer	Female	5–14	.0001	1.82
	Female	45–59	.0565	2.34
	Female	60+	.1172	2.96
Maternal Conditions	Female	15–44	.9089	2.80
	Female	45–59	.0834	2.79
Lung Cancer	Male	5–14	.0008	1.70
	Female	5–14	.0005	1.80
	Female	45–59	.0272	2.24
	Male	60+	.0577	2.54
Stomach Cancer	Male	5–14	.0005	1.74
	Female	60+	.0428	1.97
Liver Cancer	Male	5–14	.0009	1.70
Other Cancers	Females	60+	.1244	1.74
Chronic Respiratory Disease	Male	0–4	.2814	1.84
Digestive Disease	Female	60+	.2613	2.62

expectations and review of the case study material on the effects of civil wars. Topping that list is HIV/AIDS, hitting both genders for all but one age group. (The coefficient for females 15 to 44 years is also high and just misses statistical significance at $p < .06$.) Its devastating impact is concentrated in the economically most productive age groups and on very young children, striking both genders more or less equally. Not only does this disease strike virtually all groups, many of the impacts are among the highest in the table, reaching more than two years of healthy life lost among every 100 men aged 45–59. Regrettably, that is the lingering effect of civil war operating through only one disease out of 23; the misery accumulates with each of the other 22 categories of disease.

The next most damaging impact is by malaria: eight of the ten age-gender groups (all but young girls and women over 60, both at $p < .06$) are affected. Some of the highest t-values in the table are from wars raising the incidence of malaria. The very high impact coefficient for young boys indicates 1.75 years of healthy life lost in 1999 per 100, controlling for all other factors.

The three other disease groups showing great increases are tuberculosis, respiratory infections, and other infectious diseases—each reaching statistical significance with seven or eight of ten possible age and gender groups. The age and gender group effects are strikingly similar for these three diseases but, unlike malaria, for each category they affect older children and adults rather than the very young. The significant coefficients for the impact of war on tuberculosis are generally much lower (ranging from around .1 to .25) than for malaria in children. Respiratory infections hit nearly all groups other than young children about equally, with coefficients in a narrow range (.14 to about .19). For other infectious diseases — something of a catchall category — the impact is greater (with nearly all coefficients in the range of .35 to .53). Together, the five infectious disease groups account for 42 of the 64 equations with a significant effect of civil wars.

Another common effect is from transportation accidents, and may in part reflect the deterioration of roads and vehicles. But it is also consistent with our expectations of an increase in stress and a breakdown of law and order in post–civil war societies. We cannot satisfactorily map the causal relationships without detailed microlevel analysis. Nevertheless, while the impact is fairly small (.03 to .18 years), it affects four of the ten groups: mostly young and middle-aged adults. More obvious from an expectation of a breakdown of social order is the elevated homicide rate, the victims chiefly being women and younger men. (The coefficients for girls 0–4 and 5–14 and women over 60 are nearly significant, at $p <$ .06 and .07.) The substantive impact is similar to that of transportation accidents.

The entry for unintentional injuries may also derive from stress, and may include unreported suicides. With a lower threshold of statistical significance ($p <$ .10), three more adult age groups would make it into the table for unintentional injury. Chronic respiratory diseases not included elsewhere (as tuberculosis and respiratory infections) for young boys might reflect stress-induced loss of resistance.

We also find an apparent effect of civil wars on the rate of cervical cancer for three of the four female groups above age 4 (plus weakly at $p <$ .16 for women aged 15–44). While cervical cancer may develop too slowly for the time lag used in our analysis, there may be two possible connections to civil wars. First, it fits our expectation of a breakdown in social norms, here norms against forced sexual relations, though the coefficients are small (the largest is .12). Second, in poor countries infection plays an important etiologic role in cancer and civil wars increase the incidence of other infectious diseases.[11] Also, other sexually transmitted diseases in traditional societies may be recorded as cervical cancer. Women also are reported as subject to maternal ills, perhaps exacerbated by social disruption from war, or perhaps misreported sexually transmitted disease. In any event, the damage is severe, amounting to almost one year of healthy life per 100 women in the major child-bearing age group.

The four lung cancer groups are unexpected, but sharp increases in stress-induced smoking are a plausible cause, with generally small impacts in this moderate 2–8 year lag period. The six remaining statistically significant groupings show little pattern, and with this lag we have no explanation. With this many equations some will appear significant by chance, usually with rather low t-values.

Overall, females constitute 34 out of the 64 affected groups, and the two gender groups of children aged 5–14 account for 16 (chance would mean 12 or 13 groups). Whoever the actual combat deaths during the war may represent, in their long-term impact the most frequent victims of civil wars are women and children.

CONTIGUOUS CIVIL WARS

Table 5.4 shows the effect of civil war in a contiguous country, above any effect of civil war at home. Our initial analysis found that having a civil war in an adjacent country was itself a major contributor to loss of healthy life expectancy overall. In the disease-specific analysis we find about as many (66) disease-age-gender groups for which a contiguous civil war significantly increased death and disability. This too is far above the 10 or 11 categories we would expect by chance to cross the line of statistical significance in 210 equations. Of the countries in our analysis, about 75 percent of those experiencing civil wars also were affected by neighboring civil wars. Conversely, of the 83 affected by neighboring wars, fewer than 60 percent had civil wars at home. These overlaps prevent a precise accounting of the two effects, but still leave enough variation to identify differences as well as similarities in the two tables.

Here we see the impact of civil wars in neighboring countries and the consequent military, refugee, and other traffic across borders. The highly significant effect of a neighboring civil war on HIV/AIDS is immediately apparent. As with the effect of civil wars within countries, some of the most susceptible groups are very young children, infected largely through their mothers, and young and middle-aged adults. Again as in table 5.3, the other biggest post–civil war diseases are the major kinds of infections: malaria, tuberculosis, respiratory infections, and others.

Homicide once more appears as a consequence, for girls and younger women. Transportation accidents do not appear as a special problem here, likely because a contiguous civil war may do little damage to the country's own infrastructure and perhaps does not raise tensions so much. But we again see a substantial impact for maternal conditions on women of childbearing age, and of cervical cancer. Finding these for neighboring wars as well as wars within the country suggests they are not statistical flukes, even though it is not entirely clear what they are really measuring. Notable here are the reported deaths and disabilities from liver cancer in many age/gender groups, probably

Table 5.4. The Long-term Impact of Contiguous Civil Wars: DALYs Lost by Disease Categories

Cause	Gender	Age Group	Contiguous Civil War Deaths Coefficient	Contiguous Civil War Deaths T-ratio
AIDS	Female	0–4	.4807	4.37
	Male	0–4	.3891	4.32
	Female	5–14	.0213	4.32
	Male	5–14	.0208	4.26
	Female	15–44	.9654	3.84
	Male	15–44	.7399	3.82
	Female	45–59	.2289	4.11
	Male	45–59	.4278	4.26
	Female	60+	.0131	4.23
	Male	60+	.0302	4.30
Malaria	Female	0–4	.4807	3.25
	Male	0–4	.4851	3.34
	Female	5–14	.0213	4.45
	Male	5–14	.1106	4.07
	Female	15–44	.0110	4.13
	Male	15–44	.0220	4.79
	Female	45–59	.0037	4.46
	Male	45–59	.0016	3.18
	Female	60+	.0013	2.50
	Male	60+	.0009	3.30
Tuberculosis	Female	5–14	.0316	4.49
	Male	5–14	.0282	3.94
	Female	15–44	.0273	2.64
	Male	15–44	.0563	4.35
	Female	45–59	.0343	4.46
	Male	45–59	.0624	3.72
	Female	60+	.0287	2.50
	Male	60+	.0834	3.30
Respiratory Infections	Female	5–14	.0340	2.80
	Male	5–14	.0328	2.13
	Female	15–44	.0356	4.40
	Male	15–44	.0497	4.71
	Female	45–59	.0459	4.85
	Male	45–59	.0494	4.62
	Female	60+	.0528	3.17
	Male	60+	.0376	3.02
Other Infections	Female	5–14	.0974	2.87
	Male	5–14	.0853	2.71
	Female	15–44	.0823	2.31
	Male	15–44	.1861	4.41
	Female	44–59	.1117	4.33
	Male	44–59	.1139	4.70

Cause	Gender	Age Group	Contiguous Civil War Deaths Coefficient	T-ratio
	Female	60+	.0842	2.42
	Male	60+	.0559	4.08
Homicide	Female	5–14	.0018	1.93
	Female	15–44	.0068	1.90
Cervical Cancer	Female	5–14	.00002	2.09
	Female	45–59	.0090	2.35
	Female	60+	.0018	4.90
Maternal Conditions	Female	15–44	.0260	4.42
	Female	45–59	.2286	5.47
Liver Cancer	Male	5–14	.0009	1.70
	Female	15–44	.0010	2.33
	Male	15–44	.0078	3.64
	Female	45–59	.0062	3.21
	Male	45–59	.0016	2.46
	Female	60+	.0164	4.54
	Male	60+	.0270	3.73
Stomach Cancer	Male	5–14	.0002	4.03
	Female	60+	.0069	2.00
Cancer of Mouth, Esophagus	Female	60+	.0079	2.62
	Male	60+	.0169	2.60
Other Cancers	Female	60+	.0199	1.75
	Male	60+	.0498	2.59
Digestive Disease	Female	60+	.0347	1.71
	Male	60+	.0425	2.68

representing the results of epidemic hepatitis. In addition there are again scattered other conditions that affect a few groups, but not enough or strongly enough to attribute much importance to them without further research.

Tallying all the effects in this table, females (36 groups, 30 male) again predominate. Older children are also slightly overrepresented (14 entries), as with civil wars at home.

CONCLUSION

We developed the central hypothesis that civil wars produce long-term damage to public health and medical systems that extend well beyond the period of active warfare and tested it in the context of a more general political-economic model of conditions affecting death and disability cross-nationally. Using newly available data on disability-adjusted life years lost from various diseases and conditions by age and gender groups, we found that, controlling for the other influences, civil wars greatly raise the subsequent risk of death and disability from many infectious diseases, including malaria, tuberculosis, and other infectious respiratory diseases. We have evidence, though weaker, that civil wars may increase the risk of death and disability through the breakdown of norms and practices of social order, with increases in homicide, transportation accidents, other injuries, and cervical cancer. These excess war-induced deaths and disabilities followed both wars in one's own country and civil wars in contiguous countries. Women and children are the most common long-term victims.

Totaling up the sum of human misery from warfare remains subject to considerable approximation and speculation, but this kind of work begins to fill in some neglected pieces. From table 5.2 we estimated that about 12 million disability years were lost in 1999 due to civil wars in the same country, and perhaps another 3 million were suffered in neighboring countries—giving a total of about 15 million DALYs. That approaches twice WHO's estimate for the immediate loss of DALYs from all the wars fought in 1999. Moreover, both WHO's estimate and ours miss the impact of the first postwar year. Finally, it includes only those incurred in a single year of a cumulative postwar process that lasts many years, for possibly another order of magnitude in casualties, far exceeding the immediate losses. This assumes some decay function extending ten years after each civil war year, which on average our snapshot catches in a middle year.

These results are intriguing, but not conclusive. Certainly we need to comprehend better the microlevel political, social, and epidemiological processes. We also must understand better the possible complex interrelations among influences, and drive backward in the full mutually interacting system to comprehend how civil wars may interact with income, inequality, ethnic diversity, and type of political system to affect people's health and well-being. One improvement in subsequent research should be a more nuanced and medically informed consideration of appropriate lag times. Our rather crude one-size-fits-all lag, of civil war deaths from 1991 to 1997 to explain DALYs in 1999, is not a bad fit to the descriptive literature on the spread of many diseases, and gives a reasonable empirical fit overall. Still, something more fine-grained is necessary for diseases, notably AIDS and other long-term noninfectious conditions (e.g., many cancers) that are slow in developing. Cross-temporal analysis will provide better guidance when the necessary data become available.

The kind of data analyzed here must be combined with more contextual information and field reports from countries that have experienced civil wars. Further analyses could provide projections on the likely effect of major civil violence to be used by peacekeeping and postconflict peace-building missions, national governments, and nongovernmental organizations. They may suggest possible key interventions, such as in caring for refugees and assessing priorities for postconflict efforts to rebuild devastated and overburdened health care systems. They indicate the number of long-term deaths and disabilities to be anticipated from various diseases, which in turn can be used in cost-benefit analyses to estimate the price of averting each death or disability through the best postconflict allocations to prevention and treatment.

Finally, they should inform any attempted cost-benefit analysis of war. The recent invasion of Iraq, though not a civil war, permits some general points. Even before the war Iraq's public health infrastructure was well below that at the start of 1991 because of the first war and subsequent economic sanctions.[12] Clean water was in short supply even before the bombing began. The invasion itself ended quickly, and coalition forces made serious efforts to limit civilian casualties. But subsequent civil disorder and looting have done great further damage. The potential for massive additional loss of life and health over the next ten years or so is clear. Some may be prevented by prompt and extensive efforts to rebuild that country and relieve its citizens' misery.

NOTES

Authors' note: We thank the Weatherhead Initiative on Military Conflict as a Public Health Problem, the Ford Foundation, and the World Health Organization for financial support, Gary King, Thomas Gariepy, Melvin Hinich, Kosuke Imai, Jennifer Leaning, Roy Licklider, Lisa Martin, Christopher Murray, Joshua Salomon, Nicholas Sambanis, and William D. White for comments, and Sarah Croco for research assistance. This chapter is reprinted with minor changes from the authors' article with the same title in *Social Science and Medicine*, Vol. 54, Copyright 2004, with permission from Elsevier.

1. The one-year impact of infectious disease and health system breakdowns associated with refugees is well established (Toole 1997). Gustafson et al. (2001) document war-related deaths from tuberculosis during the war in Guinea-Bissau; Roberts et al. (2001) report war-derived disease deaths in Congo during the war as six times greater than those from direct violence. Effects beyond the war period are less clear, though the longer-term risk from tuberculosis, respiratory infections, and malaria is well recognized (Centers for Disease Control 1992).

2. More information on the procedures can be found in WHO (2000, 145–46); DALYs are displayed by disease category, gender, and region in WHO (2000, 170–75).

3. Fatality figures are from Doyle and Sambanis (in press), kindly supplied to us by Nicholas Sambanis.

4. We have run several sensitivity checks for the results reported in the data analysis section below. As expected, very long lag structures such as 1977–1990 produce

much weaker findings in which the coefficient for the civil war variable is only about one-fourth as large as for 1991–1997, and not statistically significant. A break between 1991–1995 and 1996–1997 shows greater impact for the latter period, but the standard error is higher. Eliminating all countries whose civil wars extended past 1997 reduces the impact of wars in 1996–1997, but not that of earlier wars.

5. We supplemented with data for two additional countries in the 2003 edition of *Human Development Report*, and for three more in Sass and Ashford (2002).

6. Despite its democracy, and leading the world in per capita income and health spending, the United States ranks only 27th in HALE ratings. This may reflect its moderately diverse ethnic composition (87th out of 177 countries) and distinctly high economic inequality (109th).

7. Other influences on the ability to sustain a dissident group at war may include rugged terrain and the availability of "lootable" natural resources. They seem particularly important for nonethnic wars (Collier and Hoeffler 2000). But since over 70 percent of all civil wars between 1960 and 1999 can be characterized as between ethnic groups (Sambanis 2001) we do not consider them here.

8. This analysis shows the effect of an adjacent civil war whether or not the country itself had a civil war, and is robust to inclusion or exclusion of countries that experienced civil war themselves (Ghobarah et al. 2003). The impact coefficient for contiguous civil wars, however, is not strictly comparable to that for wars within countries, since it depends in part on our somewhat arbitrary scaling of the interactive measure. Some alternative scalings nevertheless suggest this coefficient is reasonable.

9. This coefficient may well be a conservative estimate, since it had to be computed without data on three of the four countries experiencing the most intense civil wars.

10. Twenty-three disease groups times five age groupings and two genders would give 230 equations. Some categories, however, are empty: for males, five each for maternal conditions, breast cancer, and cervical cancer; three for maternal conditions for females under 15 and over 44; two for suicide by children under 5 years.

11. Research in sub-Saharan Africa suggests that the human papillomavirus (HPV) is linked to cancer of the cervix (Feachem, Jamison, and Bos 1991, 17). Every new sexual partner greatly increases the risk of HPV infection, which may produce low-grade squamous intra-epithelial lesions (LSIL) within the next three years (Moscicki et al. 2001). Progression from LSIL to cancer is slower.

12. Estimates of the impact of the 1991 Gulf War are deeply complicated by the effects of prewar and postwar economic sanctions and the deliberate policy of the Iraqi government to divert humanitarian food and medical assistance away from its intended recipients (Fourth Freedom Forum 1999).

6

Alliances and the Expansion and Escalation of Militarized Interstate Disputes

Brett Ashley Leeds

Commitments from outside allies affect the probability that challengers initiate militarized interstate disputes. In other words, alliances affect the success of general deterrence. But what if general deterrence fails? How do military alliances affect the evolution of disputes once they begin? Are alliance commitments associated with particularly serious violent conflicts if peace breaks down? I develop and test hypotheses about the influences of alliances on the probability that disputes expand to multilateral crises and escalate to war. When disputing states have commitments from outsiders to assist them in conflict, they are more likely to receive help in any dispute that emerges. Alliances have little direct effect on escalation, but they do have an indirect effect – alliances affect dispute expansion, and dispute expansion affects the probability that disputes escalate to war. Alliances have their greatest impact on the initial emergence of conflict, but when disputes emerge among states with allies committed to their assistance, the resulting conflicts can be particularly severe.

ALLIANCES AND MILITARIZED CONFLICT

Despite the fact that many theories of interstate conflict place military alliances in a privileged position, scholars of international relations have had a surprisingly difficult time describing, explaining, and predicting the influence of military alliances on the probability of war.[1] Alliances have been credited both with deterring military action and with spreading it. Allies have been known to restrain partners and enforce bargains, and also to

117

reduce negotiating flexibility and make conflict-avoiding agreements more difficult to reach. In this chapter, I provide evidence that both views of alliances have a basis in fact. While alliances play an important role in influencing the initiation of military conflict and have a well-deserved place in a strategy of general deterrence, when general deterrence fails and conflict emerges among states with allies committed to assist them, the resulting disputes can be particularly severe.

The primary lesson of this study, for both researchers and policymakers, is that alliances can have multiple effects on the probabilities of war and peace. By exploring the influence of different types of alliances at different stages in the evolution of militarized disputes, we can learn more about their overall impact. Those who view alliances as problematic due to their potential to involve outsiders in disputes tangential to their direct interests and to turn bilateral disputes into worldwide conflagrations (a story frequently told about World War I) must temper their indictment with a recognition of the deterrent properties of alliances. At the same time, those who champion clear alliance commitments as the route to peace must recognize that when deterrence fails, alliances may be associated with particularly intractable negotiating problems and serious military conflicts.

There are several ways in which this study represents a "new direction" in research on the relationship between alliances and international conflict. Theoretically, it builds on bargaining models of war and signaling models of alliances, both of which have been developed relatively recently (e.g., Fearon 1995; Wagner 2000; Filson and Werner, 2002; Morrow 1994; Smith 1995). Empirically, it takes advantage of analysis techniques that allow researchers to connect processes at different stages (e.g., Reed 2000). By starting with a directed dyadic research design and using modeling procedures that link dispute initiation and dispute evolution together, I am able to provide a better understanding of the complexities of the impact of alliances on conflict than has been available in the past. Finally, the study uses a relatively new dataset that provides rich information about the content of alliance agreements (Leeds, Ritter, Mitchell, and Long 2002). This allows me to match alliances explicitly to the potential conflicts where they would be relevant.

The chapter proceeds as follows. In the next section, I explain the theoretical perspective on the causes of militarized disputes and war and the role of alliances in foreign policy that underlies the argument in this chapter. I then develop specific hypotheses about the relationship between alliances and the expansion and escalation of disputes once conflict emerges. In section four, I describe the research design used to evaluate these hypotheses and the empirical evidence in support of them. Section five offers concluding observations about the influence of alliances on war and peace.

THE CAUSES OF WAR AND THE ROLE OF ALLIANCES

Under what conditions does militarized interstate conflict begin? A particularly compelling contemporary perspective views militarized conflict as emerging from bargaining failures (Blainey 1973; Fearon 1995). Because the shadow of force lies over all international interactions, force need rarely be used. Most of the time, the joint understanding of the likely outcome of any militarized conflict leads state leaders to agree on a distribution of benefits consistent with their ability to achieve gains through force without actually resorting to arms. Yet, due to uncertainty about the outcome of a conflict and the incentives to misrepresent one's power and interests to achieve a more favorable bargain, militarized disputes and war sometimes occur. They occur when the parties disagree about the bargain that is consistent with their ability to compel or resist change and believe that the benefits to be gained through the threat or use of military force exceed the costs involved in militarization.

Given this perspective, what role do alliances play in the emergence of militarized disputes?[2] Contemporary theorists have argued that alliances affect the initiation of militarized interstate disputes through the information they provide to potential challengers about the likelihood that they can gain a more favorable distribution of benefits through the overt threat or use of force (Morrow 1994; Smith 1995, 1998c; Fearon 1997). Specifically, alliances provide potential challengers with fairly reliable information about whether a dispute is likely to remain bilateral or to involve outside parties. When their potential targets have allies committed to assist them in conflict, challengers can expect that they are likely to face a multilateral force and are less likely to be successful at achieving their goals. On the other hand, when the potential challenger has allies of its own committed to join in the challenge or to remain neutral, challengers can feel more confident of their ability to gain in conflict (Leeds 2003a).

Leeds (2003a) provides evidence that alliances do affect the probability of dispute initiation in precisely this manner. Defensive alliances discourage attacks on potential targets, but offensive alliances and neutrality pacts embolden challengers and make the initiation of disputes more likely. Recent research has pointed out, however, that the initiation of military hostilities is not the end of the bargaining process, but merely a new stage in bargaining. The conflict ends once the two sides reach agreement on an acceptable division of benefits, and what they learn during the dispute influences the bargain they are willing to make. Escalation to war and longer and more costly wars are a result of particularly intractable bargaining problems (Wagner 2000; Filson and Werner 2002; Smith and Stam's contribution to this volume).

So what role should alliances play once a dispute begins? Alliances that were in place before the dispute began were already known, and the parties were willing to engage in conflict fully aware of their existence. The information provided by existing alliances about the prior commitments of outsiders should not be able to encourage a bargained solution after the conflict begins any more than it could before overt conflict emerged. As Fearon (1994a) has noted, because previously known alliances were accounted for in the calculus that led to the breakdown of general deterrence, they are unlikely to have much impact on the success of immediate deterrence; if challengers willing to initiate disputes are aware of alliances, they are unlikely to back down from escalating a dispute because of them (see also Huth and Russett 1984; Huth 1988).

Yet, some new information does become available to both the challenger and the target after the dispute begins. Just as the challenger and target are likely to learn more about the settlements that their adversaries would accept in lieu of war during the dispute process, both also learn more about what the ally views as an acceptable settlement and the actions the ally might be willing to take to encourage his or her preferred outcome.

When a leader's ally becomes involved in a dispute with an outside state, one can imagine that leader would have two competing interests. On the one hand, if the leader views involvement in war as undesirable, he or she would want to avoid allowing the dispute to escalate. If the leader were unsuccessful at moderating the demands of the adversary (which is likely if general deterrence has failed), then the leader might work to moderate the demands of the ally to avoid being drawn into an unwanted conflict. The French were unwilling to face Germany without British support in 1938, and thus encouraged their ally, Czechoslovakia, to give in to German demands for the Sudetenland rather than escalate the conflict. The Soviets and Americans similarly restrained their Arab and Israeli allies in 1973 in the interest of avoiding superpower confrontation. In this sense, allies might be able to use their influence, and particularly their power to deny assistance in the event of unmoderated demands, to resolve the crisis and avoid escalation to war. Along these lines, Gelpi (1999) has argued that allies are particularly effective mediators due to their means of influence over their partners.

Despite the fact that a leader might want to avoid involvement in war, it is not clear that leaders will always prefer to pressure their allies to give in, because allies also have an interest in the post-dispute distribution of benefits. Leaders prefer to see their allies resolve conflicts of interest peacefully and prefer not to engage in war if all else is equal, but they also have an interest in the distributional outcome of the conflict, and are likely to prefer a distribution of benefits that favors their ally. This creates a countervailing pressure to the desire to avoid war. Thus, leaders of outside powers may under some circumstances compel their allies to moderate their bargaining positions and facilitate settlement as a result, and under other circumstances may allow or even encourage their allies to maintain a tough bargaining stance that makes settlement more difficult. Thus, while Gelpi claims that allies are in the best position to encourage compromise on behalf of their partners, Smith (1995) notes that having allies committed to assist them may tend to make states particularly intransigent in their bargaining positions and increase the risk of escalation to war.

To complicate matters, any action that encourages moderation on the part of an ally may correspondingly toughen the bargaining stance of the adversary, and vice versa. It is difficult, therefore, to claim a single systematic influence of allies on the bargaining positions of states in a militarized dispute. What is probably fair to claim, however, is that the existence of alliances is likely to result in more parties being involved in the bargaining process because more states have a direct interest in the outcome of the bargaining and escalatory processes. Thus, the main effect of alliances is to turn bilateral crises into multilateral crises, and bilateral bargaining problems into multilateral bargaining problems.

This in itself is significant because political bargains become more difficult to achieve as additional actors join the bargaining process. Raiffa (1982, 257) writes, "Significant conceptual complexities arise when even a single new party is added to a two-party negotiation." This is especially true in the absence of specific institutional rules.[3] International bargaining tends to take place under ad hoc rules established by the participants themselves, and few alliance treaties specify rules for determining a joint position of a crisis coalition. While the extent to which additional parties complicate bargaining depends on the possible outcomes and the distribution of preferences over outcomes, it is reasonable to assume that all else being equal, increasing the number of parties that must be satisfied by a bargain to avoid war makes the negotiation of a successful settlement less likely, and war correspondingly more likely. This would also be commensurate with the observation that multilateral wars tend to last longer than bilateral wars.[4] It is harder to resolve a conflict that involves more actors.

EXPECTED INFLUENCES OF ALLIANCES ON THE CONFLICT PROCESS

Alliances affect dispute initiation by influencing a potential challenger's beliefs about the probability that a conflict will remain bilateral. Challengers prefer to initiate disputes when they believe they can win in military conflict, and challengers are more likely to believe they can be successful when they expect that they will receive outside support and when they believe that their targets will not receive outside support (Leeds 2003a; see also, Gartner and Siverson 1996; Morrow 1994; Smith 1995, 1998c). Recent theoretical and empirical research suggests that alliances are a fairly reliable signal of future intentions because most of the time leaders form alliances under which they are willing to fulfill their obligations (Morrow 1994; Smith 1995, 1998c; Fearon 1997; Leeds, Long, and Mitchell 2000; Leeds 2003b). It follows, therefore, that when challengers with allies committed to their assistance initiate disputes, or when challengers choose to start a dispute with a target with one or more allies committed to assist the target in defense, these disputes are unlikely to remain bilateral.[5] When alliances that provide for active assistance fail to deter challenges, they will often be associated with disputes that become multilateral crises.[6] Specifically:

H1: When a conflict initiator has an offensive alliance in place when a dispute begins, it is more likely that more than one state will be involved in the dispute on the side of the initiator.

H2: When a conflict target has a defensive alliance in place when a dispute begins, it is more likely that more than one state will be involved in the dispute on the side of the target.

Some alliances, however, are not aimed at providing active support, but instead offer a commitment to remain neutral in an emerging conflict. Through neutrality pacts, potential challengers can receive promises from outsiders not to intervene to help the potential target, clearing a path for military success (Moul 1988; Werner 2000). Neutrality pacts should be associated with a higher probability of a dispute remaining bilateral, as they make it less likely that outsiders will intervene to help a target.

H3: When an initiator has a neutrality pact in place when a dispute begins, it is less likely that more than one state will be involved in the dispute on the side of the target.

Thus, alliances that are in place before conflict emerges should affect the probability that a militarized interstate dispute becomes a larger, multilateral affair. While alliances may sometimes deter the initiation of hostilities, disputes that emerge among states with allies may be particularly severe due to their likelihood of involving multiple participants. We can imagine circumstances under which a leader's desire to avoid escalation to war would cause him or her to impose moderation on an ally's claims.

One can also imagine circumstances under which a leader will encourage increased toughness in an ally and make the ally's bargaining position more intransigent. These countervailing effects make it difficult to predict the impact of outside allies on a state's willingness to capitulate or to hold firm absent more information about the outside state's value for war and for the political settlement. It does seem reasonable to suggest, however, that regardless of the content of the preferences of outside states, adding additional states to the negotiating process who must be satisfied with a settlement for war to be avoided will make negotiated settlements harder to reach and war more likely. Thus:

H4: Multilateral conflicts are more likely to escalate to war than bilateral conflicts.

RESEARCH DESIGN AND EMPIRICAL ANALYSIS

My empirical examination of the influence of alliances on the evolution of militarized disputes begins with a model of the initiation of disputes. As Reed (2000) has shown, many of the same factors that influence how disputes evolve also influence whether they emerge in the first place, and in order to achieve a proper understanding of the evolution of disputes, we must account for the emergence of the dispute in our empirical analysis. This methodological advance is an important new direction in international relations research. In this case, using a maximum likelihood probit estimation with selection allows me to analyze the impact of alliances on dispute expansion and dispute escalation conditional on dispute initiation. It also allows me to estimate the joint impact of alliances on the failure of general and immediate deterrence.

I assemble a dataset that includes all states in interactions with the states in their politically relevant international environments in each year from 1816 to 1944 (Maoz 1996). The unit of analysis is the directed dyad-year.[7] I employ a two-stage probit technique that accounts jointly for the probability that a dispute emerges and the likelihood that it expands and/or escalates.[8] The dependent variable in the first (selection) equation is the initiation of a militarized interstate dispute (MID), defined as an instance "in which the threat, display, or use of military force . . . by one . . . state is directed towards . . . another state" (Jones, Bremer, and Singer 1996).[9] The independent variables are drawn from Leeds (2003a). That study reveals that defensive alliances to a potential target are negatively related to the initiation of militarized disputes, and a potential challenger's offensive alliances and neutrality pacts are positively related to dispute initiation. Control variables have generally predictable effects. Stronger initiators are more likely to initiate disputes against weaker targets, contiguous states are more likely to engage in military conflict, and jointly democratic dyads and states with similar alliance portfolios (and we infer, more similar foreign policy interests) are less dispute prone.[10]

The uncensored cases in the second stage of analysis are all the dyad-years in which a new militarized interstate dispute is initiated by the challenger against the target. The unit of analysis is the militarized interstate dispute. For each MID, I create three different dependent variables, all of which are coded dichotomously based on the answers to the following questions: (1) Did more than one state participate in the dispute on the side of the initiator?; (2) Did more than one state participate in the dispute on the side of the target?; (3) Did the dispute escalate to war?

I begin by evaluating the influence of alliances on the likelihood that a dispute involves more than two states. Because I have argued that alliances influence the initiation of disputes by providing information to potential challengers regarding the probability that outsiders will intervene in any emergent conflict, it follows that some types of alliances, namely, those that obligate signatories to assist their partners in the event of hostilities, should be systematically associated with the expansion of military conflict. On the other hand, neutrality pacts specifically obligate states to refrain from intervention on the opposing side and should be associated with a lower probability of outside assistance to the opponent.

In the first model, the dependent variable is whether or not, if a dispute emerges, more than one state participates on the side of the initiator. In the second model, the dependent variable represents the active participation of more than one state on the side of the target. In both cases, the dependent variable is coded dichotomously, with disputes in which the initiator or target was the only state involved on his or her side of the dispute coded 0, and cases in which multiple states are involved coded 1.

The independent variables of primary interest are variables representing outside alliances to the initiator and the target. Using the Alliance Treaty Obligations and Provisions (ATOP) dataset (Leeds, Ritter, Mitchell, and Long 2002), I coded three variables. First, I developed a dichotomous variable representing whether the target in the dispute had any alliance commitments when the dispute began that would obligate any other state to come to its assistance in a conflict with the initiator. Second, I coded another dichotomous variable representing whether the initiator of the dispute had any alliance commitments when the dispute began that would obligate any other state to assist the initiator in a conflict that the state initiated against this target. Third, I coded a dichotomous variable that indicates whether the initiator had any existing agreements when the dispute began that would preclude outside states from intervening to help the target (that is, any relevant neutrality pacts).[11]

I also include two additional control variables that may influence whether additional states participate in disputes.[12] First, I include a variable representing how strong the initiator is in comparison to her target. A long debate has ensued in international relations scholarship over the incentives for outsiders to join ongoing disputes. Some have argued that states have an interest in balancing power and should work to protect weak targets from challengers, who once they succeed in defeating their target, may seek further aggrandizement at the expense of outside states. Others claim that states have an incentive to bandwagon. By joining stronger states, they may get a chance to share in the spoils of conflict.[13] Because the strength of the initiator in comparison to the target may influence state decisions to intervene, I include a measure of relative power. It is drawn from the Correlates of War capabilities index, and is calculated as the CINC score of the initiator divided by the sum of the scores of the initiator and target (Singer 1988). The result is bounded between zero and one with higher values indicating stronger initiators, and lower values indicating weaker initiators.

Second, I include in each equation a variable representing whether outsiders join the adversary. Because it may be the case that intervention on one side of a conflict begets intervention on the other side, I control for the influence that the addition of one outsider may have on the decisions of other states to join conflicts.

Table 6.1 presents the empirical results of this analysis. The results are entirely supportive of hypotheses 1 through 3. When an initiator begins a dispute with an offensive ally, it is more likely that the initiator will receive outside assistance. When a target has a defensive ally at the time the dispute begins, it is more likely that the target will receive assistance. When the initiator has a neutrality pact, however, the target is less likely to get outside help, all else being equal. At the same time, allies to the target seem to deter assistance to the initiator, and allies to the initiator seem to deter assistance to the target.

The control variables are statistically significant as well. The power relationship between the initiator and the target influences the likelihood that outsiders will join, and these results seem to suggest more support for bandwagoning than balancing. Stronger initiators tend to attract more assistance, and weaker targets attract less. When outsiders join one side of the dispute it becomes more likely that outsiders join the other side. Intervention does seem to beget intervention.

How much influence do alliance commitments have on the probability that a dispute expands? To answer this question, I perform two analyses, both of which are reported in table 6.2.[14] First, I evaluate the impact of alliances on dispute expansion conditional on dispute initiation. If a dispute has been initiated, the average probability that outsiders help the initiator increases from 18.9 percent to

Table 6.1.   The Effects of Outside Allies on the Probability That Outsiders Help in Militarized Interstate Disputes, 1816–1944

	Outsiders Help Initiator Coefficient (s.e.)	Outsiders Help Target Coefficient (s.e.)
Power of Initiator in Relation to Target	0.447 (0.100)**	−0.352 (0.168)*
Target has Def. Ally When Dispute Begins	−0.449 (0.090)**	0.857 (0.131)**
Initiator has Off. Ally When Dispute Begins	0.229 (0.070)**	−0.466 (0.170)*
Initiator has Neut. Pact When Dispute Begins	—	−0.378 (0.172)*
Outsider Joins Target	0.331 (0.097)**	—
Outsider Joins Initiator	—	0.669 (.179)**
Constant	−3.067**	−0.822
Selection: Dispute Initiation		
Joint Democracy	−0.127 (0.053)*	−0.143 (0.059)*
Contiguity	0.530 (0.030)**	0.523 (0.031)**
Power of Challenger in Relation to Target	0.186 (0.038)**	0.185 (0.038)**
Similarity in Alliance Portfolios	−0.388 (0.038)**	−0.411 (0.040)**
Potential Target has Defensive Ally	−0.194 (0.034)**	−0.205 (0.034)**
Potential Challenger has Offensive Ally	0.189 (0.038)**	0.184 (0.038)**
Potential Challenger has Relevant Neut. Pact	0.209 (0.036)**	0.203 (0.039)**
Constant	−2.321**	−2.301**
Rho (Chi^2)	.949 (50.02)**	−0.005(0.99)
N (total, uncensored)	69730, 812	69730, 812
Chi^2	69.22**	68.93**

*p < 0.05; **p < 0.001

22.8 percent when the initiator has an offensive ally. If a dispute has been initiated, the average probability that outsiders help the target increases from 13.5 percent to 38.3 percent when the target has a defensive ally, and decreases from 20.6 percent to 12.4 percent when the initiator has a relevant neutrality pact.

In evaluating the effects of alliances on dispute expansion, we must keep in mind, however, that these alliances also have an effect on whether the dispute is initiated to begin with. Defensive alliances to targets decrease the probability of dispute initiation, and offensive alliances to initiators increase the probability of dispute initiation. Thus, I evaluate the impact of alliances on the probability of dispute expansion throughout the entire process. In other words, I examine the full impact of these types of alliances on the probability that a dispute both emerges and expands.[15] Because the probability of dispute initi-

Table 6.2. Changes in Population Risk Based on Analysis in Table 1

Dependent Variable/ Independent Variable	Risk of Dep. Var. in Sample	With Ind. Var.=0	With Ind. Var.=1	Percentage Change
Probability Conditional on Initiation				
Initiator Help/Offensive Ally	19.8	18.9	22.8	+21%
Target Help/Defensive Ally	19.1	13.5	38.3	+184%
Target Help/Neutrality Pact	19.1	20.6	12.4	−40%
Probability of Initiation and Expansion				
Initiator Help/Offensive Ally	0.31	0.25	0.49	+96%
Target Help/Defensive Ally	0.30	0.24	0.44	+83%
Target Help/Neutrality Pact	0.30	0.31	0.29	−6%

ation in the sample is very low, these probabilities are small, but the differences between them are interesting. The combined probability of initiation and expansion on the initiator's side is 0.25 percent without an offensive ally and 0.49 percent with an offensive ally. The combined probability of initiation and expansion on the target's side is 0.24 percent without a defensive ally and 0.44 percent with a defensive ally; 0.29 percent when the initiator has a neutrality pact and 0.31 percent when the initiator does not have a neutrality pact.

Thus, while offensive alliances have a relatively small impact on the probability of expansion once a dispute is initiated, they have a fairly large impact on the combined probability of dispute initiation and expansion, doubling the likelihood. Defensive alliances decrease the likelihood that a dispute will be initiated, but because they have a very large impact on the probability of dispute expansion if a dispute begins, they make larger disputes more likely on balance.

This empirical analysis provides support for the claim that alliances are good predictors of the probability that disputes will be multilateral crises; states with allies committed to assist them are more likely to receive outside help in disputes. Thus, defensive and offensive alliances do seem to be associated with the probability that disputes expand to involve additional actors. Those who have argued that alliances serve as a conduit for the expansion and diffusion of conflict will find support in this analysis (e.g., Siverson and Starr 1991).

Next I consider the influence of military alliances on the probability of particularly severe disputes—those that end in war. The dependent variable in this analysis is a dichotomous variable indicating whether the dispute is coded by the Correlates of War project as escalating to war (Small and Singer 1982; Sarkees 2000). I analyze both the direct and indirect effects of alliances on escalation. In one model, I include variables representing outside alliances to the initiator and target as independent variables. In the second, I include a variable representing whether more than two states were involved in the dispute before it escalated to war to capture dispute expansion.

I include two control variables as well. First, I include a dichotomous measure of joint democracy, coded 1 if both states score a six or higher on the POLITY democracy scale (Jaggers and Gurr 1996). While scholars tend to agree that democratic states are less likely to become involved in militarized disputes with one another (e.g., Russett and Oneal 2001), there is much less agreement on the relationship between joint democracy and the escalation of disputes to war (Dixon 1993; Senese 1997). Very few democratic disputes emerge, which makes it difficult to evaluate the phenomenon. While some argue that even once military hostilities have erupted, democratic states are better at bargaining to agreement short of war, others claim that democracies may be particularly prone to getting locked into an escalatory process and finding it difficult to back down from crises once they have begun (e.g., Fearon 1994b). Because a number of scholars have suggested, however, that jointly democratic dyads may exhibit unique tendencies, I include a control variable to isolate these effects.

Second, I include a measure of the difference in power between the initiator and the target. Many have argued that conflicts are most likely to escalate to war when both sides are uncertain who would win a war, and this is most likely when the two sides are relatively equal in power. Using the Correlates of War National Capability Index, I calculate the difference in power between the stronger state in the dyad and the weaker state. Smaller values mean that the states are relatively equal in power, whereas larger values indicate more difference in power between the two combatants.[16]

The results of this analysis are presented in table 6.3. Once we account for the factors that cause disputes to emerge in the first place, alliances have little direct influence on the likelihood that the parties bargain to a settlement before reaching the threshold of war. Defensive alliances seem to have some restraining effect (the negative coefficient is significant at the 0.10 level), but alliances to the initiator do not have a discernible effect on the probability that disputes end in war. Bilateral disputes, however, are less likely to escalate to war. Since alliances do have a clear impact on the likelihood that a dispute expands, they may be indirectly related to escalation. While jointly democratic dyads are neither more nor less likely than other dyads to end up in war once they have begun a dispute, similarities in power are correlated with a greater probability of escalation.[17]

Turning once again to the substantive importance of the primary independent variables in influencing the escalation of disputes to war (reported in table 6.4), we find that once a dispute emerges, the average probability of es-

Table 6.3. The Effects of Outside Allies on the Probability That Militarized Interstate Disputes Escalate to War, 1816–1944

	Model 1 Coefficient (s.e.)	Model 2 Coefficient (s.e.)
Joint Democracy	−0.251 (0.342)	−0.160 (0.335)
Difference in Capabilities	−1.734 (0.956)	−2.023 (0.984)*
Target has Def. Ally When Dispute Begins	−0.300 (0.180)	—
Initiator has Off. Ally When Dispute Begins	0.066 (0.186)	—
Initiator has Neut. Pact When Dispute Begins	−0.071 (0.195)	—
Bilateral Dispute	—	−0.479 (0.134)**
Constant	−1.567	−0.518
Selection: Dispute Initiation		
Joint Democracy	−0.143 (0.059)*	−0.143 (0.059)*
Contiguity	0.523 (0.031)**	0.523 (0.031)**
Power of Challenger in Relation to Target	0.192 (0.038)**	0.192 (0.038)**
Similarity in Alliance Portfolios	−0.408 (0.040)**	−0.406 (0.040)**
Potential Target has Defensive Ally	−0.191 (0.033)**	−0.193 (0.033)**
Potential Challenger has Offensive Ally	0.185 (0.038)**	0.185 (0.038)**
Potential Challenger has Relevant Neut. Pact	0.202 (0.039)**	0.202 (0.039)**
Constant	−2.306**	−2.307**
Rho (Chi^2)	0.138 (0.19)	−0.179 (0.45)
N (total, uncensored)	69730, 812	69730, 812
Chi^2	6.97	15.77**

*p < 0.05; **p < 0.001

calation to war is only 4.7 percent for a bilateral dispute, but 11.5 percent for a multilateral dispute similar in all other characteristics. It appears that bargains are more difficult to reach short of war when multiple parties are involved. Because alliances are so likely to be associated with dispute expansion, they may indirectly cause escalation as well.

While the direct effect of alliances on the probability of war once a dispute has emerged is relatively weak, there is a fairly clear impact of alliances on the combined probability that a dispute is initiated and escalates to war. The probability that a dispute will emerge and escalate to war in a given dyad averages .04 percent with a defensive ally to a target and 0.11 percent without—the risk of war is nearly tripled when a target does not have an ally. The average probability of initiating a dispute and escalating it to war is 0.08 percent for a potential challenger without an offensive ally and 0.14 percent for a potential challenger with an ally committed to assist her. Gaining a neutrality pact similarly changes the joint probability of initiation and escalation from 0.08 percent to 0.11 percent.

In the end, the data suggest that the strongest impact of alliances is on the probability that a dispute is initiated. Defensive alliances to a target make dispute initiation less likely, and offensive alliances to the initiator and neutrality

Table 6.4.   Changes in Population Risk Based on Analysis in Table 3

Dependent Variable/ Independent Variable	Risk of Dep. Var. in Sample	With Ind. Var.=0	With Ind. Var.=1	Percentage Change
Probability Conditional on Initiation				
War/Multilateral Dispute	7.5	4.7	11.5	+145%
Probability of Initiation and Escalation				
War/Offensive Ally	0.09	0.08	0.14	+75%
War/Defensive Ally	0.09	0.11	0.04	−64%
War/Neutrality Pact	0.09	0.08	0.11	+38%

pacts with the initiator make dispute initiation more likely. Once initiation occurs, however, alliances are associated with dispute expansion, and dispute expansion is in turn associated with a higher probability that a dispute escalates to war. There is reason to believe that even defensive alliances, when they fail to deter aggression, are associated with particularly severe conflicts. On balance, however, in the sample studied here, defensive alliances have made war less likely. Because they deter initiation, they reduce the overall risk of war, even if they raise the risks once a dispute begins.

CONCLUSION

International relations scholars have devoted tremendous energy to explaining the causes of war and developing effective deterrent strategies. Both in developing explanations and recommending policy, scholars have turned frequently to military alliances. Despite intense interest, however, scholars have been frustrated by their inability to discern clear systematic relationships linking alliances to deterrence success and to the probability of war. One of the primary reasons for this difficulty is that, until recently, statistical analyses of factors affecting general deterrence, and particularly those linking general and immediate deterrence, have been scarce. As some researchers have suspected, similar policies can have different effects on the probable success of general deterrence and of immediate deterrence, and a full understanding of their impacts requires a linked analysis of both (e.g., Huth 1999).

Alliances are a case in point. Defensive alliances are an effective means of general deterrence. Promises to assist a potential target in the event of overt conflict do make a challenger less likely to attack. When general deterrence fails, however, alliance commitments can serve to expand conflicts and complicate the bargaining required for successful settlement. When alliances fail to deter the initiation of disputes, they are more likely to be associated with conflicts that expand, and in turn, that escalate to full-scale war.

Overall, the appropriate conclusion to reach seems to be that most of the influence of alliances on military conflict occurs before an overt military dispute emerges. Challengers do use the information they have about the probability that they or their targets will receive assistance in deciding whether to begin a dispute, and this information seems to be fairly reliable; alliances are good predictors of the likelihood that a dispute becomes a multilateral crisis. Multilateral crises are more difficult to resolve in a low-cost manner than are bilateral crises, and thus, alliances may be indirectly associated with a greater risk of war. The evidence provided here, however, suggests that the general deterrent impact of defensive alliances is strong enough to make their overall impact pacifying.

NOTES

Author's note: This research was supported by the National Science Foundation (grant # SES-0095983). I would like to thank Vesna Danilovic, Erik Gartzke, Håvard Hegre, Jack Levy, Sara Mitchell, Cliff Morgan, Bill Reed, Jeff Ritter, Holger Schmidt, Randy Stevenson, and Ric Stoll for helpful advice on this research. Replication data is available at www.ruf.rice.edu/~leeds.

1. For a review, see Vasquez (1993).

2. For the purpose of this study, alliances are defined as "written agreements, signed by official representatives of at least two independent states, that include promises to aid a partner in the event of military conflict, to remain neutral in the event of conflict, to refrain from military conflict with one another, or to consult/co-operate in the event of international crises that create a potential for military conflict" (Leeds, Ritter, Mitchell, and Long 2002, 238).

3. For an application of this claim (based on social choice theory) to international relations, see Miers and Morgan 2002.

4. In the Correlates of War data, version 3.0 (Sarkees 2000), the mean length of multilateral wars is 552 days, while the mean length of bilateral wars is 358 days.

5. I refer to alliances that include promises of active military assistance in the event of attack on a member's sovereignty or territorial integrity as defensive alliances, and alliances that include promises of active military assistance in conflicts not precipitated by attack on a member's sovereignty or territorial integrity as offensive alliances. Some alliances, because they include promises of active assistance in both of these situations, are both defensive and offensive alliances. See Leeds et al. (2002, 241) for a discussion of this categorization, and Leeds (2003a, 432–33) for examples of treaty language characteristic of defensive alliances, offensive alliances, and defensive and offensive alliances.

6. Additional evidence in support of this claim is provided by Huth (1998), who shows that major powers are more likely to intervene in crises when they have alliance commitments to participants (see also Huth and Russett 1988), and Siverson and Starr (1991) who identify alliances as agents of conflict diffusion. An alternative argument, however, is offered by Smith (1995). Smith suggests that because reliable alliances deter conflict initiators, the observed cases in which challengers attack targets with allies should be biased toward targets who will not receive support. It is worth noting that the question addressed here—are disputes involving challengers and targets with allies more likely to expand?—is a slightly different question than that addressed in studies that demonstrate that allies are more likely to join conflicts than non-allies (e.g., Huth 1998; Werner and Lemke 1997).

7. I assembled this dataset using the EUGene computer program (Bennett and Stam 2000a). The indicators for my dependent variables and most of my independent variables are not available for the pre-1816 era, and the data for my primary independent variables are only available through 1944, so my temporal domain is constrained to the years between 1815 and 1945. The directed dyadic research design allows one to distinguish factors leading to the initiation of a dispute from factors conducive to being the target of a dispute. Limiting the spatial domain to interactions among states who are plausible candidates for military conflict restricts the sample in a way that appears not to threaten proper inference (Lemke and Reed 2001).

8. All analysis was performed using the *heckprob* command in STATA 7.0; this is a probit model with sample selection.

9. This study uses the dyadic version of the MID data (version 1.1) provided by Zeev Maoz. Only pairs of states that engage one another directly are included as disputing dyads, and only original initiators and original targets are included at this stage of analysis. Decisions to join ongoing disputes are studied separately. Original initiators are states that are coded as original participants on side A (the side to take the first militarized action), and original targets are those that are coded as original participants on side B. The data can be obtained at http//spirit.tau.ac.il/~zeevmaoz (January 29, 2001).

10. See Leeds (2003a) for discussion of the expected influence of these variables and their operationalization. There are two changes in the analysis presented as the first stage of the selection equation here from the analysis reported in Leeds (2003a). First, since the variable representing membership in a common alliance never reaches conventional levels of statistical significance in any of the models, I have eliminated it from the analysis. This has no effect on the interpretation of the other variables. Second, in the two-stage format, I am unable to adjust the analysis to account for temporal dynamics. Without accounting for the cross-sectional time series nature of the data, one inference does change. Joint democracy, which was negative but statistically insignificant in the original analysis (using a population-averaged panel data model), is negatively related to the initiation of disputes here.

11. Many alliance treaties state that the obligations arise only under clearly specified circumstances. I have been careful to include only alliances that would be applicable to conflicts arising in the dyad in question. I also checked the dates of alliance

formation and of dispute initiation and only included alliances that were in effect on the date the dispute began. It is important to note that obligations were coded in the Alliance Treaty Obligations and Provisions (ATOP) dataset based solely on the texts of the written alliance agreements and independent of the behavior that followed them. Please see Leeds, Ritter, Mitchell, and Long (2002) for further discussion of the distinctions among different types of obligations in the ATOP dataset and the specific nature of alliance commitments.

12. In designing my statistical models, I have included different control variables in my models of different aspects of dispute evolution. While there are a number of variables that prior research has shown to have some empirical effect on disputes or war, our theories tell us that different variables affect different parts of the dispute process. For instance, while contiguity has a relatively strong effect on the probability that a dispute is initiated since contiguous states find it easier to fight one another and tend to interact on a great number of issues over which disputes might arise, we have no compelling theories that suggest that once a dispute has begun contiguous states are more or less likely to engage in multilateral disputes or to escalate their disputes to war. Contiguity, therefore, is included as a control variable in the model predicting dispute initiation, but not in models of dispute expansion or escalation. The fact that the control variables in my models of dispute initiation are different from the variables in my models of various aspects of dispute evolution has the additional benefit of identifying the joint probit models.

13. For a discussion of this debate, see Walt (1987).

14. What I report here is the change in the average risk for the population given changes only in the characteristics of interest. In other words, I reanalyze predicted probabilities retaining all the same characteristics of the observations except for their alliances. Thus, the figures represent the average risk for a population where targets do have defensive allies versus one in which targets do not have defensive allies.

15. In the case of assistance to the initiator, we see a clear statistical connection between the initiation and expansion stages. The rho (the correlation between the error terms of the selection and outcome models) is highly significant. In fact, most of the influence of offensive allies is on the decision to initiate. In the case of assistance to the target, however, the error terms of the initiation and expansion equations are not significantly correlated. Empirically, it may be possible to study the two stages independently, and an independent test of the expansion model leads to similar inferences. Because there is theoretical reason to believe that a joint estimation is warranted, however, I choose to report the two stage model.

16. Please note that this measure of dyadic power relations is different from the measure included in the models of dispute expansion. In the models of dispute expansion, I include control variables that measure whether the initiator is stronger than the target. Larger values indicate the initiator is strong and the target is weak in comparison, and smaller values indicate that the target is strong in comparison to the initiator. In this analysis, the measure of dyadic power relations does not indicate who is stronger, but rather how much difference there is between the power of the stronger and weaker actors. Large values indicate that one state is much stronger than the other

(but not who is the stronger state) and smaller values indicate that the two states are fairly equal in power.

17. These models have extremely poor predictive ability—neither predicts any wars, and thus neither improves on a null model. Because the outcome models are so poor, it is not surprising that the rhos are insignificant—the error terms in the outcome equations surely include much more than the unobservable relationship to the initiation model.

7

Separation of Powers, Lawmaking, and the Use of Military Force

William G. Howell and Jon C. Pevehouse

Although investigations of the domestic politics of international relations have proliferated, studies of the use of force in American foreign policy regularly overlook the partisan struggles that erupt between presidents and Congress. We examine whether two government functions—writing laws and coordinating military ventures abroad—have common domestic institutional linkages. Specifically, we explore the possibility that partisan alignments between executive and legislative branches simultaneously augment the production of laws and the president's discretion to respond militarily to foreign crises; or, alternatively, whether inter-branch dynamics reverse course when presidents move away from advocating their legislative agenda, and toward contemplating the exercise of military force abroad. We show how international relations research can usefully adapt theories developed in American politics and suggest ways in which separation-of-power theories might incorporate other empirical investigations of international relations.

Almost twenty-five years after Kenneth Waltz proclaimed that "domestic systems are centralized and hierarchic" and hence are functionally "like units," international relations is rediscovering domestic political institutions, both the struggles that occur among them and the implications they have for the state's behavior in the international system (1979, 88). The rediscovery began with the advent of two-level games, which effectively linked the domestic political order to the international (Putnam 1988). Subsequently, scholars demonstrated that legislatures critically affect the capacity of states to commit to international agreements (Martin 2000; Milner 1997). In the United States, Congress's fundamental relevance in negotiating trade policies and tariffs appears well established (Lohmann and O'Halloran 1994; Karol

2000; Sherman 2002; Schnietz 2003). Within the democratic peace literature, scholars have begun to explore the ways in which legislatures help states signal resolve and act as conduits for public opinion (Huth and Allee 2003; Reiter and Tillman 2002; Prins and Sprecher 1999).

A concern for domestic political institutions, however, has yet to penetrate the quantitative literature on the use of force. Although the Constitution vests Congress with the power to raise and support armies, to provide and maintain a navy, to regulate the military, and to appropriate funds, the existing empirical literature on the use of force continues to overlook Congress's capacity to influence when, and whether, the president deploys troops abroad. Rarely are measures of congressional relations with the president included in statistical models on the use of force; and when included, they are crudely specified, typically nothing more than indicator variables for divided government (Gowa 1998, 1999; Fordham 2002), the post–War Powers Resolution period (DeRouen 1995), or for eras of "cold war consensus" (Meernik 1993).

Here too, however, there are signs that change is afoot. According to Milner, international political-economy arguments about legislatures' influence over the possibilities for, and content of, international cooperation fully extend to security studies: "In general, the more groups internally with which an executive must share power and the more preferences of these groups differ, the less likely it is that cooperation *or* conflict will occur. Polyarchy can prevent both cooperation *and* conflict" (Milner 1997, 259, emphasis added). Democracies that are internally divided—what Milner calls polyarchies— should be less likely to initiate military conflict abroad.[1] For as the number of parties vying for power proliferates, and as ideological divisions across branches of government intensify, the anticipated costs of military initiatives abroad increases, making heads of state less prone to initiate international conflict.

To test Milner's specific claim that ideological convergence within systems of separated powers paves the way for coordinated military ventures, we recently revisited the event-count models used to predict U.S. uses of force, adding appropriate measures of congressional support for the president (Howell and Pevehouse forthcoming). Our findings ran directly against the notion that politics stop "at the water's edge" (Gowa 1998). Between 1945 and 2000, no relationship was observed between the partisan support for the president within Congress and the total number of foreign military engagements each quarter. Large impacts emerged, however, when distinguishing minor from major military initiatives. While Congress did not appear to constrain the president's capacity to initiate low-level military maneuvers, sizeable effects were observed for major military ventures—the very events that can have electoral consequences for presidents *and* members of Congress. As partisan support within Congress increased, presidents engaged in major military initiatives more and more often; but, as support within Congress waned, so did the frequency with which presidents conducted significant acts of military force abroad.

This chapter advances the argument one step further, connecting the logic of inter-branch relations in security matters back to more traditional legislative concerns—namely, writing laws. We examine whether the institutional forces that promote the production of laws also support the president's discretion to respond militarily to foreign crises; or, alternatively, whether inter-branch dynamics reverse course, or are suspended altogether, when presidents move away from advocating on behalf of their legislative agenda and toward contemplating the exercise of military force abroad. Doing so, we show how processes that are typically studied in isolation from one another have common institutional linkages, suggesting that international relations may benefit from adapting theories developed in American politics.

We proceed as follows. The first section reviews the quantitative literature on the use of force in the international relations subfield and the theoretical literature on presidential-congressional relations within the American politics subfield. The second section applies these theoretical insights about executive-legislative relations to presidents' decisions about whether to deploy military troops abroad. The third examines the empirical relationships between the partisan composition of Congress, the number of uses of force during the post-war eras, and the enactment of important laws. The final section identifies additional synergies in international relations and American politics and recommends paths for future research.

INTERNATIONAL RELATIONS AND THE USE OF FORCE

Military deployments short of war (such as the Berlin airlift, the Cuban missile crisis, and interventions in the Middle East, Africa, and Central America) represent some of the most potent expressions of executive authority. Not surprisingly, the practice has garnered a large academic following, beginning with the pioneering work of Barry Blechman and Stephen Kaplan in 1978. Blechman and Kaplan were principally concerned with the international conditions (e.g., whether the Soviet Union or China was a party to a crisis, whether troops were already deployed in the region, the relative nuclear capabilities of the United States and the Soviet Union) that led presidents to initiate lower-level military ventures, what they termed "force without war." Blechman and Kaplan identified 226 such incidents between 1946 and 1976 and tracked when, and whether, U.S. presidents achieved their strategic objectives.

Beginning in the mid-1980s, scholars built upon Blechman and Kaplan's database to test international relations theories about interstate conflict and the political psychology of executive decision making. Charles Ostrom and Brian Job's study (1986) added an important set of domestic variables to the study of the use of force short of war. According to Ostrom and Job, U.S. presidents must create simple decision rules to balance the competing demands of the presidency. As commander in chief, chief executive, and "political leader," presidents "monitor salient dimensions in the domestic, international, and political arenas" before committing U.S. forces abroad. Domestic politics, however, retains special significance (1986, 555). Indeed, in Ostrom and Job's empirical analysis, the substantive impacts of domestic variables (public aversion to war, a weighted economic misery index, presidential approval, "overall presidential success," and national elections) were consistently as strong if not stronger than their international counterparts.

The Ostrom and Job findings spurred a number of quantitative studies that examined how the economy and public opinion influence presidents' decisions to deploy troops abroad. Patrick James and John Oneal (1991) introduced a new variable that tapped international threats to U.S. interests, yet still found that the same domestic political factors that Ostrom and Job introduced were largely responsible for the use of force. Benjamin Fordham (1998b) subsequently argued that economic factors and public opinion do not directly shape presidential choices, but instead influence how the president views his external environment. The president, according to Fordham, perceives international crises as particularly troublesome when the domestic economy is poor. When inflation is low and employment high, however, presidents have few incentives to imperil their reelection prospects with foreign military ventures and, hence, are more likely to overlook such crises.

Other scholars have reached very different conclusions, holding that purely external factors drive decisions to use force. Meernik (1994), for instance, finds that domestic economic forces played little to no role in predicting American use of military force (see also Meernik and Waterman 1996). Joanne Gowa (1998) contends that between 1875 and 1992 neither the partisan nature of Congress, electoral cycles, nor the state of the economy was a significant predictor of U.S. involvement in militarized disputes. In a slightly different vein, Mitchell and Moore (2002) and Fordham (2002) raise important issues of data comparability (scholars use different years in analyzing their hypotheses) and temporal dynamics (uses of force may be clustered together in time), both of which potentially compromise previous statistical findings.

While much divides the protagonists in the use of force literature, one assumption is dominant: Congress is weak.[2] Indeed, legislative impotence has achieved the status of conventional wisdom. According to James Meernik:

The literature on U.S. foreign policymaking unambiguously demonstrates that because of his constitutional prerogatives and political incentives as well as congressional weaknesses in foreign policy, it is the president who exercises supreme control over the nation's military actions. (1994, 122–23).

Joanne Gowa, one of the few scholars to use event count data actually to test Congress's influence on the use of force, concludes that:

The use of force abroad is invariant to both the domestic political calendar and the partisan composition of government. . . . The use of U.S. military power abroad responds only to changes in national power and to the advent of the world wars. (1998, 307).

Because the president is commander in chief of the military, Congress cannot (or will not) try to constrain his freedom to pick battles, define the scope and duration of conflict, or set the terms by which a conflict ultimately is resolved. While Congress may direct domestic policymaking, its hold over foreign policy is tenuous; and when the president decides to exercise military force abroad, members of Congress can only complain on Sunday morning talk shows. According to these scholars, the president's authority over military matters is beyond reproach.

Consider, by way of examples, the work on two of the causal mechanisms that underlie the use of force literature: the diversionary war hypothesis and the rally around the flag effect. The diversionary war hypothesis suggests that heads of state deploy troops abroad in an effort to distract attention away from domestic strife, most commonly a flagging economy (see, e.g., Richards et al. 1993). Advocates of the theory assume that Congress, the bureaucracy, and the public are blind to a leader's true intentions and, as a consequence, regularly accept on faith proffered justifications for conflicts (for critiques, see Meernik and Waterman 1996; Blainey 1988; Levy 1989; Morgan and Bickers 1992). By sending troops abroad, it is supposed, presidents can shift public attention away from a failing economy and rally widespread support, as members of Congress (very much including the opposition party) naturally and automatically fall behind their chief executive.

Congress, again, is largely absent from most quantitative tests for rally around the flag effects (Mueller 1973; Ostrom and Simon 1985; Wittkopf and Dehaven 1987; Lian and Oneal 1993). Congress's stance on military ventures conducted abroad, it is assumed, does not mediate the size or direction of changes in the president's public approval ratings (for exceptions, see Brody 1991; Brody and Shapiro 1989). While "aggressive foreign behavior [may be] a useful tool for dealing with domestic political problems," domestic political institutions do not hinder the president's ability to engage in aggressive foreign behavior (Morgan and Bickers 1992, 26). Quite to the contrary, members of Congress are just as susceptible to the rally phenomenon as is the general public (Stoll 1984). As Barbara Hinckley argues, "The use of force shows the clearest conventional pattern: presidents are active and Congress accedes to what the presidents request. On these occasions both Congress and the public rally around the President and the flag" (1994, 80).

We believe scholars overstate executive supremacy over the use of force and overlook opportunities for congressional influence. Presidents, to be sure, are not empty vessels responding to the whims of Congress. They retain profound informational and tactical advantages over Congress that make them the most powerful actors in U.S. foreign policy generally, and over security matters specifically (Peterson 1994). But we question the "unambiguous demonstration" that domestic political institutions do not, or cannot, impede the presidential use of force. Presidents cannot easily and automatically dupe their political opponents, especially when doing so entails putting American troops in harm's way. To strip away the institutional setting in which presidents operate is to dismiss the institutional politics associated with the use of military force.

THE AMERICAN POLITICS LITERATURE

While the existing use of force literatures occasionally gesture toward domestic political institutions (DeRouen 1995; Morgan and Campbell 1991), the treatment consistently is fleeting. This is unfortunate given the tremendous volume of research on executive-legislative relations within the American politics subfield (see, e.g., Binder 2003; Jones 1994; Mayhew 1991; Peterson 1990; Bond and Fleisher 2000; Krehbiel 1999). Scholars of American politics have developed ample theories with strong micro foundations on interactions between the executive and legislative branches. This work examines the conditions under which presidents successfully guide their legislative agendas through Congress (e.g., Rudalevige 2002); the ability of presidents to rally public opinion in support of particular bills, and the impact this has on Congress (Canes-Wrone forthcoming; Edwards 2003); the respective powers presidents wield in foreign versus domestic policy when negotiating with Congress (Wildavsky 1966). When discussing presidential power within the American politics subfield, Congress cannot be avoided. Yet within the extant use of force literature, the legislative branch, along with theory required to explain its behavior, is wholly absent.

A burgeoning body of work examines when presidents will unilaterally set public policy given that Congress and the courts may subsequently undo his actions (Cooper 2002; Howell 2003; Mayer 2001). Using executive orders, proclamations, memoranda, and administrative orders, presidents have managed to impose a wide array of public policies that never would have survived the legislative process. This work demonstrates that the president's powers of unilateral action—which very much encompass the option to deploy troops abroad—are critically defined by the capacity and willingness of Congress to subsequently overturn him.

Presidents rarely exercise their unilateral powers when large and unified majorities govern Congress. As shown elsewhere (Howell 2003), when strong majorities stand in support, the president would do better to engage the legislative process and set policy with firm legislative footings; and when such majorities stand in opposition, presidential efforts to unilaterally set public policy of consequence may provoke a congressional response. But when small and divided majorities govern Congress, presidents have incentives to strike out on their own. Just as an internally divided legislature cannot enact the president's agenda, nor can it overturn, post hoc, policies written and issued within the executive branch. In this sense, congressional strength marks presidential weakness, and congressional weakness presidential strength. The outcome is hardly accidental, for it is the checks that each institution places on the other that determines the overall division of power.

With regard to the use of force, inter-institutional dynamics shift as a clear asymmetry defines the relationship between Congress and the president. While members of Congress can punish the president for deploying troops abroad (Grimmet 2001), they cannot readily impel military action in the face of presidential resistance. In this realm—unlike policymaking generally, where Congress has the option of legislating when the president refuses to issue a unilateral directive—Congress's impact manifests itself principally as a constraint on presidential power. Not since the Spanish-American War has an activist, interventionist Congress forced a president into a foreign conflict that he would have just as soon avoided. Historically, the norm has been for presidents to identify foreign crises that they believe warrant military action, and subsequently (occasionally simultaneously) for members of Congress to support, abstain, or demur.

Unfortunately, while ready-made theories on the institutional foundations of unilateral powers are easily applied to presidents' decisions to use military force, the American politics and U.S. foreign policy literatures are devoid of systematic quantitative tests on this issue. Instead, scholars have offered up little more than isolated case studies, some of which herald Congress's impotence in foreign affairs (e.g. Hinckley 1994; Weissman 1995), while others celebrate examples of Congress successfully asserting its authority in foreign policy (Auerswald and Cowhey 1997; Freedman and Karsh 1993; Hall 1978; Lindsay

1994; Lindsay and Ripley 1993). Assuredly, scholars can point to instances of executive dominance (Nixon's expansion of the Vietnam War into Cambodia, Clinton's decision to invade Haiti in 1994 despite widespread congressional reluctance, Bush's uncontested exercise of military might in the immediate aftermath of September 11, 2001), just as others can selectively cite assertions of congressional prerogatives (the War Powers Resolution, Republicans' refusal to appropriate funds in 1976 for an invasion of Libya, the contentious debates that preceded invasions of Iraq in 1991 and, to a lesser extent, 2003). It remains unclear, however, whether Congress systematically figures into presidential decision making; or whether military deployments proceed irrespective of preference alignments across the legislative and executive branches.

Rarely are the limits of one subfield's treatment of a topic so well complemented by the strengths of another's. While American politics scholars have developed rich institutional theories that delineate the conditions under which presidents exercise their unilateral powers, uniformly they have overlooked the presidential decisions to deploy troops abroad. Meanwhile, international relations scholars have constructed impressive datasets on the use of force, but most overlook interactions between Congress and the president. Indeed, the international relations treatment of the use of force assumes away legislative constraints on presidential power, just as American politics scholars remain captivated by them.

EMPIRICAL TESTS

Congressional influence should vary according to the relative size and cohesiveness of the president's party and its opposition.[3] Without enough seats in Congress, and enough discipline within its ranks, the opposition party can do little to derail presidents' decisions to use force abroad—for as the international relations literature rightly insists, decisions regarding when and where the military intervenes ultimately reside with the commander in chief. But when the opposition party is unified and large, it can credibly threaten to punish presidents who pursue misguided military ventures. Although such punishments will not derail or stall all military initiatives, congressional opposition should decrease the likelihood that presidents will exercise force abroad.

Elsewhere, we demonstrate that the partisanship of Congress does in fact significantly affect the frequency with which presidents deploy troops abroad (Howell and Pevehouse forthcoming). As the size and unity of their party grows in Congress, presidents exercise force with rising frequency; but when support wanes, so too does their proclivity to engage in major military ventures. These effects, we show, hold for multiple time periods during the post–

World War II era, using multiple datasets on troop deployments, including a wide variety of background controls, and operationalizing congressional support in different ways. The willingness of presidents to assume the substantial risks (political and otherwise) associated with sending troops abroad appears to depend critically on the partisan support they enjoy within Congress.

It remains unclear, however, whether the politics that surround the creation of public policy differ markedly from those that surround military deployments; that is, whether inter-branch dynamics shift abruptly when discussions of proposed legislation turn to preparations for military engagements. For two reasons, this issue is consequential. First, and foremost, it raises the possibility of trade-offs occurring across policy spheres. If factors that positively contribute to the president's capacity to respond militarily to foreign crises negatively influence the prospects for enacting laws, then heretofore unrecognized tensions are built into systems of separated powers. Presidents may enjoy influence over the creation of public policy or discretion over the deployment of troops abroad, but not both—suggesting that the legacies they leave are confined to a single area of governance. Just as the administration begins to direct the military abroad, its ability to govern effectively at home becomes mired in gridlock; and just when the president and Congress begin to find common ground on domestic policy, tensions flare over security matters.

Consider the following scenario. Assume for the moment that Democratic members of Congress (but not Democratic presidents) are more dovish, and hence more skeptical of arguments on behalf of military deployments; while Republican members of Congress (but not Republican presidents) are more hawkish, and hence more willing to support foreign military ventures.[4] Further assume that Democrats and Republicans generally disagree with one another about the content of public policy. To see the trade-offs between lawmaking and military force, let us fix the president's partisanship while allowing Congress's to vary. During periods of divided government, a Democratic president should find ample opportunities to enact sweeping policy reforms, but precisely because his co-partisans in Congress generally oppose military campaigns, his discretion to respond militarily to foreign crises will be significantly reduced. Conversely, a Democratic president who faces a Republican Congress will enjoy widespread discretion to use force abroad, just as negotiations over policy matters bog down. Either way, agreement in one policy sphere implies opposition in the other, and presidents—by virtue of the distribution of parties across branches of government, rather than independent choices made while in office—must focus on those areas of governance where possibilities for coordinated action reside.

The "Partisan Divide" argument, however, could be wrong. Indeed, institutional arrangements may promote (or undermine) government action more generally, in both the creation of public policy and the initiation of military campaigns. Presidents and Congress, accordingly, are either productive or idle, just as policies and military ventures proliferate or languish. If true, then the success political actors enjoy in one area of governance need not be weighed against the failure they inevitably confront in another. The same factors supporting the passage of domestic laws may support the deployment of U.S. troops abroad.

The second reason for exploring inter-branch dynamics across policy spheres relates to the work of scholars in American politics and international relations, and the degree to which existing theories of legislative-executive relations can be transported to topics involving security matters. If the domestic politics of military engagements are completely unrelated to those of lawmaking, then American politics scholars have little to offer international relations scholars, except to remind them that Congress might deserve recognition. On the other hand, if these politics proceed in tandem, then much of the work of specifying inter-branch relations has already been accomplished, and the immediate job at hand involves linking up two literatures that, until now, have developed independently from one another. Just as encouraging, if the domestic institutional politics of policymaking and the use of force do in fact coincide, then, we may make strides toward unifying theories of systems of separated powers. Rather than constructing separate institutional theories for domestic policymaking and military engagement, scholars may begin to identify those opportunities that contribute to, or hinder, government action and gridlock more generally.

In this section, we examine whether those institutional dynamics that support the enactment of legislation also contribute to the propensity of presidents to use force in the international arena. Specifically, we estimate a seemingly unrelated negative binomial model, with the use of force and the enactment of significant laws as the two dependent variables. The seemingly unrelated (SUR) class of models is appropriate for our empirical test. Although we have proffered that the same underlying institutional arrangemenets inform both the enactment of key laws and the deployment of U.S. forces abroad, there is nothing to suggest a strictly simultaneous process, vitiating the need to move to a set of simultaneous equations. SUR models, however, account for correlations in residuals between equations and yield efficiency gains.[5]

Our model specification is as follows:

(1) $\text{FORCE} = \beta_0 + \beta_1 \text{CongressSupport} + \beta_2 \text{Unemployment} + \beta_3 \text{CPI} + \beta_4 \text{Approval} + \beta_5 \text{Election} + \beta_6 \text{War} + \beta_7 \text{ColdWar} + \beta_8 \text{Hegemony} + \beta_9 \text{WorldDispute} + \Sigma \beta_i \text{President} + \epsilon_1$

(2) $LAWS = \gamma_0 + \gamma_1 CongressSupport + \gamma_2 Approval + \gamma_3 Election + \gamma_4 War + \Sigma \gamma_i President + \epsilon_2$

Equation 1: Use of Force

In equation 1, the dependent variable (FORCE) is a yearly count of major deployments of force directed by the president. We update data from Fordham (1998b), Fordham and Sarver (2001), and Zelikow (1987), who extended the original Blechman and Kaplan time series that ended in 1976.[6] The dependent variable, as such, is the number of times each year that the president initiates major force abroad.[7] Table 7.1 includes descriptive statistics for all variables.

Our key explanatory variable measures the convergence of preferences between Congress and the executive. This variable, *CongressSupport*, is operationalized three ways. First, we employ a simple indicator variable (*Unified*) that equals 1 when the House, Senate, and president are led by the same political party, and zero otherwise. Second, we compute the average percentage of seats held by the president's party in the House and Senate and label this variable *Percent President Party*.[8]

Southern Democrats present obvious problems for partisan-based measures of presidential support. While Democrats enjoyed large majorities in the House and Senate in the 1960s, they also faced strong divisions within their ranks. To address this shortcoming, David Brady, Joseph Cooper, and Patricia Hurley (1979) constructed "legislative potential for policy change" (LPPC) scores. They base LPPC scores on four factors: (1) the size of the majority party; (2) the majority party's internal cohesiveness; (3) the size of the minority party; and (4) its cohesiveness.[9] To generate our third measure

Table 7.1. Descriptive Statistics

	Mean	Std Dev.	Min.	Max.
Force	2.52	1.95	0.0	7
Laws	46.88	17.02	18.0	103
Unified	0.39	0.49	0.0	1.0
President Percent Party	0.50	0.09	0.35	0.68
President Party Power	−0.46	13.98	−23.63	26.96
Unemployment	5.51	1.61	2.03	9.70
CPI	4.22	3.38	−0.95	14.65
Approval	55.19	12.16	28.25	85.25
Election	0.25	0.44	0.0	1.0
Ongoing War	0.25	0.44	0.0	1.0
Cold War	0.80	0.40	0.0	1.0
Hegemony	0.33	0.06	0.26	0.52
World Disputes (non U.S.)	22.14	7.77	4.0	38.0

of congressional support for the president, we modify these scores only slightly, substituting the president's and opposition parties for the majority and minority parties, respectively. When the president's party is relatively large and unified and confronts a relatively small and divided opposition party, the president should be able to use force with considerable freedom. Conversely, when the president's party is relatively small and divided, and the opposition party is larger and more unified, the president's freedom to use force abroad should decline substantially. We label this variable *President Party Power*.

Upon reflection there is good reason to expect that the impact of *Percent President Party* and *President Party Power* could be nonlinear. Incremental changes at the tails of the distribution may not have an appreciable impact on the frequency with which presidents exercise force abroad. Shifts around the center of the distribution, meanwhile, may induce large changes in the use of presidential force. To test for the possibility of nonlinear effects, we take the logistic transformations of *Percent President Party* and *President Party Power* and reestimate the statistical models (these transformations are noted in each table with an "e" prefix). Thus, for both *Percentage President Party* and *President Party Power*, the first set of estimates in tables 7.3 and 7.4 contains only a linear term of each variable, while the second set contains their logistic transformations.

As previously discussed, scholars have focused almost exclusively on other domestic and international factors that shape the president's ability to use force abroad. To mitigate concerns about omitted variable bias, we incorporate controls for many of the alternative hypothesized influences on the use of force. To begin, consistent with a burgeoning literature on the political economy of the use of force (Ostrom and Job 1986; Fordham 1998b), we control for the yearly unemployment rate and the inflation rate (CPI), both of which were taken from the Bureau of Labor Statistics. Past research, for the most part, finds that poor economic performances encourage presidents to act aggressively in foreign policy affairs (James and Oneal 1991; Fordham 2002).

Because much of the literature on the use of force draws upon theories of diversionary war, we control for the president's public approval rating (*Approval*). The impetus for much of the original quantitative work on the subject was Ostrom and Job's (1986) finding that approval ratings were a highly significant determinant of the use of force—though subsequent research has proven less definitive on the matter. We measure the first Gallup presidential approval rating at the beginning of each year.[10]

A related body of work examines whether elections usher in additional uses of force (Stoll 1984; Gaubatz 1991). This research contends that rally around the flag effects establish incentives for presidents to use force during the months immediately preceding an election. As such, we control for presidential election years (*Election*).

The next four variables capture facets of the international environment that may impinge on the president's autonomy in foreign policy. Due to contemporaneous military commitments, there should be a tendency for presidents to employ force for bargaining purposes less often during times of war. We introduce the *War* variable to control for periods of international wars in which the United States was involved (here, Korea, Vietnam, and the 1991 Gulf War). The Cold War was also a period of heightened concern over international engagement of U.S. forces. To account for its influence, we include a dummy variable coded 1 during the 1945–1989 period (*ColdWar*).

To account for systemic forces that have been linked to the onset of both interstate wars and disputes (Mansfield 1994; Mansfield and Pevehouse 2000), we include a measure of U.S. hegemony during the period of analysis (*Hegemony*). The measure is the percentage of international military capabilities held by the United States and derives from the Correlates of War Capabilities dataset (Small and Singer 1993). With hegemonic power may come responsibilities (and incentives) to monitor, and possibly intervene, in conflicts. If true, then hegemony ought to be positively associated with the use of force. Finally, we include a measure of the number of world military conflicts beginning in each year of observation (*WorldDispute*). Presumably, a higher number of world conflicts provides more opportunities for the United States to respond with the use of force (Meernik 1994; Fordham 1998b). The data here aggregates non-U.S. militarized interstate disputes (MIDs) over the period of observation (on the MIDs data, see Jones, Bremer, and Singer 1996).

Finally, we include presidential fixed-effects in our model to account for individual differences in each president's leadership style, military experience, and policy agendas.

Equation 2: Nontrivial Laws

In equation 2, the dependent variable (*LAWS*) represents the number of "nontrivial" laws enacted each year. Nontrivial laws encompass all "landmark," "important," and "ordinary" laws enacted by each Congress. Landmark enactments consist of the "Sweep One" laws identified by David Mayhew (1991). By measuring the amount of coverage laws received in the *New York Times*, the *Washington Post*, and the annual *Congressional Quarterly* almanacs, Howell et al. (2000) categorized all of the remaining laws as important, ordinary, or trivial. Between 1945 and 1995, 17,830 total laws were enacted, 1 percent of which they deemed landmark, 1 percent important, 10 percent ordinary, and 87 percent trivial.[11] Here, we combine the 12 percent of landmark, important, and ordinary laws and extend the time series through 2000.

The remaining control variables in the *LAWS* equation draw from those used in the *FORCE* equation. As no one, to our knowledge, argues that changes in the economy, the number of international disputes, the relative power of the United States vis-à-vis the rest of the world, or the Cold War systematically affect the production of laws, we exclude these variables from the model. Background controls for election years, periods of war, and presidential approval ratings regularly are included in statistical models of legislative productivity, and hence are kept here as well. Finally, as in the *FORCE* model, we include presidential fixed-effects to account for differences across administrations that may contribute to their baseline propensity to enact laws.

Results

The estimates of each model across the versions of our independent variable of interest are presented in three tables. Table 7.2 shows the results for our simple dummy variable indicating the presence of unified government. *Unified* is positive and significant in each equation, suggesting that during periods of partisan alignment between the legislative and executive branches, both the use of force and the enactment of important laws become more likely. Specifically, for the *FORCE* equation, the presence of unified government increases by over 80 percent the predicted count of the use of force. For the *LAWS* equation, unified government induces a nearly 20 percent increase in the predicted number of nontrivial laws.

The models utilizing *Percent President Party* (Table 7.3) and *President Party Power* (Table 7.4) also show strong support for our hypothesis. In fact, in only one case (the logistic transformation of *President Party Power* in the *LAWS* equation) is our explanatory variable of interest not statistically significant. For the estimates using the *Percent President Party* measure, an increase in one standard deviation from the mean of that variable produces a 17 percent increase in the number of predicted uses of force and a corresponding 15 percent increase in the predicted number of nontrivial laws. An equivalent shift in *President Party Power* induces a 24 percent increase in the number of military deployments and a 10 percent increase in the predicted number of laws.

The overwhelming balance of evidence from these models suggests that there is a strong link between the partisan composition of the legislature and

Table 7.2. Seemingly Unrelated Count Model of Use of Major Force by the United States and the Enactment of Nontrivial Laws: 1945-2000

	FORCE	*LAWS*
Unified	0.603***	0.170**
	(0.161)	(0.079)
Unemployment	0.229***	—
	(0.079)	
CPI	0.061**	—
	(0.028)	
Approval	0.001	0.001
	(0.016)	(0.002)
Election	0.089	0.052
	(0.242)	(0.112)
Ongoing War	−0.739***	−0.108***
	(0.119)	(0.041)
Cold War	0.655***	—
	(0.135)	
Hegemony	3.264	—
	(3.270)	
World Disputes	0.013	—
	(0.023)	
Constant	−2.889*	3.183***
	(2.006)	(0.147)
ln(α)	−16.623	−3.525

NOTE: N = 56 for both equations. For all table entries: *** = p< .01; ** = p< .05; * = p< .1; one-tailed tests. Each model is estimated using negative binomial regression with Huber/White/sandwich clustered standard errors. Each model also contains fixed effect terms for each presidential administration, which are not reported to conserve space.

the president's ability to act in both the domestic and international realms. These models lend no support for the notion that presidential influence is consigned to either foreign or domestic policy initiatives, but not both. Quite the contrary, increased legislative activity implies greater freedom for presidents to exercise military force abroad, and vice versa. The American politics literature helps explain why: when the president enjoys strong support in Congress, he is less constrained in both foreign and domestic policy. Stronger congressional support leads to a comparatively easier road for the president to pursue his legislative agenda, just as it affords greater discretion to send troops abroad. The very institutional structures that support the enactment of numerous laws—namely, widespread support within Congress for the president—also lend the chief executive considerable discretion to exercise force abroad.

Table 7.3. Seemingly Unrelated Count Models of Use of Major Force by the United States and the Enactment of Nontrivial Laws: 1945–2000

	(Model 1)		(Model 2)	
	FORCE	LAWS	FORCE	LAWS
Percent President Party	1.785**	1.571*	—	—
	(0.969)	(0.963)		
e[Percent President Party]	—	—	7.565**	6.583*
			(4.191)	(4.108)
Unemployment	0.239***	—	0.239***	—
	(0.090)		(0.090)	
CPI	0.039*	—	0.039*	—
	(0.026)		(0.026)	
Approval	−0.003	0.0002	−0.003	0.0003
	(0.016)	(0.002)	(0.016)	(0.002)
Election	0.057	0.081	0.057	0.081
	(0.252)	(0.118)	(0.253)	(0.118)
Ongoing War	−0.575***	−0.077***	−0.575***	−0.077**
	(0.182)	(0.030)	(0.182)	(0.030)
Cold War	0.679***	—	0.678***	—
	(0.158)		(0.157)	
Hegemony	5.030*	—	5.025*	—
	(3.265)		(3.281)	
World Disputes (non U.S.)	0.009	—	0.009	—
	(0.024)		(0.024)	
Constant	−3.725*	2.497***	−7.544**	−0.816
	(2.198)	(0.530)	(3.986)	(2.597)
ln(α)	−17.248	−3.589	−17.496	−3.586

NOTE: N = 56 for both equations in both models. For all table entries: *** = p< .01; ** = p< .05; * = p< .1; one-tailed tests. Each model is estimated using negative binomial regression with Huber/White/ sandwich clustered standard errors. Each model also contains fixed effect terms for each presidential ad- ministration, which are not reported to conserve space.

Regarding the control variables, the presence of war depresses both the number of times force is used as well as the number of laws enacted. When both institutions are preoccupied with ongoing conduct of a full-scale war, the nation's ability to extend the military to other parts of the globe and the resources required to enact important legislation undoubtedly decline.

In the *FORCE* equation, both unemployment and inflation correlate positively with uses of force. In nearly every model, these estimates are statistically significant, which is consistent with the existing use of force literature's emphasis on economic predictors of foreign policy (Fordham 1998b, 2002; Ostrom and Job 1986). The Cold War saw consistently more activity in terms of the use of force. As predicted, higher levels of hegemony are positively as-

Table 7.4.   Seemingly Unrelated Count Models of Use of Major Force by the United States and the Enactment of Nontrivial Laws: 1945–2000

	(Model 1)		(Model 2)	
	FORCE	LAWS	FORCE	LAWS
President Party Power	0.015***	0.007*	—	—
	(0.005)	(0.004)		
e[President Party Power]	—	—	0.393***	0.098
			(0.105)	(0.096)
Unemployment	0.222**	—	0.231***	—
	(0.088)		(0.084)	
CPI	0.041*	—	0.036	—
	(0.028)		(0.030)	
Approval	−0.003	0.001	−0.003	0.001
	(0.016)	(0.002)	(0.016)	(0.002)
Election	0.078	0.070	0.066	0.044
	(0.252)	(0.117)	(0.235)	(0.110)
Ongoing War	−0.645***	−0.085*	−0.692***	−0.072**
	(0.160)	(0.033)	(0.150)	(0.043)
Cold War	0.660***	—	0.682***	—
	(0.159)		(0.136)	
Hegemony	4.257*	—	4.848*	—
	(3.103)		(3.064)	
World Disputes (non U.S.)	0.011	—	0.012	—
	(0.024)		(0.024)	
Constant	−2.600*	3.266*	−2.979*	3.224
	(1.781)	(0.124)	(2.037)	(0.132)
ln(α)	−19.990	−3.554	−17.116	−3.497

NOTE: N = 56 for both equations in both models. For all table entries: *** = $p < .01$; ** = $p < .05$; * = $p < .1$; one-tailed tests. Each model is estimated using negative binomial regression with Huber/White/sandwich clustered standard errors. Each model also contains fixed effect terms for each presidential administration, which are not reported to conserve space.

sociated with increases in the use of force in four out of five sets of estimates. The state of public approval of the president, the presence of elections, and the number of disputes in the world have no discernible bearing on the use of force.

A Note on the Possibility of Direct Trade-offs

Our previous statistical tests showed that there was nothing inherent in the assignment of preferences across branches of government that forces presidents to choose between an aggressive foreign or domestic policy agenda. Nonetheless, it could be the case that time and resource constraints during a presidential administration establish more direct trade-offs between the enactment of laws and the use of force, implying a negative relationship between the two. This question is important to consider for two reasons.

The first is substantive in nature. Efforts to address foreign policy crises may erode the president's ability to pursue his domestic policy agenda, just as ongoing negotiations over domestic policy may distract a president from attending to foreign crises. While presidents may choose to pursue foreign or domestic policy successes during periods of unified government (an eventuality that the Partisan Divide argument does not allow for), as a practical matter, they may not always be able to secure both. No one, perhaps, has been more aware of this eventuality than Lyndon Johnson, who witnessed his Great Society stall as developments in Vietnam dominated the news, and who eventually decided to forego reelection in 1968 because of mounting domestic protest against the war.[12]

Second, the existence of trade-offs would indicate that our previous statistical models are miss-specified. Rather than seemingly unrelated processes, we would be dealing with related processes. Such a relationship would require a modeling strategy that accounts for systems of simultaneous equations wherein the endogenous variable in one equation represents the dependent variable in the other—the common stock of three-stage estimators. Unfortunately, simultaneous count models using three-staged estimators are not well developed in the econometrics literature. We attempted to estimate the simultaneous count models a number of other ways, including instrumental variable maximum-likelihood approaches, two-stage least squares, and three-stage least squares. Each of these sets of estimates yielded wildly diverging estimates of the effects of uses of force on the enactment of nontrivial laws, and vice versa. No strong evidence emerged that a consistent trade-off exists between the use of force and the enactment of laws, but given the fragile nature of these models, we do not place much weight on these results and leave the issue for future research.[13]

CONCLUSIONS, FUTURE DIRECTIONS

Given extant theories from the American politics subfield, our own empirical findings are not surprising. Just as the composition of Congress has clear, and profound, implications for the president's legislative agenda, so too does it affect executive discretion to use force abroad. When the president confronts a hostile Congress, he is less likely to initiate large-scale military forces; when he enjoys widespread support in Congress, meanwhile, he is more likely to do so. The levels of partisan support presidents inherit when they assume office crucially defines their capacity to govern, and set in motion legislative processes or military campaigns that address any number of domestic or foreign problems.

Let us be clear, however, about our argument's boundaries and structure. We do not claim that the influence Congress exerts over domestic public policy carries over, in full, to deliberations over military engagements; plainly, Congress gives considerable ground when policy discussions turn from farm subsidies and welfare reform to armed conflicts in Libya and border disputes between Ecuador and Peru. Similarly, we are not arguing that presidents need to seek Congress's formal or tacit consent every time that they consider military action; clearly, presidents often send troops abroad with little regard to Congress's wishes. Our argument is probabilistic in nature, suggesting that Congress, all else being equal, plays an important role in defining the political costs of a military venture, and determining the chances that presidents will have to pay them.

In the immediate future, three matters require attention. The first concerns issues of measurement and model specification. Admittedly, the statistical models estimated here are crude. The dependent variables are annual frequencies of enacted laws and military deployments. Nothing in the *FORCE* models identifies the duration of time troops are deployed, the eventual success or failure of the missions, or the kinds of foreign crises to which the United States is responding. Similarly, the *LAWS* models do not differentiate legislation by policy type or the margins by which they were enacted. The key explanatory variables, meanwhile, could also benefit from improved measurement. The models presented here assume that the number of copartisans within Congress strictly determines support for the president. Consequently, members of each political party are assumed to have identical preferences (both in form and intensity) across multiple policy realms. Democratic members of Congress are presumed always to oppose Republican presidents, just as Republicans are presumed to uniformly oppose Democratic presidents. Little in these models allows us to explore intra-party disputes, instances when opposition to the president rises as the revealed costs of a military engagement materialize, or possibilities for bipartisan alliances when a military engagement succeeds.

Second, empirical studies of the use of force should move beyond simple event-count models, and begin to examine the ways in which Congress influences not only decisions to deploy troops but also the timing, duration, scope, and ongoing conduct of military exercises. Witness, for example, the decision to authorize the use of force against Iraq in the fall of 2002, an event which would seem to disprove our argument as the president confronted a House controlled by his own party, but a Senate very much divided and (weakly) controlled by his opposing party. Why did the processes outlined in this chapter ultimately fail to check the prospects of an Iraq invasion? We would first remind the reader that our argument is probabilistic—we do not claim that partisan politics influence every military deployment. Rather, on balance, a president facing a hostile Congress will be less likely to deploy troops. Still, the Iraq episode indicates various ways in which congressional-executive dynamics shape decisions to exercise military force. After weeks of insisting that prior resolutions granted him the required authority to exercise military force, Bush nonetheless relented in October 2002 and formally requested from Congress authorization to use force in Iraq. As the existing literature presumes, Bush could have easily ignored Congress; and while it is possible that Bush asked for a vote knowing that it would be favorable, a vast array of voices (especially among Democrats) pushed for a formal vote. Then, during congressional debates over Iraq, many questioned the lack of international support for the Iraq operation, establishing further impetus for the Bush administration subsequently to seek United Nations approval.

In the end, Congress did not stop the administration from attacking Iraq, nor did it convince the administration to act exclusively through the UN, substantiating Louis Fisher's argument that "the decision to go to war cast a dark shadow over the health of U.S. political institutions and the celebrated system of democratic debate and checks and balances" (2003, 390). But even amidst these extraordinary events are undercurrents of congressional influence—most prominently, over the invasion's timing. Had the Bush administration not felt impelled to seek congressional approval, nor go to the UN, we might well be discussing the December 2002 invasion of Iraq. None of the existing empirical tests in the use of force literature (nor our own) capture such procedural developments and hence overlook additional manifestations of congressional influence.

The final task for future research involves the incorporation of other empirical studies in international relations with domestic policymaking and the use of force. As previously mentioned, limited work has investigated how divided government influences trade policy (Lohmann and O'Halloran 1994; Sherman 2002), the escalation of military disputes (Huth and Allee 2003), and aggressiveness in foreign policy (Clark 2001). As it does for the production of laws and the initiation of military force, the structure of partisan preferences across branches of government should have implications for treaty ratification, signing preferential trade agreements, military spending, foreign aid allotments, immigration policy, and economic sanctions, among others.

Having accomplished these three objectives, the groundwork may be set for the identification of a unified theory of systems of separated powers. Some efforts to specify such a grand theory are already underway. Bruce Bueno de Mesquita and colleagues (1999a, 1999b, 2000) have developed a general model of domestic institutions and international conflict that high-lights differences in institutional rules guiding the election of leaders. Their argument suggests that the size of the "selectorate" (those who participate in the selection of government leaders) and the proportion of the selectorate that is required to hold positions of government leadership have a direct influence on foreign policy behavior, very much including the propensity to use force in the international system. They argue that as the size of a winning coalition increases (more support is needed to sustain leadership), leaders will want to fight more effectively since "the prospects for survival increasingly hinge on successful policy performance" (Bueno de Mesquita et al. 1999b, 804). Thus, Bueno de Mesquita and colleagues deduce that democracies are more likely to win wars and credibly deter those who would challenge them.

This theory of political institutions, however, largely ignores the alignment of preferences across political institutions *within each country*. For example, what is the role of those individuals outside of the winning coalition, but within the selectorate? What happens when the winning coalition must "win" in more than one powerful institution (e.g., executive and legislative branches)? We suggest that what may drive leaders in democracies to fight ef-fectively (and selectively) is not only concern with the winning coalition size but concern over winning coalitions in other institutions.

George Tsebelis has articulated an alternative theory that better accounts for political actors' preferences across a governing system (2002). Tsebelis focuses on the number of veto players in a political system and their impact on possibilities for major policy change. Veto players, Tsebelis argues, en-hance policy stability just as they inhibit innovation; and where multiple veto players with divergent ideological orientations preside over legislative and executive branches, policy change can be expected to come almost exclu-sively through independent bureaucracies and judiciaries. A unified theory of domestic institutions, however, need not specify a set of conditions under which activity in all branches of government increases, or decreases, concur-rently and in equal proportion. Howell (2003), for instance, argues that there are clear trade-offs between the production of laws and the issuance of uni-lateral directives from presidents (e.g., executive orders, executive agree-ments, national security directives). A unified institutional theory need not predict that all indicators of government activity point upward or downward, either across branches of government or policy spheres. Such a theory, in-stead, should identify the key underlying institutional configurations that link the various processes of enacting laws, issuing unilateral directives, deploy-ing troops, and negotiating trade agreements.

In any discipline, a certain division of labor emerges. As grand theories (e.g., selectorate and veto-player models) are asserted and modified, so too are finer measures of executive and legislative preferences developed, datasets that capture particular features of domestic policy, trade, and military campaigns are assembled, and statistical modeling techniques that allow for the estimation of systems of equations based upon event-counts are specified. From our perspective, however, the time is long overdue for scholars across subfields to speak directly to one another. As we demonstrate here, processes that appear to play out on entirely different dimensions (writing laws and deploying troops) in fact have important institutional linkages; and, as a consequence, theories in American politics may well benefit scholars in international relations. Eventually, we hope, the boundaries across (and within) subfields will continue to dissipate as scholars edge toward a unified theory of systems of separated powers that generates predictions about *both* the presence or absence of cooperation between states (in dyadic analyses) and the likelihood of different policies being enacted within states (in monadic analyses).

NOTES

We thank the Center for American Political Studies, the Weatherhead Center for International Affairs, and the Wisconsin Alumni Research Foundation for financial support; Doug Kriner for research assistance; and the participants at the New Directions for International Relations seminar at Yale for helpful feedback. Standard disclaimers apply.

1. Milner's (1997, 11) definition of polyarchy (the nature of power sharing arrangements among domestic groups) differs from Dahl's (1971) definition (amount of democracy within a country).

2. For a partial exception, see Morgan and Campbell (1991) and Morgan and Bickers (1992).

3. Consistent with George Edwards's observation that "members of the president's party almost always form the core of the president's support in Congress" (2003, p. 10), we focus on partisan support for the president within Congress. There is, at present, a sizeable literature in American politics that examines the effects of partisan divisions across the legislative and executive branches on lawmaking (Mayhew 1991; Coleman 1999; Howell et al. 2000; Rudalevige 2002; Binder 2003; Lewis 2003). Concurrently, there is an ongoing debate about whether parties represent mere proxies for members' preferences (see, e.g., Krehbiel 1993), or whether party leaders independently influence legislative processes (e.g., Cox and McCubbins 1993). On this particular issue, we remain agnostic. Given that the unilateral presidency literature consistently finds that the partisan composition of Congress influences executive discretionary authority, however, we choose in this chapter to use partisan measures of congressional support.

4. Many scholars assume that Republicans and Democrats have divergent preferences concerning the use of force. Among others, see Gowa 1998; Fordham 1998a; Fordham 2002.

5. On seemingly unrelated models, see Pindyck and Rubinfeld (1991, 308-11); Kennedy (1992, 164, 170).

6. For a description of our modifications and extensions of the Blechman and Kaplan data, see Howell and Pevehouse (forthcoming). We use only major uses of force in this investigation. Note that the classification of major versus minor force is *ex ante* to the crisis and is based on initial deployment size. For a further discussion of this choice, see Howell and Pevehouse (forthcoming) and Mitchell and Moore (2002).

7. Following those who have investigated the determinants of legislative productivity, we use annual event counts (see, e.g., Coleman 1999; Peterson 1990). Those who have not used annual event counts, for the most part, have aggregated to each Congress (Howell et al 2000; Mayhew 1991). Because many of the influences on the legislative calendar do not vary within the year, there is good cause for using annual data; it is worth noting, however, that observed impacts attenuate when relying upon quarterly data on the nontrivial law time series. For more on issues of temporal aggregation, see Mitchell and Moore 2002.

8. Versions of the key explanatory variables that consider only the partisanship of the Senate generate virtually identical results.

9. The LPPC score for either chamber in any given term is calculated as follows: Chamber LPPC = [(majority party size in percent) x (cohesion of majority party)] - [(minority party size in percent) x (cohesion of minority party)]. *Congressional Quarterly*'s party unity scores are utilized.

10. Some research, including Ostrom and Job, does not measure approval at the outset of the period of observation, but throughout the period. This specification invites endogeneity problems (on this issue, see DeRouen 1995; DeRouen 2000b; De-Rouen and Peake 2002), as rally around the flag effects emanating from exercises of force may influence popularity ratings.

11. For a further description of these data, see Howell et al. (2000).

12. Johnson's experience, in fact, reveals an important limitation to our analyses. Neither the original Blechman-Kaplan series nor its extensions includes major, protracted conflicts (e.g., Vietnam and Korea), which may derail presidents' domestic agendas. Because our event data concerns uses of force short of war, and because our analyses focus only on initial deployment decisions, our empirical test are poorly equipped to detect these trade-offs. (More on this below.)

13. Another possibility is that while military campaigns conducted abroad may disrupt negotiations over certain public policies (e.g., those over welfare or social security reform), they may actually facilitate others (e.g., adjustments to military appropriations and the creation of new administrative agencies). Given that the *LAWS* equation above distinguishes legislation by its significance but not its policy type, these kinds of trade-offs should not affect the estimates presented.

8

Democracies Prefer to Negotiate: Institutionalized Democracy, Diversion, and Statecraft during International Crises

Karl DeRouen Jr. and Shaun Goldfinch

We analyze statecraft choices during international crises from 1918 to 1994. When a crisis erupts, leaders can choose to negotiate, use coercive policies such as threats or sanctions, or resort to violence. One literature suggests that democracies are less likely to use violence to resolve crises. Another literature argues that domestic unrest makes violence more likely. These findings have not been looked at within a range of policy choices. Studies tend to ignore the negotiation or coercion outcomes. We hypothesize, drawing on the new institutional literature, that leaders of democracies prefer nonviolent measures to resolve crises, whether or not opponents are democratic. We specify a model with an ordered dependent variable: negotiation, coercion, or violence, and test it using joint democracy, monadic democracy, relative capabilities, contiguity, trigger of crisis, domestic unrest, and whether ethnicity is a component of the crisis. Both joint and monadic democracy increase the probability that actors will select negotiation over coercion or violence during crises. When states are experiencing domestic unrest, the use of violence is more likely than either negotiation or coercion, but either monadic and dyadic democracy increases the use of negotiation and decreases the use of violence.

A large and growing body of research has shown that democracies seldom, if ever, go to war with other democracies (c.f. Russett and Oneal 2001). It is argued, however, that democracies are as likely to fight wars as nondemocracies (Dixon 1993). Another body of research suggests democracies may engage in military action to divert attention from internal problems (Gelpi 1997; Levy 1989). Drawing on Brecher and Wilkenfeld's (2000) International Crisis Behavior (ICB) dataset of international crisis actors from 1918 to 1994, we assess these discrepant findings and show that democracies are less likely to engage in violent crisis management, both against other democracies and nondemocracies. Even during periods of social unrest, democracies are less likely to attempt to divert attention by military adventurism; indeed, democracy provides a framework in which to better manage domestic unrest. However, our most significant finding is that democracy increases the probability that a state will engage in diplomatic efforts to manage international crises. That is, rather than calling out the armies, democracies are more likely than nondemocracies to try to negotiate and manage their way through difficult periods. This is true when both parties in a dispute are democracies. It is also true when a democracy faces a nondemocracy.

This research represents a new direction in international relations research. We go beyond traditional views of statecraft, and, drawing on the new institutional literature, we hypothesize that the institutions of democracy socially construct individuals who prefer to use nonviolent means of dispute resolution. In other words, humans are different in a democracy. The new institutional model goes beyond the division made in much of the literature, between institutional constraints in a democracy on one hand, and democratic norms on the other. We see this division as largely untenable. Instead, institutions, formal and informal, contain, construct, and condition norms and behaviors. The new institutional approach also moves beyond treating policy actors and political leaders simply as rationally optimizing agents, arguing rather that norms and behaviors are to some extent internalized. This new institutional view forms the basis for our explanations of crisis statecraft behavior by both democratic dyads and monadic democracy behavior toward nondemocracies.[1] In these latter cases, we provide evidence that democratic leaders will still prefer to use nonviolent measures of dispute resolution. This is in large part counter to Dixon (1994) who argues much of the democratic peace can be explained by a shared conception of "bounded competition" between democracies and as such does not apply to disputes between democracies and nondemocracies. It is also counter to a similar argument of "policies of reciprocity" (Huth and Allee 2002) used by actors in international disputes. Relatedly, we argue democracy provides a structure for managing and accommodating social unrest, thereby reducing the incentives for democratic leaders to divert public attention from internal problems.

A second novel contribution is that this study of diversion and democratic peace looks at more than two outcomes (i.e., violence/no violence). Bennett and Nordstrom (2000) note that oversimplifying to the dichotomous level can mask important information. This needs some explanation. Our ordered logit analysis approximates a complete range of statecraft: negotiation, coercion, and violence. By looking at the full range of policy choices, we are able to show not only that democracy diminishes violence, but also that the likelihood of negotiation increases in the presence of both joint and monadic democracy. We are most interested in the use of cooperative statecraft. The use of negotiated settlement by joint democracies described, inter alia, by Dixon (1993; 1994) has direct relevance to the democratic peace theory. We use the negotiation outcome to describe a basket of cooperative behaviors including negotiation, mediation, arbitration, and adjudication. We show that democracies are more likely to rely on compromise to resolve crisis situations.

The next form of statecraft on our ordinal continuum is nonviolent coercion. We expand on the negotiation/military escalation policy options described by Huth and Allee (2002) to include the use of nonviolent coercive statecraft. Coercive statecraft describes those actions between negotiation and violence. It can include sanctions, withholding aid, and threats of violence. For example, military and economic aid can be used as a reward or inducement by donor countries. Krause (1991, 314) asserts that the United States has used military aid as a vital form of foreign policy statecraft since World War II. More specifically, Krause (1991) detailed this form of statecraft in terms of superpower arms transfers. He suggests that a power relationship can obtain when a superpower uses military assistance to prevent regional shifts away from their respective spheres of influence. The use of incentives, such as tied aid, in conflict prevention has increased (Cortright and Carnegie Commission on Preventing Deadly Conflict 1997). The distinction between incentive and coercive measures can become blurred. Providing a loan or granting aid vital to saving an economy or a population only if certain conditions are met is to all intents and purposes a coercive action. Explicitly coercive measures such as sanctions can include trade embargoes or arms bans. Due to collateral damage and their effect on sometimes innocent populations, sanctions have increasingly been of a targeted type. These include bans on travel for leaders, their families and associates, the freezing of leaders' or elites' funds in foreign bank accounts, and expulsion from such international organizations as the Commonwealth (George 1999).

The final form of statecraft is the use of violence. This form of crisis management involves combat, casualties, military operations, and in some cases war (Hewitt and Wilkenfeld 1996, 129). The realist perspective portrays the use of violence as an extreme though acceptable form of statecraft. The diversionary force literature also suggests that the force option is more likely during social unrest (Levy 1989).

Over the course of this chapter we will discuss the theoretical underpinnings of the democratic peace and diversionary behavior. We will then outline our model, methods, data sources, and results before concluding and drawing some implications for further research.

DEMOCRACY AND DISPUTE RESOLUTION

There are typically two explanations for the democratic peace. First, democracies provide institutional constraints on governmental action (Huth and Allee 2002). It is assumed that the consent of citizens is required for democracies to go to war. Drawing on Kant, it is also assumed that citizens will resist war because it is they who will bear the burden of casualties, paying for the military, suffering economic disruption, and rebuilding after war (Russett and Oneal 2001). Democracies have competitive elections, separation of powers, upper houses, "loyal oppositions," constitutional limits on government power, public expression of preferences, and competing and overlapping interest groups, amongst other things. These provide constraints on government, and, reflecting the will of citizens to some extent, limit the ability of governments to engage in military adventurism. Governments can be removed if they do not fulfill voters' preference for peace, and democratic leaders (assuming they want to be reelected) thus avoid wars, particularly those they might lose. Democratic institutions also limit the speed and increase the transparency of the policy-making process so that issues of mobilization of troops or allocation of resources to military spending can be monitored by those inside and outside the state, and are therefore better responded to and constrained (Enterline and Sobek 2001), although there are examples of democracies engaging in subterfuge and misinformation regarding their military intentions (Rosato 2003). Nonviolent measures of dispute resolution can be better appraised as such in the face of this transparency. Such openness also decreases the likelihood of policy moves being misinterpreted as potentially violent, and responded to, possibly preemptively, with seemingly appropriate levels of force. Opponents will also be aware that democratic constraints will also make it less likely that the state in question will engage in violent activity, and are thus less likely to fear attack, again reducing the likelihood of preemptive strikes.

Second, it is argued that democracies embrace a series of norms and behaviors that facilitate the peaceful resolution of conflicts and disputes. According to Rummel (1995, 4), democracies encourage an environment where social conflicts that may become violent are resolved by "voting, negotiation, compromise and mediation." Political leaders are accustomed to using these nonviolent measures to achieve their aims. Indeed, democratic politics often rewards those better able to manage and convince constituencies, political opponents, and colleagues without resorting to aggressive or belligerent behavior (Dixon 1994). At the same time it socializes leaders to use these methods (Rousseau et al. 1996). Political leaders unable to use these nonviolent methods to resolve disputes may be seen as lacking the requisite statecraft and therefore suffer in elections (Geva, DeRouen, and Mintz 1993). Leaders of democracies facing other democracies in a dispute will be aware that other democratic leaders share the same conception of "bounded competition" or "rules-of the–game" that privileges nonviolent methods of dispute resolution and thus respond in kind (Dixon 1994).

However, a strong distinction between institutional (or structural) constraints, and norms and behaviors (or cultural constraints) is difficult to maintain. Instead, behaviors and norms are constrained and to some extent formed within and by formal and informal institutions and institutional structures. Existing cultural norms and beliefs might foster the development of certain formal institutions. This is the argument of the growing literature known as "new institutionalism" (c.f. March and Olsen 1996). For Goodin (1996, 19–20), "individual agents and groups pursue their respective problems in a context that is collectively constrained." These constraints include institutions—which are "organised patterns of socially constructed norms and roles and socially prescribed behaviors expected of occupants of those roles which are created and recreated over time." These constraints have historical roots as "residuals of past actions and choices" and "also shape the desire, preferences and motives" of agents. They "embody, impart and preserve" different power relations and resources. However, individuals and groups are not the near automatons of structuralist approaches but this individual and group activity, socially constrained as it may be, "is the engine that drives social life." Distinguished here are the concepts of organization and institution. As Brennan and Castles (2002, 5) note "an institution is to be viewed as some amalgam of norms, practices, structures and organizations, an organization like a university or a large corporation can only be understood 'institutionally' when all the norms and habits and structures governing the actual relationship of players within the organization are filled in."

In sum, democratic institutions constrain, channel, influence, and, to some extent, form preferences, values, and behavior. While there may be a formal element to democratic institutions—either organizational structures, laws, or written rules—these become "institutionalized" when the accompanying norms and behaviors become embedded and routinized. We argue that different sorts of people arise in democracies. Rather than the asocial, ahistorical, rationally optimizing agent of more extreme rational actor models, or the simple realist assumptions made regarding state behavior, individuals and leaders in democracies are influenced, constrained, and, to some extent, socially constructed within and by institutions to behave and think in certain ways. These norms and behaviors are to a considerable extent internalized, and even to some extent become automatic. In democracies these norms and behaviors include a preference toward nonviolent means of conflict resolution, and particularly toward the accommodation and negotiation of settlements. As Dixon (1994, 16) argues, democracies foster "the internalization of norms for regulating and reconciling different interests and values in public affairs in ways that are neither violent nor coercive." Moreover, democratic leaders facing other democratic leaders in a crisis are aware that these institutionalized constraints against the use of violence are shared. In his study of conflict from 1945 to 1979, Dixon (1994, 29) finds that the "democratic states embroiled in disputes will be more likely than others to achieve peaceful settlements." As Dixon concludes elsewhere, "the more democratic a state the more likely its political leadership will maintain conciliatory norms of dispute resolution, and leaders with conciliatory norms are more likely than others to adopt or at least accede to conflict management efforts" (1993, 46).

This discussion leads to our first hypothesis based on joint democracy:

Hypothesis 1: Democracies are less likely to use violence and coercive statecraft and more likely to pursue negotiated settlements to international crises if their principal adversary is another democracy.

Monadic Democracy

While it seems clear that democracies are less inclined to use violence against other democracies, it is argued that they do not engage in war any less often than nondemocracies (Dixon 1993; Rousseau et al. 1996). A nondemocracy might see the constraints on democratic states' war-making ability as giving an opportunity to force concessions or capitulations, although Huth and Allee (2002) found little evidence to support this. On the other hand, democracies are likely to respond vigorously if attacked, as history shows. If losing a war or facing capitulation is seen to have greater electoral costs than fighting a war, there may be incentives for democracies to engage in preemptive strikes (Bueno de Mesquita and Lalman 1992), although there are few cases of preemptive strikes starting wars (Reiter 1995). Due to the greater transparency of support (or dissent) within populations or within political and governmental actors for military action, and the greater availability of information on the intent and ability of democratic governments to engage in war, opponents are better able to gauge whether threats of military force are credible or whether such threats will be undermined and constrained by possible lack of electoral and/or political support (Fearon 1994b; Huth and Allee 2002; Schultz 2001). Correspondingly, democratic governments are less able to "bluff" by threatening violence in international disputes and crises, but threats of force are given reluctantly, and can be taken more seriously, and so can be effective deterrents.

On the other hand, as Schultz (2001) argues, once democratic governments commit to engaging in violence to settle an international crisis, particularly in the face of widespread electoral and political support for such a stance, there are considerable incentives not to back down. This is due to the possibility of being seen as indecisive and weak and the consequent diplomatic, status, electoral, and other costs that may be faced (c.f. Fearon 1994b; Schultz 2001). Consequently as Fearon (1994b, 586) theorizes, "democratic leaders have a structural incentive to pursue more escalatory, committing strategies when they face authoritarians than when they face fellow democrats, and this can generate a greater overall chance of war." However as Huth and Allee (2002, 281) found in military disputes between democracies and nondemocracies, nondemocracies were more likely to initiate and escalate military threats and "military conflict generally resulted from the more aggressive policies [and norms] of non-democratic leaders."

Bueno de Mesquita et al. (1999b) theorize that due to the demands of electoral politics that will more immediately punish leaders for their losses, democracies are more likely to shift extra resources to fighting wars and will therefore be more successful in their execution. Assuming (rather heroically) that nondemocratic leaders are more or less rational actors and will suffer to some extent by losing a war, if this widely held (Reiter and Stam 2003; Bueno de Mesquita et al 1999b) but disputed (Desch 2002) belief that democracies are better at winning wars is correct, this should dissuade attacks by nondemocracies upon democracies, ceteris paribus. On the other hand, as Bueno de Mesquita et al. (1999b) theorize, due to the electoral costs to democratic leaders for lost wars, democracies are less likely to initiate wars they do not expect to win—and will be aware that fighting other democracies provides a greater eventuality of this occurring. At the same time, however, the possibility of defeat for democracies is not as great in the case of nondemocratic opponents, ceteris paribus, and so there lower disincentives in initiating wars against nondemocracies. As Bueno de Mesquita et al. (1999b) argue then, the democratic peace is explained by a combination of these incentives and disincentives and democracies are not by nature any less warlike.

In a different vein Dixon (1994, 17–18) argues that the proposition that shared norms between democracies leads to less war between democracies does not imply that democracies are any less warlike. Instead, his democratic norms model only holds when both parties to a dispute share norms of peaceful settlement and "bounded competition," i.e., the rules of the game. To this extent, his normative model contains realist assumptions regarding nondemocracies whose behavior is thought to be primarily determined by standard realist notions of anarchy and power seeking (see also Maoz and Russett 1993).

There may, however, be some reasons why democracies are less likely to go to war, whatever the regime of the opponent. If the new institutional constraints model provides justification for the dyadic democratic peace (i.e., between two democracies), we suggest it will hold to some extent for monadic (i.e., single) democracies. That is, the norms and constraints that encourage nonviolent behavior between democracies are also likely to encourage democracies and democratic leaders to seek to engage in nonviolent crisis management with nondemocracies. These nonviolent values are seen as internalized by democratic actors. That is, rather than statecraft being a purely instrumental (or realist) selection of appropriate means in a crisis, democratic actors chose from the norms and toolbox of solutions they are socialized or institutionalized within—namely, they have a preference for using nonviolent means of dispute resolution if at all possible, even if the opponent does not share this preference and does not hold to "the rules of the game." We argue such internalized preferences for nonviolence may not always be entirely overridden by the exigencies of immediate electoral politics, even if there is some current electoral support for belligerence (c.f. Schultz 2001). Relatedly we suggest political actors are not simply or entirely focused on office seeking, although this will likely be a major factor in their behavior (c.f. Bueno de Mesquita et al 1999b). Indeed, such rational choice approaches, while parsimonious, are reductionist and evidentially challenged, and we argue our assumption of complex, somewhat conflicted, and socially constructed humans is considerably more compelling (c.f. March and Olsen 1996). In any event, electoral politics in democracies will sometimes (or most often) support nonviolent dispute resolution for reasons already outlined.

This preference for nonviolence amongst democratic actors is not, however, a naive Panglossian view of statecraft. It will take into account opponents and their values and behavior. Such preferences for nonviolence will be subject to corrosion in the face of failure—that is, institutions, values, and constraints are not immutable and may develop and change over time, particularly in the processes of policy and international disputes and electoral battles. Given the possible lack of trust of, and transparency of, policy processes of nondemocracies, and the awareness that nondemocratic states may not share norms and behaviors facilitating nonviolent resolution, democracies and democratic leaders may be more circumspect in using nonviolent measures when dealing with nondemocracies. Moreover, if the opponent is not a democracy, this lack of shared norms of compromise means negotiation is probably less likely to be successful, and democracies will more likely use or escalate to nonviolent coercive measures to resolve disputes. However, we argue that these new institutional constraints are such that democracies and democratic leaders will still be reluctant to resort to violence, whether or not the opponent is a democracy. This leads us to our second hypothesis:

Hypothesis 2: Democracies are less likely to use violence and more likely to employ negotiation to manage international crises, whether opponents are democracies or nondemocracies.

Diversionary Behavior

A vast body of literature has asked whether state elites engage in diversionary behavior. That is, do they attempt to divert attention from domestic problems by engaging in external violence? This diversionary behavior argument has been theorized in a number of different ways. Sociological literature on group dynamics has focused on in- and out-group models, whereby cohesion within the in-group can be increased through manifestation of a threat from, or conflict with, an external out-group (Coser 1956). Others have developed rational actor models including agency models, game theory, and other approaches. Attention is focused on the incentives for leaders to engage in military adventurism (Gelpi 1997). Compelling as many theoretical models may be, empirical evidence of diversionary behavior is mixed, but some studies suggest democracies engage in diversionary behavior (Gelpi 1997). This section will discuss the role of democracy and diversion, and ask whether the democratic peace hypothesis is threatened by the existence of diversionary behavior by nondemocracies.

DeRouen (1995; 2000b) has shown that the use of quarterly military force by U.S. presidents increases as a function of unemployment. Meernik and Waterman (1996) are skeptical of diversionary action by U.S. presidents. In contrast, others have argued that politicians are likely to use force when they are popular (Morgan and Anderson 1999). Drawing on principal-agent models, Gelpi (1997) argues that this diversionary behavior can be shown across democracies. As he argues, a leader's support can be shaken by social unrest as it undermines the efficiency of the state in extracting resources and so its ability to reward supporting coalitions. Uprisings can also provide a direct threat to that leader's hold on power. An autocracy can use violence directly to suppress unrest. However, this response is usually denied to democratic leaders, who, instead, are more likely to initiate external violence in the face of social unrest. Gelpi (1997, 227) finds strong support for these beliefs drawing on 180 crises between 1948 and 1982, concluding that the "diversionary initiation of force is generally a pathology of democratic states." Russett (1990) finds that the United States may respond with force if the economy is bad, but that other democracies such as France and Britain do not; nor do autocracies. Miller (1999) finds that autocracies, not democracies, are more likely to engage in diversionary behavior, while Leeds and Davis (1997) in their study of eighteen advanced industrial democracies find that conflict-initiating behavior is unrelated to electoral cycles and economic performance. Oneal and Tir (2003, 14) "found no evidence that poor economic performance affected the incidence of fatal militarized disputes, 1886–1992." As Oneal and Tir (2003, 8) note, "it is unusual to find so little consistency in empirical studies on a topic that has received so much theoretical attention."

There are reasons why democratic leaders and democracies might be less inclined to engage in diversionary behavior. As democracies have greater transparency of policy-making structures, greater freedom of information, greater levels of press freedom, and greater levels of open debate, the costs and benefits, risks and uncertainties of war are likely to be better able to be established, or at least disputed (c.f. Oneal and Tir 2003; Smith 1996; Schultz 2001). Pluralist democracies that allow and even facilitate debate and disagreement will allow different and competing views to be presented and heard—that is, the population is less likely to be "fooled" by simplistic appeals by opportunistic leaders to nationalism, tribalism, to them and us in-group/out-group responses, or the myriad fears that diversionary tactics play upon, at least compared to regimes where information and debate is more tightly controlled. This does not imply that information (see Rosato 2003) will be perfect or even entirely "manageable," only that more information will be available and that opinion and "facts" are better able to be debated within a democracy, even if this information is filtered, debated, and even misrepresented by, at very best, individuals with only bounded or even limited rationality.

Similarly, democratic actors may be more cynical (or able to express this cynicism) of the motives of their leaders than actors in more authoritarian regimes—engaging in "wag the dog"-type responses to international crises and diversionary tactics. Opposition parties may also point out problems and offer alternatives. We have already hypothesized that voters in a democracy are generally not in favor of war, following Kant, and that leaders democracies construct are also more likely to favor nonviolent measures of dispute resolution. The possible risk to electoral success and immediate loss of power of engaging in war-like behavior is greater in democracies—i.e., voters may punish diversionary behavior, particularly if they are not convinced of its legitimacy (Geva, DeRouen, and Mintz 1993). Indeed, democratic voters are more likely to reward leaders who handle a crisis in a manner that fits with democratic norms—such as through negotiation. At best, the boost to electoral popularity through diversion is likely to be short lived (Oneal and Tir 2003). Institutional constraints and checks and balances on executive action in democracies can also limit the use of force for partisan gain (Oneal and Tir 2003). While leaders in an autocracy are possibly as likely to face sanctions in the face of diversionary efforts and costly wars, particularly failed military adventures, these are generally less immediate (or at least perceived as less immediate) than electoral losses, although sanctions for non-democratic leaders if they are successfully removed from power can be considerable and even fatal (Goemans 2000; Schultz 2001).

This leads us to two conclusions. First, assuming political leaders are focused on maintaining power at least to some extent, we argue that political leaders in democratic regimes are less likely to engage in diversionary behavior as they risk electoral sanctions. Second, restating the new institutional characterization of democracies, war-like behavior is constrained in both the values and the characteristics of leaders that democracies produce and in the formal and informal institutional constraints on the behavior of leaders that will allow initiation of force without a significant degree of support. Moreover, as the reasons for force initiation may be better contested in a democracy, it is less likely that this support will arise in a democratic system.

Democracies also provide structures and institutions in which to accommodate and constrain social unrest, particularly if it is channeled within the "rules of the game." Gelpi (1997) argues that regimes can respond to unrest in three ways. First, leaders may grant the demands of the demonstrators. Second, they may suppress dissent by force. Third, they may divert attention through external conflict. However, Gelpi misses the point of how democracies constrain, channel, and accommodate dissent (cf. Lai 1999; Moore 2000). That indeed is their strength. Democracies also see dissent as legitimate within certain boundaries. The institutions of democracy develop, construct, and constrain individuals to work with the "rules of the game" or what Dixon (1994) calls "standards of bounded competition"—that is, dissent is usually expressed within certain norms of behavior. While there may be criminal elements to dissent using terrorism or assassinations, the majority of dissent in democracies—including common forms of dissent such as demonstrations or strikes—is likely to be expressed within a range of behaviors that accept, more or less, the legitimacy of the system and its dispute-resolution mechanisms and is not usually aimed at overthrowing the social order. State responses to dissent are also conditioned by these same institutional constraints and tendency to play within the rules of the game. Dissent outside these boundaries is likely to be contained through legitimate criminal sanctions, constrained by the rule of law and independent judiciaries and police forces. To sum, there is a fourth and more likely group of options that democratic regimes may follow if faced with dissent—negotiation, accommodation, and compromise. Democratic institutions allow disagreement and dissent and allow settlement of disputes through such things as the rule of law, independent courts, employment tribunals, the processes of democratic government and political parties, interest groups, and the role of a free media. While such mechanisms may not grant all that dissenters wish, and may, on the other hand, grant more than the leadership is comfortable with, some accommodation may be reached that is seen as legitimate (more or less) by all parties.

Containing and accommodating dissent and social fragmentation through the strong institutions found in a democracy is also likely to reduce the threat to economic performance. Rodrik (1999) found economic growth was worse in countries with social conflict—measured by indicators of inequality and ethnic fragmentation—if institutions of conflict management were weak. These institutions were proxied by indicators of the quality of governmental institutions, rule of law, democratic rights, and social safety nets. Even apart from the ability of democracies to accommodate social unrest, some social unrest and social movements may be associated with the development of more stable and democratic societies in the future and possibly have a positive impact on the reduction of violence. This is because social unrest may be in response to genuine problems and may contribute to their resolution. Political leaders of the future may develop skills and knowledge through their involvement in social disputes. To conclude, social unrest is a lesser threat to the political and economic order under democracy and therefore less likely to propel leaders toward extreme measures such as diversion to maintain their power. Indeed, some social unrest may be seen as legitimate and even positive.

In sum, we hypothesize that diversionary behavior is less likely for three reasons. First, as democracies allow the questioning of claims of the benefits of diversionary behavior and these doubts can be expressed through the ballot box, and, in any event, electoral benefits to leaders are at best likely to be small and short, democratic leaders face disincentives to engage in diversionary behavior. Second, the institutions of democracies condition and constrain any warlike tendencies of leaders and the ability to express these. Indeed, democratic actors, including leaders, are likely to be less warlike in general. Third, democracies allow for accommodation of social unrest. Such internal conflict is seen as a legitimate activity (if it is played within the rules of the game), and is less a threat to the political and economic order, so that there is less incentive to divert attention during unrest.

This leads us to our next group of hypotheses based on the linkage between joint and monadic democracy and domestic unrest:

Hypothesis 3: States experiencing domestic unrest are more likely to use violence and coercion and are less likely to employ negotiation during international crises.

Hypothesis 4: Both monadic and joint democracy reduce the likelihood that states experiencing domestic unrest will use violence and increase the likelihood of negotiation.

RESEARCH DESIGN

Data

Brecher and Wilkenfeld's (2000) ICB data are rich in contextual information and contain crises from minor disputes, through civil war, to interstate war. In contrast, many studies focus only on interstate war or civil war thus limiting their generalizability. The ICB data has been widely used elsewhere, making our finding comparable to other published research. Among others, ICB data have been used by Gelpi (1997), Gelpi and Griesdorf (2001), Maoz and Russett (1993), and Rousseau et al. (1996). Unless otherwise stated, the data below are derived from Brecher and Wilkenfeld (2000).[2]

The ICB dataset defines an international crisis as having two hallmarks:

1. a change in type and/or an increase in intensity of *disruptive*, that is hostile verbal or physical, *interactions* between two or more states, with a heightened probability of *military hostilities*; that, in turn,
2. destabilizes their relationship and *challenges* the *structure* of an international system.

Some of the crises escalate to violence but most do not. Most are less than 100 days and the longest is 1,359 days. Our observations are the state actors in these crises (1918–1994).[3] This dataset is not explicitly dyadic in nature. In order to capture the dyadic component needed to create some of the independent variables below we turned to the ICB "source of threat variable." This variable identifies the state that poses the greatest threat to the values of the actor during a crisis.[4] This state is usually, but not always, the same as the triggering entity (Brecher and Wilkenfeld 2000, 49). Hereafter we refer to the state that poses the greatest threat to the actor as the opponent.

Dependent Variable

We specify an ordered, ordinal-dependent variable that ranges from negotiation to coercion to use of violence. This variable is created from the ICB variable Crisis Management II: Principal Technique (CRISMG). This scaled ICB measure captures the primary crisis management technique used by actors.

The values range from negotiation, adjudication, mediation, multiple without violence, nonmilitary pressure, nonviolent military, multiple including violence, and violence. As mentioned previously, we collapsed this variable into three outcomes by collapsing the first three CRISMG values into a negotiation outcome, the middle three become the coercion outcome, and the final two become the violence outcome.

Independent Variables

Contiguity. Bremer (1982) showed that contiguous states are more likely to fight than noncontiguous ones. Brecher and Wilkenfeld (2000) find that contiguous dyads are more likely to use violence in resolving crises than are "near neighbors" or dyads separated by distance. Following this line of reasoning, a shared border might increase the likelihood of the violence option. On the other hand, neighbors might share norms that more readily lend themselves to negotiation outcomes (Dixon 1994).

We created our own contiguity variable (CONTIG) by looking at each actor-opponent dyad and coding as 1 instances where the two are contiguous and 0 otherwise. In cases involving separation by water, we coded states closer than 100 miles as contiguous (e.g., Cuba and the United States would be considered contiguous).

Democratic dyads. Rousseau et al. (1996, 526) found that "the democratic peace is primarily a dyadic process when addressing the escalation of international crises." We posit that the "prevalence" of democracy among crisis actors diminishes the use of violence and increases the use of negotiation to resolve crises (Dixon 1993; 1994). More relevant for our purposes, Hewitt and Wilkenfeld (1996) extended the democratic peace argument to crisis behavior. They showed that the more democracies there were in a crisis, the less the overall violence in the crisis and the diminished likelihood that actors will use violence as a crisis management technique.

We constructed a democratic dyad (DYADDEM) score based on the actor and its opponent's democracy scores. These scores range from 1 to 10. These data are from the Polity IV project (Marshall and Jaggers 2002).[5] DYADDEM is coded as 1 when both actors have a polity score of 6 or above (Senese 1997).

Monadic democracy. There is some evidence that regime type impacts the propensity for actors to use force. Rummel (1997) and Benoit (1996), for instance, have shown that democracies are more pacific *in general*. Gelpi (1997) has shown that democracies are more likely to use diversionary force while Oneal and Tir (2003) find to the contrary. We create a measure of monadic democracy (MONADIC DEMO) that is simply the Polity score of the actor.

Trigger. It is reasonable to expect states to respond to a trigger with a factor-appropriate level of force (Brecher and Wilkenfeld 2000, 174–75). In other words, if a crisis is triggered by a verbal action, we should not expect a full-scale invasion in response. We control for this contingency by modeling a trigger variable (TRIGGER). In the ICB data, the "trigger to foreign policy crisis" variable ranges from verbal act to violent act. The trigger is the "catalyst" to the crisis as it invokes a heightened sense of "threat, time pressure, and the likelihood of war" (Brecher and Wilkenfeld 2000, 9). We expect that non-violent triggers will diminish the use of violence and enhance the likelihood of coercion or negotiation. Violent triggers will have the reverse effect.

We collapse the ICB variable into a dichotomous variable and code as 1 those triggers involving the military (ICB categories 7-9; e.g., show of force, manoeuvres, mobilization, border clash, war) and 0 those that did not entail direct military activity (ICB categories 1-6; e.g., verbal protest, treaty violation, sanctions, alliance formation by adversary, withholding aid, embargo).

Social unrest. When social unrest is high, we might expect leaders to attempt to divert attention and respond more forcefully to a crisis trigger (Brecher and Wilkenfeld 2000, 176). In other words, if an actor has domestic problems, it may be more willing to use violence and less likely to seek peaceful resolution of crises (see Bennett and Nordstrom 2000). We use the ICB variable "Social Unrest" to create SOCUN. This variable captures assassinations, general strikes, terrorism, demonstrations, and riots. It is coded as 1 when there is evidence of unrest *prior* to the crisis and 0 otherwise.

Capability differences. Standard realist assessments of conflict incorporate measures of the power ratio of the adversaries. Decision makers are not expected to initiate violence against much more capable adversaries (Bueno de Mesquita 1981). Brecher and Wilkenfeld (2000, 177) suggest that crisis behavior based on power balance essentially follows general conflict behavior. Russett and Oneal (2001) find that dyadic preponderance decreases the likelihood of militarized interstate disputes because strong states do not need force to achieve goals. Thus capability advantage should decrease chances of violence. However Dixon (1994) notes that stronger states should be less likely to agree to negotiated settlements. On balance, we expect states that command a greater share of capabilities than their adversary to opt for violence or coercion rather than negotiation.

We create a variable called RELCAP based on the ratio of actor to opponent capabilities.[6] The capability data are from the Correlates of War project and are based on population, urban population, military personnel, military spending, and iron and steel production (Singer and Small 1999).[7]

Ethnic conflict. Ethnic crises are particularly violent and difficult to resolve peacefully (see Bercovitch and DeRouen forthcoming; Brecher and Wilkenfeld 2000; Brogan 1989; Carment and Harvey 2001). The ICB system-level dataset provides information on whether the crisis is ethnicity related in its variable "Ethnicity Related Crisis" (ETHNIC). Using this we create a variable called ETHNIC and code it as 1 in cases where there is evidence of secessionist or irredentist issues and 0 otherwise.

Territorial conflict. Territory is another issue that can lead to escalation and longer, more intractable crises (see Vasquez 1993). The ICB system-level dataset provides information on whether the crisis had border or other territorial issues in its "Territoriality" (TERR) variable. We create a variable called TERR and code it as 1 in cases where the crisis had these issues present and 0 otherwise.[8]

Method

Because our dependent variable is an ordinal outcome with more than two values, we employ the ordered logit form of maximum-likelihood estimation.[9] Ordered logit assumes that the values of the dependent variable represent increasingly higher outcomes (Long 1997). In our case, the three outcomes represent a set of three increasingly proactive forms of statecraft states use to manage crises. Negotiation is a cooperative venture, while the middle value of coercion captures sanctions and other punitive diplomatic measures. Finally, the third value represents the actual use of violence. Since some crises have multiple actors, we estimate the model with robust standard errors adjusted for crisis.

FINDINGS

The results of the ordered logit analysis can be seen in table 8.1. The first model is specified with monadic democracy scores. Social unrest, relative capabilities difference, ethnic issues, and violent triggers each increase the probability of more aggressive crisis management policy. Monadic democracy has a negative impact on the use of violence. The findings for the joint democracy model are similar except that the negative effect of joint democracy is much greater. Thus far our evidence supports democratic peace and diversionary theory.

The ordered logit results become easier to interpret upon the estimation of predicted probabilities of the three outcomes. Table 8.2 contains several simulations based on the equations contained in table 8.1. We first consider the joint democracy model. With all covariates set to their mean (baseline model), the model predicts a 24 percent likelihood an actor will use negotiation, a 34

Table 8.1. Ordered Logit Estimates: Actor Crisis Management Technique during International Crises

Variable	(1)	(2)
Monadic Democracy	−.0337	
	(.0112)**	
Joint Democracy		−1.1726**
		(.3801)
Social Unrest	.3385*	.3882*
	(.1735)	(.1752)
Contiguity	.1841	.2750
	(.1775)	(.1790)
Relative Caps	1.1350***	1.0000***
	(.2584)	(.2457)
Ethnic	.5511*	.5238*
	(.2400)	(.2423)
Trigger	.6568***	.6889***
	(.1850)	(.1878)
Territorial	−.1025	.0919
	(.2139)	(.2188)
Ancillary Parameters		
Cut1	.1021	.0644
	(.2282)	(.2344)
Cut2	1.5853	1.5453
	(.2258)	(.2338)
Number of obs	653	653
Wald chi2(7)	67.36	60.27
Prob > chi^2	0.0000	0.0000
Log likelihood	−667.9427	−668.6801

Note: dependent variable is ordered from negotiation (1) to coercion (2) to violence
(3); numbers under coefficients are robust standard errors adjusted for clustering on
crisis; monadic democracy scores are treated as missing in interregnum, transition,
and transition years.

percent likelihood coercion will be employed, and a 41 percent likelihood violence will be used. Specifying social unrest in the model (all others at mean) increases the likelihood of violence to 48 percent and decreases the likelihood of negotiation. Specifying joint democracy in the model increases the likelihood of negotiation to 50 percent and reduces chances for violence to 19 percent. Setting joint democracy to 0 and social unrest to 1 diminishes negotiation to 19 percent and raises violence to 49 percent. Finally, with social unrest and joint democracy, the likelihood of negotiation is 43 percent and violence is down to 23 percent.

Several important findings emerge. Social unrest seems to reduce the probability of coercion and negotiation in favor of violence. Shifts in policy as a result of regime type or domestic unrest seem to have more impact on vio-

Table 8.2. **Predicted Probabilities after Ordered Logit**

Scenario	Outcome		
	Negotiation	*Coercion*	*Violence*
Joint Democracy Model			
Baseline	24(%)	34	41
Social Unrest	20	32	48
Joint Democracy	50	32	19
Social Unrest, No Joint Democracy	19	32	49
Social Unrest, Joint Democracy	43	34	23
Monadic Democracy Model			
Baseline	24	34	41
Social Unrest	21	33	47
Monadic Democracy = 10	32	35	33
Social Unrest, Democracy = 10	27	35	38
Social Unrest, Democracy = −10	16	29	55

Note: probabilities may not sum to 100% due to rounding; variables not manipulated are set to mean.

lence or negotiation. Changes in the likelihood of one of these outcomes seem to come at the expense of the other. We present moderately strong evidence for hypothesis 3 that supports the diversionary argument. States experiencing social unrest appear to select the violence option at the expense of negotiating and acting tough diplomatically through the use of coercion.

The effect of joint democracy is quite strong, thus supporting hypothesis 1. It clearly increases the likelihood of negotiation rather than violent management of crises. This is consistent with the findings of Dixon (1993; 1994) who used different data, methods, and time frame. Relatedly, we find support for hypothesis 4 that joint democracy diminishes the effect of social unrest. This is consistent with Oneal and Tir (2003) who report that the democratic peace diminishes diversionary force rather than the reverse. Their data, methods, and time frame also differ markedly from ours. This finding differs from Gelpi's (1997) main conclusion that democracies are more likely to divert attention from domestic problems. Indeed, we argue that one of the great strengths of democracy is that it provides a framework within which to accommodate and manage dissent.

Monadic democracy is also an important determinant of whether a state will choose negotiation or conflict. This also supports hypothesis 2. In particular, when a state is a "full" democracy, the probability of using negotiation to manage a crisis goes up 8 percent and the probability of using violence goes down by 8 percent. This is not as dramatic as the effect of joint democracy but is nonetheless an important addition to the democratic peace literature as it parallels the findings of Benoit (1996) and Rummel (1997) on monadic democracy. It also provides some support for Huth and Allee (2002) who show that there is little evidence for the belief that democracies are generally more belligerent toward nondemocracies, instead arguing that violence they discover in mixed dyads is usually caused by democratic states responding to military threats and escalation of nondemocracies. Further, monadic democracy also seems to diminish the diversionary incentive (hypothesis 4). Monadic democracy in the presence of domestic unrest reduces the probability of violence by almost 10 percent and increases that of negotiation by about 6 percent. As a corollary to hypothesis 4, nondemocracies appear more likely than democracies to use violence in the presence of domestic unrest.

CONCLUSION

This analysis of crisis management techniques provides additional evidence for the literatures on democratic peace and diversionary force. We show that the democratic peace actually hinders the use of diversionary force and that both monadic and joint democracy enhance the likelihood that an actor will pursue a negotiated settlement to a crisis. Our finding that democracies prefer to negotiate provides some support to Huth and Allee's (2002, 15) findings that democracies do not "aggressively escalate to high levels against non-democracies" in territorial disputes, although Huth and Allee use different datasets, methods, and time frames and focus on territorial disputes. Our findings go beyond simply stating that democracies do not fight or escalate disputes. Rather than simply a realist view of statecraft or an instrumentally rational view of the motivations of democratic and other leaders, drawing on the new institutional literature, we hypothesize that the institutions of democracy socially construct individuals who prefer to use nonviolent means of dispute resolution—that humans are different in democracies. There may of course also be incentives for nondemocratic leaders not to use force, but these incentives proceed in part from new institutional factors that construct, encourage, and reward nonviolence in political actors in general. This new institutional view accords with our finding that democracy has a positive impact on the probability of negotiation even if the adversary is not a democracy. This is counter to Dixon (1994) who argues much of the democratic peace is explained by a shared conception of "bounded competition" between democracies and as such does not apply to disputes between democracies and nondemocracies (see also Huth and Allee 2002). We also argue that democracy provides a structure for managing and accommodating social unrest so that there is less incentive for democratic leaders to divert attention.

Future research can also approach the analysis of statecraft choices as a function of foreign policy substitutability (see Starr 2000; Gelpi 1997). For example, one could examine whether democracies begin with negotiation strategies, and only move to coercion or violence in the event of failure. In other words, is there a sequential element beginning on the cooperative end of the scale for democracies? The alternative is that in dealing with non-democracies the norms of the latter prevail (Maoz and Russett 1993) and democracies might not begin by seeking negotiated settlement in the first instance. We would expect to find that democracies are more likely to choose negotiation as the initial strategy, persist with it for longer, and be more reluctant to move to coercive and violent stages of crisis resolution than non-democracies, for the institutional reasons we have already discussed. Such a prediction is also suggested by Huth and Allee's (2002) findings on territorial disputes. It would also be instructive to ascertain whether nondemocracies are more likely than democracies to shift from cooperative to antagonistic crisis management policies in disputes other than territorial ones.

NOTES

1. The 1975 Cod War between the United Kingdom and Iceland is an example of a crisis between two democracies that was resolved via negotiation. The North Korea nuclear crisis of 1993–1994 contained two mixed dyads—United States–North Korea and South Korea–North Korea. This crisis provides an example of democracies pursuing negotiation to resolve a crisis with an autocratic adversary. These examples are from the Brecher and Wilkenfeld (2000) ICB data.

2. The ICB data were downloaded from web.missouri.edu/~polsjjh/ICB/ (January 2002).

3. We deleted 178 intra-war crises. Brecher and Wilkenfeld (2000, 145; see also Gelpi 1997; Rousseau et al. 1996) argue that intra-war crises should be excluded as they "have already escalated to violence and war and hence their inclusion would confound the results." We also deleted two crisis actors (Hijaz and Najd from crisis number 29, Hijaz-Najd War) because of missing data. We deleted 11 cases where there were no data available for duration. We also deleted China as an actor in the China civil war because its principal adversary was listed as China. From this we lose 70 cases due to missing data on our social unrest measure. This left us with a sample size of 653 observations representing actors/states that had a foreign policy crisis during an international crisis.

4. There were two missing cases of the ICB "source of greatest threat" variable. The first was Germany's greatest threat in the German reparations crisis of 1921. We therefore consulted Rousseau et al.'s (1996) dyadic data where the opponent was shown to be France. The second missing opponent came in the Iraqi no-fly zone crisis of 1992. As the Rousseau et al. data end in 1988, we could not use this source. Based on widely reported information, we coded Iraq's main adversary in the crisis to be the United States.

5. The data are available at www.bsos.umd.edu/cidcm/polity/index.html (September 2003).

6. The ICB data have a variable based on "power discrepancy" between the actors in each crisis but there were too many missing observations to be useful.

7. The data are available at www.umich.edu/~cowproj/capabilities.html (September 2003).

8. This variable and contiguity are only weakly correlated (r = .05).

9. See Long (1997) for a technical description of the estimation of ordered logit models.

9

When Likely Losers Choose War

Alastair Smith and Allan C. Stam

Why would a state start a war knowing that it will lose every battle? Standard bargaining theories of war built around the assumption that war is a lottery cannot account for this possibility. To understand this phenomenon, which is common in guerrilla campaigns and wars over hard to divide issues, we model warfare as a series of battles, in each of which A captures a fort from B, or vice versa. The war continues until either one side decisively defeats the other by capturing all the forts, or they reach a negotiated settlement. We examine how war aims and disagreement about the cost of fighting affect the nature of these settlements. Negotiated settlements are hard to reach when nation-states have territorial ambitions. Yet when nation states fight over issues unrelated to the possession of forts, then agreement over the prospects of victory (the probability of capturing additional forts) and the cost of fighting ensures a negotiated settlement. We examine how disagreements over the likely cost of fighting can delay negotiated settlements and show how conflict resolves informational differences between states.

Why would a nation-state fight a war that it knows it is bound to lose? Standard bargaining theories of international relations built around war as a lottery cannot account for this possibility. While standard formal theory approaches cannot explain this phenomenon, it is fairly common in guerrilla campaigns and wars over hard to divide issues. For example, in 1973 the Egyptian army initiated a war that many of its leaders believed they would lose. They did so in the hopes of improving their chances at the bargaining table with Israel, where the two sides had been previously unable to reach a negotiated settlement over the future of the Sinai Peninsula.

While many contemporary rationalist explanations for war hinge on potential uncertainty about the outcomes of war, there is clear evidence that the Egyptian political and military leadership were well aware that the Israeli military was the superior force (Slantchev 2003a; Filson and Werner 2002; Smith and Stam 2004; Fearon 1995; Blainey 1988). Nevertheless, the Egyptians felt that waging war, even in a losing effort, would bring them positive gains at the negotiating table as well as serving to help reclaim a perceived drop in national honor following the Israelis' stunning victory in the 1967 war. Viewing the decision to wage war from the perspective of current theories of bargaining and war, typically we would assume that states, once aware that they are unlikely to win an impending war, would likely make needed concessions in order to avoid war. For example, in the clash over influence in Egypt, France backed down during the 1898 Fashoda crisis when facing the prospect of war with Britain, after the French leadership realized the considerable military inferiority it faced on the ground in Egypt and at sea against the British navy (Bates 1984, 151–59).

While at first glance it might appear to be a purely hypothetical question, there are numerous examples of wars in which nation-states have been willing to fight fully aware that they have little or no prospects of winning. For example, consider Belgium's choice at the outbreak of World War I. In the first days of the war, Germany presented Belgium with an ultimatum: allow us to move peacefully through your territory to get to France, and we will honor Belgian sovereignty after the war and recompense any damages; oppose such movement, and face destruction. Even with this relatively attractive offer in hand and facing the prospect of annihilation on the battlefield, the Belgians still fought (Tuchman 1962, 124). In 1991, Saddam Hussein believed the United States would fight to try to liberate Kuwait, but chose war and likely defeat over more peaceful negotiations (Pollack 2002a). One story that explains away many of these interstate cases of likely losers choosing to fight relies on the pernicious effects of autocratic institutions. In this story the losers either misjudged the likely outcome of the war due to poor information processing, could not risk the political fallout from a forced concession, or were risk acceptant and insulated from the costs of anything short of catastrophic failure (Reiter and Stam 2002; Goemans 2000).

In each of the above instances, the target nation-state faced the choice either to fight or back down. Are there instances in which the initiating nation states choose to start a war knowing they will most likely lose? In the classic case, weak guerrilla fighters take on the powerful states and win concessions. Algerian freedom fighters knew their forces were quantitatively and qualitatively weaker than the French forces, but chose to fight regardless. During the Vietnam War, the United States clearly controlled the preponderance of power, and yet the North Vietnamese and the Viet Cong chose to fight anyway. In 1961, America's president, John F. Kennedy, told the nation in his inaugural address that Americans should "(l)et every Nation know, whether it wishes us well or ill, that we shall pay any price, bear any burden, meet any hardship, support any friend, oppose any foe to assure the survival and success of liberty." If this statement had proven true, the outcome of the Vietnam War would likely have turned out far differently than it did. In the end, the United States was unwilling to bear the hardship and the costs of an unpopular war thousands of miles away against a seemingly overmatched foe. Many in the policy-making and military communities seemed perplexed by the inability of the United States to defeat a clearly weaker foe. The following conversation between Colonel Harry G. Summers and one of his North Vietnamese counterparts sums up the thoughts of many on both sides of the war:

"You know," he (Summers) boasted to a North Vietnamese colonel after the war, "you never defeated us on the battlefield." To which the communist officer replied, "That may be so, but it is also irrelevant" (Karnow 1983, 19).

Ultimately, the decisionmakers in a state at war must ask themselves if the potential gains from victory are worth the costs of continuing to fight. This is precisely the problem that the United States faced in Vietnam, where the insurgents in the South and their allies in the North were prepared to accept substantial punishment rather than abandon their goal of destroying the U.S.-backed regime in Saigon.

Much of the current literature on the rational origins of war points to the fact that a majority of war initiators win the wars they start. However, what of the wars the initiators went on to lose? Are those wars the result of psychological pathologies on the part of the losing initiators or are they perhaps simply cases that went against the odds, being the proverbial exceptions that prove the rule? In this chapter, we construct a model of war in which initiators can rationally start a war, fully expecting to lose every battle. The incentive to begin the losing effort lies in the belief that they will be able to impose unexpected costs on the winner, thereby gaining an advantage in the wartime bargaining process.

In short, we believe the answer to the puzzle of losing initiators may lie in disagreements over the relative costs of fighting. In this chapter, we model warfare as a series of battles between nation-states A and B. We begin by assuming that states are sensitive both to the outcomes of wars as well as their costs and durations. By relaxing the standard assumption that states want to maximize their chances in war, we open a new avenue of research into the literature on bargaining and war (Reiter 2003). States whose goals focus on altering their opponent's expectations may ultimately improve their bargaining position, even while losing the battles in which they engage. In effect, by taking a new approach to the puzzle of the origins of war, we show how losers can win. In doing so, we complicate many standard approaches to war outcomes and duration.

The logic behind our relaxing the assumption that states only want to maximize their chances for victory is straightforward. While winning is preferred to losing, winning at all costs may not be. Some victories may be pyrrhic if the costs associated with gaining the victory exceed the hoped for gains accomplished by defeating the opponent on the battlefield. In our model, during each battle, Nation A[1] might capture a strategically important objective, which we refer to as a fort, from Nation B, or vice versa. Once under way, the war continues until one side defeats the other by capturing all the forts, or the nation-states agree to a negotiated settlement. Given shared expectations of the war's likely nature, nation-states might forgo the cost of actually fighting and reach a settlement prior to fighting. Unfortunately, whether peaceful bargaining between the two nation-states can succeed depends both on what the two nation-states are fighting for as well as the level of disagreement about the costs of war. Although we present a general model, we illustrate our results with the case in which one nation knows it will lose every battle, yet still perpetuates the war.

A RANDOM WALK MODEL OF WAR

During most wars, nation-states bargain while fighting. If they cannot reach a settlement, they continue fighting. Rather than treat war as a one-time event as is common in the extant literature,[2] we develop a model of war characterized by a series of struggles. During each of these battles, both sides hope to improve their advantage relative to the other. To reflect this we assume nation-states fight battles over forts. We use the metaphor of "forts" to reflect strategically significant objectives. Although historically wars often revolved around the capture of fortified towns, this is less frequently the case in modern conflicts. However, we continue to use the heuristic of the fort since its meaning is intuitively clear.

In our model, nation-states battle over forts with probabilistic outcomes for each battle. In each period, Nation A might capture a fort from Nation B. Alternatively B might capture one from A. We assume there is a fixed total of N forts, and that initially A holds X_0 of them. We denote the number of forts that A holds at time t as X_t. In the context of the stochastic processes literature, X_t is referred to as a state variable. Eventually, A might capture all of the forts ($X_t = N$) driving Nation B out of the system. At this point, B is no longer able to prosecute the war; A has decisively defeated B and may impose whatever settlement it wishes. Alternatively, B might decisively defeat A by capturing all the forts and leaving A with no means to continue the war, $X_t = 0$. These two outcomes, $X_t = 0$ and $X_t = N$, reflect what Clausewitz refers to as an absolute war: One that is fought until one side is completely disarmed or no longer able to prosecute the war.

While some wars continue until one side is completely disarmed, such as the defeat of Germany in World War II or the South in the American Civil War, in practice most nation-states reach a settlement short of complete victory for one side. Commonly, civil wars end in negotiated settlement with the government sometimes making concessions to a rebel group demanding greater autonomy (Walter 2001). As Clausewitz stresses, war being the continuation of politics, most wars do not involve the elimination of one side or the other, although this is the reality facing nation-states unable to reach a negotiated political settlement.

In each period, one battle takes place. With probability p Nation A captures a fort from Nation B and with probability $q = 1-p$ B captures a fort from Nation A.[3] This probability distribution describes the possible paths of war. After a single period either A has captured an additional fort ($X_1 = X_0+1$) which occurs with probability p or A has lost an additional fort ($X_1 = X_0-1$) which occurs with probability $(1-p)$. After two periods of fighting, the state is $X_2 = X_0+2$ with probability p^2, $X_2 = X_0$ with probability $2p(1-p)$, and $X_2 = X_0-2$ with probability $(1-p)^2$, and so on.

One might argue the probability of winning the next battle depends upon the state. As A captures more forts it might have more resources to draw upon and hence improve its prospects in the next battle. Alternatively, as A captures many forts its resources become stretched and its supply chain longer. Under this reasoning, we might assume the prospects of winning the next battle decline. There are anecdotal cases to support either of these arguments. Although elsewhere we have examined these implications (Smith 1997), here we assume p is fixed.

We assume fighting is costly. In particular, we assume Nation A pays a cost K_A for each battle fought and Nation B pays costs K_B. These costs reflect any financial, economic, social, and physiological losses of armed conflict. In this chapter, we pay particular attention to the costs of fighting. However, our setup is general and elsewhere we focus on different aspects of the model (Smith 1997, 1998a; Smith and Stam 2004). In particular, we assume the Nation B might face high or low costs from fighting a war: $K_B \in \{k_l, k_h\}$. With probability θ B's costs are high: $K_B = k_h$. With probability $(1-\theta)$ costs are low: $K_B = k_l$. Without loss of generality, let $k_h = k_l +1$. Nations disagree as to the likelihood of high- and low-cost conflict. In the fall of 2002, the U.S. government seriously considered war with Iraq over Iraq's intransigence at the negotiating table. Both Saddam Hussein and George Bush could be sure that the U.S. military would be able to prevail on the battlefield. Nevertheless, Pollack (2002b) and others suggest that Hussein in 1990 and 2002 believed that the United States would be particularly sensitive to casualties, to the extent that if the Iraqi army could inflict sufficient costs on the United States, the U.S. government would be willing to accept a deal significantly short of total defeat for the Ba'ath regime. We might think of K_B as the number of U.S. casualties. During the insurgency campaign in 2003 and 2004, although the Iraqis anticipated losing battles, they believe they can inflict high casualties on the United States. In contrast, the United States believes it can keep casualties to "acceptable" levels. As we shall see, if the United States suffers high casualties in a battle and hence increasingly believes that Iraq can inflict future high casualties, then Iraq's bargaining position can strengthen even as it loses battles and moves closer to eventual defeat.

The random walk model of war continues either until one side decisively wins and imposes a settlement or until the nations reach agreement. We have described how the process of battling shifts the strategic balance as nations capture forts and consequently move closer to a decisive victory. However, to explain negotiations we need to understand over what issues the two nations are fighting.

WAR AIMS

What are the fundamental goals of states? For instance, do they care about capturing forts per se or is the possession of forts simply instrumental to obtaining concessions on some other dimension? For the purposes of the formal model in this chapter, we assume the latter. Specifically nations fight over the division of a prize worth V. This prize might reflect choices on some policy dimension or a transfer, such as reparations, from one state to another. The essential assumption is that nations' payoffs depend upon the state variable, the number of forts, only instrumentally. However, before considering bargaining over the prize, we pause to examine why bargaining is impossible if nations care only about the forts themselves.

When nations' ambitions are exclusively territorial, then negotiations will likely fail. Under this scenario nations care about the number of forts they possess. Suppose Nation A is unhappy with its share of forts and is willing to fight to obtain more. Nation B might be willing to transfer additional forts to Nation A in order to mitigate A's desire for war. Unfortunately, rather than diminishing A's wants, transferring forts increases A's demand. With additional forts, A is closer to a decisive victory in which it obtains everything.

Therefore A increases its demands. Since further concessions create further demands, nations negotiating territorial issues typically need to resolve the disagreement with force. Unless nations can credibly commit not to demand additional forts following a territorial transfer, negotiated settlements are difficult to reach.

We might suppose nations care more about their "heartlands" than their peripheries (Goemans 2000). As forts become more remote they drop in value. Hence although obtaining additional forts makes nations closer to complete domination and control of all territory, if the value of additional forts drops off sufficiently then nations can commit not to increase demands following territorial gains. Without such assumptions, when nations care primarily about the forts themselves, territorial transfer cannot produce stable settlements.

Although assuming nations value forts per se is a valuable research enterprise, the current focus is on forts being instrumental to obtaining a negotiated settlement on an alternative dimension. Nations battle over a prize, which is worth V. Should A decisively defeat B then A takes the whole prize. Similarly, should B become the absolute victor, it takes the whole prize. Yet, if nations can agree to a division of the prize then they divide the prize accordingly and forgo the cost of fighting the war.

NEGOTIATIONS

As Clausewitz is commonly noted observing, "War is the continuation of politics by other means"; consequently, if both nations agree to a division of the prize then they can end the fighting. We model negotiations using the take-it-or-leave-it protocol. This format dominates the bargaining literature in most of the social sciences (Rubinstein 1982; Muthoo 1999).

In each period, Nation A proposes a potential division of the prize, $b_t \in [0,V]$. If in period t, B accepts the division b_t, then A receives a payoff of $V-b_t-K_A t$, where $V-b_t$ represents A's share of the prize and $K_A t$ is the cost of fighting for the t periods before reaching an agreement. B's corresponding payoff is $b_t - \sum_{i=0}^{t} K_{B,i}$, in which the second term represents the sum of B's costs over t periods.[4] At time t we denote the number of high-cost battles via the state variable h_t. Hence B's total costs of fighting t battles are $h_t k_h + (t-h_t)k_l$.

If the nations fail to reach agreement, then they fight a battle in which either A captures a fort from B or vice versa, as described above. The game continues until either a decisive winner emerges ($X_t = 0, N$) or a negotiated settlement is reached.

BARGAINING DELAY: RESOLVING
DISAGREEMENTS THROUGH FIGHTING

If both nations are in full agreement as to the parameters of the model and there is no commitment problem such that a settlement today increases demands tomorrow (as was the case when nation cared about forts per se), then nations can immediately reach a negotiated settlement negating the need for conflict. Unfortunately, disagreement about relative strength (p) or costs (K) can necessitate fighting to resolve these differences. Elsewhere we examine the implications of disagreeing over relative strength (Smith and Stam 2003a). Here we examine the consequences of disagreement over the relative costs of fighting.

As already briefly discussed above, while both sides agree that A's cost is K_A, they disagree about B's costs. To keep the model as simple as possible while reflecting these differences, we assume B pays either a high or a low cost for fighting any particular battle (k_h, k_l). We assume the probability that B's cost is high is θ, $\Pr(K_B = k_h) = \theta$.

Consider the situation in which nations A and B differ in their beliefs about θ. In particular, we suppose A believes the likelihood of B experiencing high casualties is higher than B believes it to be.[5] We model A and B's beliefs over the value of θ using the beta distribution. This distribution is characterized by two parameters, α and β. The probability density function is $f(\theta;\alpha,\beta) = \frac{\Gamma(\alpha+\beta)}{\Gamma(\alpha)\Gamma(\beta)}\theta^{(\alpha-1)}(1-\theta)^{(\beta-1)}$ where $\Gamma(\alpha) = \int_0^\infty e^{-x}x^{\alpha-1}dx$. The beta distribution has mean $\frac{\alpha}{\alpha+\beta}$, variance $\frac{\alpha\beta}{(\alpha+\beta)^2(\alpha+\beta+1)}$, and mode $\frac{\alpha-1}{\alpha+\beta-2}$ (if α, $\beta>1$).

Nations A and B have different prior beliefs about θ, represented in the case of the beta distribution through different α and β parameters. In particular A's prior beliefs about the distribution of θ are represented by the parameters α_{A0} and β_{A0}. B's prior beliefs are α_{B0} and β_{B0}. For the running example we discuss below, $\alpha_{A0} = 6$, $\beta_{A0} = 1$, $\alpha_{B0} = 1$ and $\beta_{B0} = 6$, which implies A thinks the probability of B experiencing high costs is 6/7, while B believes it has only a 1/7 chance of suffering high costs in each battle.

As a running example, we focus on the special case of $p = 0$, $N = 10$, $X_0 = 9$, $V = 3$, $K_A = 0.01$ and $K_B \in \{k_l = 0.1, k_h = 1.1\}$. We use this example for both substantive and presentational reasons. First, from a presentational perspective, characterizing the game requires tracking both the number of forts captured (the state variable X_t) and costliness of battles over time, h_t. For the general case, plotting the evolution of the system involves displaying three dimensions (X_t, h_t, t), which is difficult to present in two dimensions. By fixing $p = 0$, the dimensions of X_t and t collapse to a single dimension making representation of the systems much easier.

Second, we began by posing the question, why would a nation ever fight when it was certain to lose every battle? In particular we ask why in 1991 Iraq refused to cut a deal with the United States preceding the war when once war began each battle it lost placed it in a worse strategic circumstance. Our running example addresses this problem. In both the 1991 Gulf War and its 2003 reiteration, the United States experienced casualties up to the tens of soldiers per battle. The Iraqis hoped to be able to inflict casualties in the order of hundreds or thousands. We reflect these difference magnitudes in k_l and k_h.

LEARNING THROUGH FIGHTING

While A and B initially disagree as to B's cost of fighting, war provides them learning opportunities. During war, both sides get the opportunity to observe B's actual costs and so update their beliefs, learning whose beliefs were the more accurate. To explicate the learning process, we introduce h_t the history of the costs of fighting. In our simple setting, this takes the form of the number of high-cost battles that occur by time t.

At the start of the war, A thinks the expected value of θ is $E_{A, t = 0}[\theta] = \dfrac{\alpha_{A0}}{\alpha_{A0} + \beta_{A0}}$. We use the subscripts A and t to indicate expectations that are from the perspective of A's beliefs given its available information at time t. After t battles, if h_t of these battles have been high cost, then A's beliefs shift such that θ is beta distributed with parameters $\alpha = \alpha_{A0} + h_t$ and $\beta = \beta_{A0} + t - h_t$. Hence, $E_{A,t}[\theta] = \dfrac{\alpha_{A0} + h_t}{\alpha_{A0} + \beta_{A0} + t}$. As B experiences a greater proportion of high-cost battles, A's expectations about θ increase. B's beliefs about the probability of war being high cost given a history of h_t high-cost battles are $E_{B,t}[\theta] = \dfrac{\alpha_{B0} + h_t}{\alpha_{B0} + \beta_{B0} + t}$.

EXPECTATIONS OF WAR OUTCOME AND DURATION

Nations bargain in the shadow of absolute war (Wittman 1979; Powell 1999; Slantchev 2003a). It is therefore useful to characterize the properties of this absolute war and nations' beliefs about it since these factors shape the bargaining that occurs in the background to the fighting. Starting from state X_τ in period $\tau \geq 0$, we define the resolution time, $R(X_\tau) = \min\{(t - \tau) \geq 0 | X_t = 0 \text{ or } X_t = N\}$, as the time taken until either Nation A or Nation B attains complete victory (states $X_t = N$, 0, respectively). We define the probability that Nation A will eventually lose the war if fought to the end while starting in state X_t as $\lambda(X_t) = \Pr\{X_R = 0|X_t\}$. With complementary probability, A will emerge the eventual winner.

In state X_t, the expected number of battles that occur before one side emerges as eventual winner is $D(X_t) = E[R(X_t)]$. Fortunately, the calculation of $\lambda(X_t)$ and $D(X_t)$ are well-known results in the stochastic processes literature (See, for example, Taylor and Karlin 1994; Grimmett and Stirzaker 1992).

The probability that B will be the eventual winner is,

$$\lambda(X_t) = \begin{cases} \dfrac{(q/p)^{X_t}-(q/p)^N}{1-(q/p)^N} & \text{if } p \neq 1/2 \\[2ex] \dfrac{(N-X_t)}{N} & \text{if } p = 1/2, \end{cases}$$

where $q = 1-p$. The expected number of additional periods of fighting required until one side wins an all out war is,

$$D(X_t) = E[R(X_t)] = \begin{cases} \dfrac{1}{q-p}[X_t - N(\dfrac{1-(\frac{q}{p})^{X_t}}{1-(\frac{q}{p})^N})] & \text{if } p \neq 1/2 \\[2ex] X_t(N-X_t) & \text{if } p = 1/2, \end{cases}$$

where $q = 1-p$.

THE VALUE OF FIGHTING

Nations A and B each hold beliefs about the likelihood of each side winning and how long any war between them is likely to last. From this information, they can calculate the value of fighting a war until the end. Knowing the expected consequences of fighting, nations might choose to negotiate a settlement that reflects these expectations rather than fight the actual war.

Suppose, starting at state X_t with cost history h_t, nations A and B fight the war until an eventual winner emerges. A's expected value from this absolute war is $E[U_A \text{ (fight indefinitely} |X_t, t, h_t)] = C_A(X_t, t, h_t) = V(1-\lambda(X_t))-K_A D(X_t)$. The first term is A's probability of emerging the eventual winner, in which case A receives the whole prize, V. The second term reflects the cost of fighting an addition $D(X_t)$ battles, each at cost K_A.

B's expected value from the all-out war is $E[U_B \text{ (fight indefinitely} |X_t, t, h_t)] = C_B(X_t, t, h_t) = V\lambda(X_t)-D(X_t)E_{B,t}[K_B]$. B's cost for fighting out the war depends on the probability that battles are high cost. Hence the total cost of fighting, $D(X_t)E_{B,t}[K_B]$, depends upon B's beliefs about the likelihood of a high-cost battle. Since A's beliefs about the likelihood of high-cost battle differ from B's, A thinks that B's expected value of fighting an absolute war is $\overset{\frown}{C_B^A}(X_t, t, h_t) = V\lambda(X_t) - D(X_t)E_{A,t}[K_B]$. This is to say, from A's belief perspective, B can obtain a payoff worth $\overset{\frown}{C_B^A}(X_t, t, h_t)$ from absolute war, while B believes that it can obtain a payoff $C_B(X_t, t, h_t)$ from fighting it out. These expectations about what each side believes it can obtain from fighting the war to its conclusion form the basis for what each side can extract at the bargaining table.

Figure 9.1 shows B's continuation value from fighting an absolute war from state (X_t, t, h_t) for the numerical example. As the war continues, B captures more of A's forts which makes continuing the war more attractive. As B experiences high-cost battles (h_t increases), and hence anticipates a higher probability of high-cost battles in the future, the value of an all-out war declines. For instance, following eight battles ($X_8 = 1$), if B has experienced no high-cost battles then $E_{B,8}[\theta] = \dfrac{1}{7+8} = \dfrac{1}{15}$. Given $p = 0$ and $X_8 = 1$ then B expects to capture the whole prize ($V = 3$) from a single battle, the expected cost of which is $\dfrac{1}{15}k_h + (1-\dfrac{1}{15})k_l = 0.167$. In this setting, the continuation value of an absolute war is $3 - 0.167 = 2.83$. In contrast, if B has experienced eight high-cost battles, $h_8 = 8$, then $E_{B,8}[\theta] = \dfrac{1+8}{7+8} = \dfrac{9}{15}$, so the expected cost of the final battle is $\dfrac{9}{15}k_h + (1-\dfrac{9}{15})k_l = 0.7$. Hence, B's continuation value is 2.30.

	t=0	t=1	t=2	t=3	t=4	t=5	t=6	t=7	t=8	t=9
8									2.30	3
7								1.66	2.37	3
6							1.08	1.80	2.43	3
5						0.60	1.32	1.94	2.50	3
4					0.23	0.93	1.55	2.09	2.57	3
3				0.00	0.68	1.27	1.78	2.23	2.63	3
2			-0.03	0.60	1.14	1.60	2.01	2.37	2.70	3
1		0.20	0.74	1.20	1.59	1.93	2.24	2.51	2.77	3
0	0.81	1.20	1.52	1.80	2.05	2.27	2.47	2.66	2.83	3
time, t	0	1	2	3	4	5	6	7	8	9
forts, X_t	9	8	7	6	5	4	3	2	1	0

Number of high cost battles, h_t

Figure 9.1. B's Continuation Value for an Absolute War: $C_B(X_t, t, h_t)$

B can expect to obtain the payoff $C_B(X_t, t, h_t)$ by continuing the war. Therefore, B never accepts less than this from the bargaining process: By dominance, B never accepts $b_t < C_B(X_t, t, h_t)$. Therefore, the maximum that A can extract from B at the bargaining table is $M_A(X_t, t, h_t) = V-\max\{0, C_B(X_t, t, h_t)\}$. The max part of this expression indicates that A cannot extract more than everything, that is, deals are restricted to the interval $[0, V]$.

Dominance also asserts that the only deals A offers (that B would accept) give A at least as great a payoff as indefinite fighting: $V-b_t \geq C_A(X_t, t, h_t)$. Peaceful agreements are possible only when agreements exist that both sides prefer to indefinite fighting. We present this formally below.

Proposition 1: A necessary condition for a negotiated settlement is $C_A(X_t,$ $t, h_t) \leq M_A(X_t, t, h_t) = V-\max\{0, C_B(X_t, t, h_t)\}$. Thus, a sufficient condition for continued conflict is $C_B(X_t, t, h_t)+C_A(X_t, t, h_t) > V$.

If the sum of A and B's expected value from fighting an all-out war is greater than the total value of the prize they are fighting over, then there is no division of the prize that they both prefer to war. When the nations disagree about the cost of fighting, and in particular when B thinks its costs are low, but A believes B's costs are high, then each side expects to gain more from the negotiations than the other side is willing to concede, thereby leading to fighting.

This is precisely the situation in which Anwar al-Sadat found himself and the Egyptian army in 1973. On 1 October 1973, five days before war, Sadat provided Ahmad Ismail, Egypt's chief military planner, with a strategic directive for the war. The purpose of waging war against Israel would not be to achieve an outright military victory, but rather, to "challenge the Israeli Security Theory by carrying out a military action . . . aimed at inflicting the heaviest losses on the enemy and convincing him that continued occupation of our land exacts a price too high for him to pay." Sadat believed that Israel's "theory of security—based . . . on psychological, political, and military intimidation—is not an impregnable shield of steel which protects (the Israelis) today or in the future" (Gawrych 2000, 146). Sadat maintained that to challenge Israel successfully, the Egyptians would have to impose costs higher than the Israelis believed possible. In doing so, however, Sadat believed that even a losing war effort would have definite short-term and long-term consequences. "In the short term, by contesting the Israeli's theory of war, the Egyptians would make it possible for an honorable solution for the Middle East crisis to be reached. In the long term, a challenge to the Israeli Security Theory can produce changes which will, following on the heels of one another, lead to a basic change in the enemy's thinking, morale and aggressive tendencies" (Ibid, 146).

Unfortunately, while the existence of a division of the prize that both sides prefer to absolute war is necessary for successful negotiation, it is not sufficient. As we shall see, even though A loses every battle, it believes it can improve its bargaining leverage and extract more from B by fighting in the hope of convincing B that B's costs of fighting are high. Fighting is attractive because the sides disagree and each believes that by fighting it is likely to convince the other that its view of the world is correct and hence to extract a better settlement. The following lemma shows that beliefs converge as fighting continues. Proposition 2 uses this result to show that after some finite time, beliefs converge sufficiently that nations always reach agreement.

Lemma: For all $\epsilon > 0$, there exists a $\bar{t}$ such that for all $t \geq \bar{t}$, and for states $X_t \in \{1, \ldots, N-1\}$, $|C_B(X_t, t) - \widehat{C_B^A(X_t, t)}| < \epsilon$ and $|E_{A,t}[K_B] - E_{B,t}[K_B]| < \epsilon$.

Proof: This is a standard limit argument. Take ϵ fixed.

$$C_B(X_t, t, h_t) - \widehat{C_B^A(X_t, t, h_t)} =$$

$$V\lambda(X_t) - D(X_t)E_{B,t}[K_B] - (V\lambda(X_t) - D(X_t)E_{A,t}[K_B]) =$$

$$D(X_t)(E_{A,t}[K_B] - E_{B,t}[K_B]) =$$

$$D(X_t)\left(\frac{\alpha_{A0} + h_t}{\alpha_{A0} + \beta_{A0} + t} - \frac{\alpha_{B0} + h_t}{\alpha_{B0} + \beta_{B0} + t} \right) \leq D\left(\frac{\alpha_{A0} + h_t}{\alpha_{A0} + \beta_{A0} + t} - \frac{\alpha_{B0} + h_t}{\alpha_{B0} + \beta_{B0} + t} \right)$$

where $D = \max_{Xt} D(X_t)$. Since $\lim_{t \to \infty} \left(\frac{\alpha_{A0} + h_t}{\alpha_{A0} + \beta_{A0} + t} - \frac{\alpha_{B0} + h_t}{\alpha_{B0} + \beta_{B0} + t} \right) = 0$, there exists $\bar{t}$. Specifically, since $\left| \left(\frac{\alpha_{A0} + h_t}{\alpha_{A0} + \beta_{A0} + t} - \frac{\alpha_{B0} + h_t}{\alpha_{B0} + \beta_{B0} + t} \right) \right|$ is maximized for either $h_t = 0$ or $h_t = t$ then $\bar{t}$ is the smallest integer that solves both $\left| \left(\frac{\alpha_{A0}}{\alpha_{A0} + \beta_{A0} + t} - \frac{\alpha_{B0}}{\alpha_{B0} + \beta_{B0} + t} \right) \right| < \epsilon/D(X_t)$ and $\left| \left(\frac{\alpha_{A0} + t}{\alpha_{A0} + \beta_{A0} + t} - \frac{\alpha_{B0} + t}{\alpha_{B0} + \beta_{B0} + t} \right) \right| < \epsilon/D(X_t)$ for all X_t. Since $D(X_t) \geq 1$ for $X_t, \ldots, N-1$ this also ensures the second condition of the lemma. ?

Proposition 2: For $t \geq \bar{t}$, A offers $b_t = \max\{0, C_B(X_t, t, h_t)\}$, which B accepts.

Proof: If $C_B(X_t, t, h_t) < 0$ then A attains the whole prize. Hence, we consider only the more difficult case of $C_B(X_t, t, h_t) \geq 0$.

Suppose A offers $b_t = C_B(X_t, t, h_t)$ in every period $t \geq \bar{t}$ then B's expected value of rejecting A's offer is $C_B(X_t, t, h_t)$. Hence, B accepts if $b_t \geq C_B(X_t, t, h_t)$ and rejects if $b_t < C_B(X_t, t, h_t)$. In common with many similar games there are not subgame perfect equilibriums in which B accepts $b_t > C_B(X_t, t, h_t)$ and rejects $b_t \leq C_B(X_t, t, h_t)$, since for any offer $b_t > C_B(X_t, t, h_t)$ Nation A can always find an offer b'_t such that $b_t > b'_t > C_B(X_t, t, h_t)$. Given A's offer $b_t = C_B(X_t, t, h_t)$, B's strategy is a best response.

We now consider A's strategy. Since B accepts all deals, $b_t \geq C_B(X_t, t, h_t)$, A never offers any deal greater than $C_B(X_t, t, h_t)$. If A offers $b_t = C_B(X_t, t, h_t)$ then A's expected payoff is $M_A(X_t, t, h_t) = V - \max\{0, C_B(X_t, t, h_t)\}$. If A offers $b_t < C_B(X_t, t, h_t)$ then A's expected payoff is $Q(X_t, t, h_t) = -K_A + V - pE_{A,t}[\theta]C_B(X_t+1, t+1, h_t+1) - p(1-E_{A,t}[\theta])C_B(X_t+1, t+1, h_t) - (1-p)E_{A,t}[\theta] C_B(X_t-1, t+1, h_t+1) - (1-p)(1-E_{A,t}[\theta])C_B(X_t-1, t+1, h_t)$, where $E_{A,t}[\theta] = \dfrac{\alpha_{A0} + h_t}{\alpha_{A0} + \beta_{A0} + t}$. But this payoff is less than

$$J = -K_A + V - pE_{A,t}[\theta]\overline{C_B^A(X_t+1, t+1, h_t+1)}$$

$$-p(1-E_{A,t}[\theta])\overline{C_B^A(X_t+1, t+1, h_t)} - (1-p)E_{A,t}[\theta]\overline{C_B^A(X_t-1, t+1, h_t+1)}$$

$$-(1-p)(1-E_{A,t}[\theta])\overline{C_B^A(X_t-1, t+1, h_t)}.$$

Intuitively J is the expected amount A could extract from B tomorrow if by a single additional battle B's beliefs were to converge to A's beliefs, less the cost of an additional battle. By lemma 1 as $t \to \infty$ then $M_A(X_t, t, h_t) \to J(X_t, t, h_t)$. Thus, for $t > \bar{t}$, $|M_A(X_t, t, h_t) - J(X_t, t, h_t) + K_A| < \epsilon$. Since $J > Q(X_t, t, h_t)$, $M_A(X_t, t, h_t) > Q(X_t, t, h_t)$. Hence, A offers $b_t = \max\{0, C_B(X_t, t, h_t)\}$, which is accepted.

Proposition 2 ensures that the game ends within some finite time, either because one side decisively defeats the other, or at time $\bar{t}$ beliefs have sufficiently converged that a negotiated settlement is inevitable. Given that the game is finite, we can solve the game by simple backwards induction. We characterize A's continuation value, $Z_A(X_t, t, h_t)$, from being in state X_t at time t given the history of costs h_t. These continuation values are the expected payoff from playing the game starting at state X_t at time t given a cost history h_t. In the absorbing state 0, A has already decisively lost the war so A's continuation value is $Z_A(0, t, h_t) = 0$ for all t. Similarly, if A has already decisively won the war $Z_A(N, t, h_t) = V$ for all t. Proposition 2 also allows us to assign continuation values for all time periods $t \geq \bar{t}$, since we know that a deal will be reached without further conflict: $Z_A(X_t, t, h_t) = M_A(X_t, t, h_t) = V - \max\{0, C_B(X_t, t, h_t)\}$ for all $t \geq \bar{t}$. Proposition 3 characterizes the continuation values in all periods and states via backwards induction.

Proposition 3: For $t \geq \bar{t}$, $Z_A(X_t, t, h_t) = M(X_t, t, h_t)$. For $t < \bar{t}$, A's continuation values are defined by backwards induction:

$$Z_A(X_t, t, h_t) = \max\{M_A(X_t, t, h_t), -K_A + pE_{A,t}[\theta]Z_A(X_t+1, t+1, h_t+1)$$
$$+p(1-E_{A,t}[\theta])Z_A(X_t+1, t+1, h_t)$$
$$+(1-p)E_{A,t}[\theta]Z_A(X_t-1, t+1, h_t+1) + (1-p)(1-E_{A,t}[\theta])Z_A(X_t-1, t+1, h_t),$$

where $E_{A,t}[\theta] = \dfrac{\alpha_{A0}+h_t}{\alpha_{A0}+\beta_{A0}+t}$.

Proof: By proposition 2, we know that for $t \geq \bar{t}$, $Z_A(X_t, t, h_t) = M_A(X_t, t, h_t)$.

For $t < \bar{t}$, consider the following strategy: B accepts b_t if $b_t \geq C_B(X_t, t, h_t)$ and rejects otherwise. A offers $b_t \in \{C_B(X_t, t, h_t), 0\}$. We now show these are best responses. Given $b_t \in \{C_B(X_t, t, h_t), 0\}$, B never receives an offer greater than $max\{C_B(X_t, t, h_t), 0\}$ in any future period. Hence, accepting b_t is a best response in every subgame if $b_t \geq C_B(X_t, t, h_t)$. We now consider A's optimal strategy. Given B's acceptance strategy, any offer $b_t \geq C_B(X_t, t, h_t)$ is accepted. Offering $b' > max\{C_B(X_t, t, h_t), 0\}$ is dominated by offering b'' such that $b' > b'' > max\{C_B(X_t, t, h_t), 0\}$. Therefore, any offer strategy by A must be either $b_t = max\{C_B(X_t, t, h_t), 0\}$, or an offer that is rejected.

Consider $t = \bar{t}-1$. If A offers $b_t = max\{C_B(X_t, t, h_t), 0\}$, then A's payoff is $M(X_t, t, h_t)$. We have already shown that A never makes a larger offer, so the only other case to consider is an offer that will be rejected, $b_t < C_B(X_t, t, h_t)$. In this case A's payoff is $-K_A + pE_{A,t}[\theta]Z_A(X_t+1, t+1, h_t+1) + p(1-E_{A,t}[\theta])Z_A(X_t+1, t+1, h_t)$ $+(1-p)E_{A,t}[\theta]Z_A(X_t-1, t+1, h_t+1) + (1-p)(1-E_{A,t}[\theta])Z_A(X_t-1, t+1, h_t)$, where $E_{A,t}[\theta] = \dfrac{\alpha_{A0}+h_t}{\alpha_{A0}+\beta_{A0}+t}$. A's continuation value is the larger of the expected value from an additional battle or a negotiated settlement today.

Next, consider $t = \bar{t}-2$. By the same logic as above $Z_A(X_t, t, h_t) = \max\{M_A(X_t, t), -K_A + pE_{A,t}[\theta]Z_A(X_t+1, t+1, h_t+1) + p(1-E_{A,t}[\theta])Z_A(X_t+1, t+1, h_t)$ $+(1-p)E_{A,t}[\theta]Z_A(X_t-1, t+1, h_t+1) + (1-p)(1-E_{A,t}[\theta])Z_A(X_t-1, t+1, h_t)\}$, where $E_{A,t}[\theta] = \dfrac{\alpha_{A0}+h_t}{\alpha_{A0}+\beta_{A0}+t}$. Repeating this argument for $t = \bar{t}-3, \bar{t}-4,$ $\ldots, 0$ defines the continuation values for each nation and time period.

Figure 9.2 illustrates immediate bargains and continuation values for the numerical example. After four battles, A would always settle, offering B exactly what B would anticipate from continuing the war. The size of the settlement A can obtain depends heavily on the cost of previous battles. If, for example, B has suffered four high-cost battles then A can extract nearly the whole prize $M_A(5, 4, 4) = 2.77$. Although B will win every battle, recent evidence suggests the cost of winning the war means B is happy to let A extract the lion's share of the prize rather than risk the (what is now increasingly

A's best immediate settlement, $M_A(X_t,t,h_t)$ (upper figure)

Number of high cost battles, h_t	t=0	t=1	t=2	t=3	t=4	t=5	t=6	t=7	t=8	t=9
8									0.70	0
7								1.34	0.63	0
6							1.92	1.20	0.57	0
5						2.40	1.68	1.06	0.50	0
4					2.77	2.07	1.45	0.91	0.43	0
3				3.00	2.32	1.73	1.22	0.77	0.37	0
2			3.00	2.40	1.86	1.40	0.99	0.63	0.30	0
1		2.80	2.26	1.80	1.41	1.07	0.76	0.49	0.23	0
0	2.19	1.80	1.48	1.20	0.95	0.73	0.53	0.34	0.17	0
time, t	0	1	2	3	4	5	6	7	8	9
forts, X_t	9	8	7	6	5	4	3	2	1	0

A's continuation value, $Z_A(X_t,t,h_t)$ (lower figure)

Number of high cost battles, h_t	t=0	t=1	t=2	t=3	t=4	t=5	t=6	t=7	t=8	t=9
8									0.70	0
7								1.34	0.63	0
6							1.92	1.20	0.57	0
5						2.40	1.68	1.06	0.50	0
4					2.77	2.07	1.45	0.91	0.43	0
3				3.00	2.32	1.73	1.22	0.77	0.37	0
2			3.00	2.40	1.86	1.40	0.99	0.63	0.30	0
1		2.90	2.26	1.80	1.41	1.07	0.76	0.49	0.23	0
0	2.77	2.08	1.60	1.22	0.95	0.73	0.53	0.34	0.17	0
time, t	0	1	2	3	4	5	6	7	8	9
forts, X_t	9	8	7	6	5	4	3	2	1	0

Figure 9.2. Nation A's payoff from an Immediate Deal $M_A(X_t, t, h_t)$ (upper figure) and its Continuation Value $Z_A(X_t, t, h_t)$ (lower figure). The shaded cells represent states where A prefers to fight rather than settle.

likely) chance of more high-cost battles. In contrast, if B has experienced no high-cost battles, then A can extract much less, $M_A(5, 4, 0) = 0.95$.

For all periods $t > 4$, A prefers to settle rather than fight. Given these deals, we calculate A's expected value in earlier periods. To illustrate A's motivation consider $t = 3$ and $h_3 = 0$. Given that B has fought three battles and all have been low cost, $E_{A,t}[\theta] = \frac{6}{7+3} = .6$ and $E_{B,t}[\theta] = \frac{1}{7+3} = .1$. Given these beliefs, B's continuation value from fighting the absolute war is $V-D(X_3)(E_{B,t}[\theta]k_h+(1-E_{B,t}[\theta])k_l) = 3-6(.1*1.1+.9*.1) = 1.8$. Offering B a settlement equal to this amount, allows A to retain the remaining 1.2 of the prize for itself. Yet, A believes it can do better by fighting another battle, even though it knows it will lose. In particular, if A offers B a deal which is unacceptable ($b_3 < 1.8$), then war results. Although A always loses the battle, it believes with probability $E_{B,t}[\theta] = \dfrac{6}{7+3}$ that B will suffer high costs. If B does suffer these high costs, then A can extract a deal worth 1.41. With probability $1 - E_{B,t}[\theta] = 1 - \dfrac{6}{7+3}$, B's casualties are small, in which case B can only extract 0.95 by bargaining in the next round. Since A pays the cost K_A for fighting an additional battle, A's expected value from an additional battle is $-K_A + 1.41 E_{B,t}[\theta] + 0.95(1 - E_{B,t}[\theta]) = 1.22$.

Although a deal exists that both sides prefer to fighting, Nation A continues the war because it believes the gains it expects to make in future bargaining from altering B's beliefs about the costs more than offset the actual cost of additional fighting. This algorithm of comparing the best deal A can obtain today with the lottery over the continuation values in the next period enables the calculation of all the continuation values.

THE EGYPTIAN CASE IN THE 1973 WAR

To make the case that the model above presents a plausible story about losing states' motives for initiating a war, we need to address the question of why would Sadat be willing to lose? Saad Shazly, the chief of staff of the Egyptian military during the 1973 War, claims in his memoirs that the Egyptian political leadership, under Sadat's direction, intentionally subverted (and endangered) the Egyptian military forces. Shazly argues that the Egyptian army deliberately halted after crossing the Suez and did not capture the two Sinai passes—which he maintains they could have done. Instead, Shazly argues that the Egyptians allowed the Israeli westward counter attack to develop day by day. He argues that the political leadership vetoed plans to defend the westward flank, which in turn led to the encirclement of the Egyptian Third Army. While this encirclement led to defeat on the battlefield, it also led ultimately to significant political gains for the Sadat regime at the bargaining table with Begin and Carter (Princin 1992) and within the so-called Arab street.

While aspects of this story strain credulity (Pollack 2002a), others claim that Sadat did not want to conquer the Sinai back by force because then he could lose it again to another superior Israeli attack (Shazly 1980; Gawrych 2000). Better to get it by more secure "legitimate" means. As Nasser before him had been prone to say, "What is taken by force can be retaken by force" (Shazly 1980, 307). The purpose of the war was as much to alter the conditions at the negotiating table with the Israelis as it was to regain lost territory through military means. Sadat's sympathizers claim that Sadat wanted to leave the Sinai on the table so he would be able to exploit it in negotiations with Israel. Recognizing that any long-term peace would be brokered by the United States, and recognizing that the Israeli army was superior to the Egyptian army, Sadat recognized that he could regain and hold the Sinai only through negotiations, but would be unlikely to be able to do so through force. The war in 1973 would serve to change the bargaining dynamic following the conclusion of active fighting (Stein 1999). Sadat recognized that if he were to bargain with the Americans and the Israelis, having recently invaded Israel and reclaiming part of the Sinai by force, his claim to pose no security threat to the Israelis would be without foundation. He would have effectively traded away the ace in his hand with Carter—his desire for peace and willingness to negotiate (Princin 1992). Alternatively, by losing, but at the same time imposing unexpectedly high costs on the Israeli military, Sadat's use of militarily unsuccessful tactics changed the bargaining calculus in Israel, forcing the Israelis to recognize that they would not be able to retain the Sinai without cost (Smith and Stam 2003a).

By failing to win the war, but by changing Israel's beliefs about the costs of holding the Sinai, Sadat believed that he could signal his resolve by showing that he was going to continue the fight even if Israel had the superior military capability. From the perspective of the Egyptians, the 1973 war demonstrated to Israel that it would have to negotiate or face continued hostility and substantially larger costs than it had believed previously. This type of change in the Israelis' beliefs would in turn strengthen Sadat's power at the bargaining table. By fighting, losing, and then fighting again, the Egyptians managed to demonstrate to Israel that there would never be peace without Israeli concessions, no matter how much stronger Israel was (Ibrahim 1996a).

Sadat's predominant aim in the war was to impose significant casualties in the process, which would weaken Israel's leadership position and increase the costs of occupation and defense. Sadat states in his memoirs that imposing unexpected costs on Israel was the primary aim of the war. Sadat was of the view that following Israel's stunning defeat of the Egyptians in 1967, Israel did not have accurate beliefs about their opponents—they underestimated the Arabs. Sadat believed, correctly, that the 1967 war caused a divergence in beliefs: the Israeli leadership had begun to believe they were more powerful than they actually were. In doing so, Golda Meir and Mosha Dyan underestimated the costs they would have to pay for their own security. Sadat wanted to demonstrate that the Israeli leadership needed to revise their beliefs of the likely costs of war with Egypt. The two sides agreed about the likely outcomes of the battles that would take place, but disagreed substantially about how costly those battles would be for the Israelis.

As is the case in our model, Sadat recognized that a large, forced transfer of territory, or forts, would likely be a pyrrhic victory because in doing so the Egyptians would heighten or legitimize Israel's security concerns. Had the Egyptians managed to defeat the Israelis in the Sinai, the Egyptians might have provoked Israel to utilize their military superiority as they had in 1967. Israel would be more likely to make concessions if they felt sure that the results of the 1967 War were not a fluke, and they could therefore afford to give territory back. Sadat's primary claim that he carried to the negotiating table in 1978 was not that the Arabs could ever win, but that they could simply make winning so costly that Israel would prefer to negotiate (Princin 1992).

CONCLUSION

Although nations that initiate conflict typically win, some nations choose to fight even when they have no hope of winning an *absolute* victory. They do so because, paradoxically, losing enhances their bargaining leverage if they can inflict causalities on the other side. Nations, like people, often disagree. If the weaker side believes the cost to the stronger side of winning battles is higher than the stronger side believes the cost to be, then nations can fail to agree to a negotiated settlement. War provides a mechanism to find out whose beliefs are correct. As the cost of each battle is revealed, nations base their assessment on a common knowledge base that ensures that, even though their prior beliefs differed, their beliefs become increasingly similar over the course of the war. Once beliefs have converged sufficiently that any gain in future bargaining leverage from a shift in the opponent's beliefs closer to your beliefs fails to compensate for the cost of additional fighting, both sides can reach an agreement that they will prefer continued fighting. An *absolute* war is not required. As fighting proceeds, nations learn what the absolute war looks like and this shapes their bargaining positions.

This chapter is part of a growing literature that examines war as a bargaining process (Wagner 2000; Smith 1997, 1998a; Slantchev 2003a; Filson and Werner 2002; Smith and Stam 2004; Powell 2003; Wittman 1979, 2001). Unlike most traditional bargaining models that treat war as the failure of bargaining, these new approaches follow Clausewitz's dictum that "war is the continuation of politics by other means." Extant approaches that treat war as a single roll of the dice can offer little explanation for why those destined to lose choose to fight. Yet, in the context of bargaining, war resolves informational differences that inhibit both sides from agreeing on what the resolution of the dispute should be. When the weaker side believes the stronger side is mistaken in its beliefs about the ease and costs of victory, then the weaker side fights to strengthen its position at the bargaining table. Through fighting, nations learn both which is the stronger side as well as how much it costs to fight.

NOTES:

1. We use the term "nation" to refer to nation-states and the term "state" to refer to the "state space," or underlying distribution of material resources presented in the formal model.

2. See Wagner (2000) and Smith (1998a) for discussion.

3. The extension to allow for draws is straightforward but not developed here.

4. Payoffs are not discounted. This presents a potential problem in that payoffs are unbounded. Fortunately, as we show next, from any given point in the game, the game ends in a finite expected time for any strategy by the players.

5. The model does not require this restriction; rather, this is the interesting case.

10

Enforcing Peace: Suppressing Extremists without Losing the Moderates

Suzanne Werner and Amy Yuen

To enforce a peace agreement, third parties often must sanction and otherwise control spoiler groups that wish to disrupt the peace process. While the capacity and willingness of the third party to act can often be a significant problem, we show that the strategic dynamic among the third party, the extremists, and the moderates on both sides can undermine the effectiveness of third-party enforcement. Rather than sanction minority groups that wish to disrupt the peace, third parties often must demonstrate their neutrality by doing nothing. Since tactics to suppress extremists can generate mistrust among moderates, third parties are forced to accept a much weaker peace settlement for fear of losing the moderates and returning to all-out war. We demonstrate this dynamic in a formal model of the interactions among a third party, and extremist and moderate groups on one side, and an opposition group on the other. We derive some testable hypotheses and discuss the implications of the model for third-party intervention, emphasizing that third-party resolve is not always the fatal problem of failed peace agreements.

"General Clark," [President Milosevic] said, speaking very directly and conversationally, "it would not be good if more actions were taken against Serbs. Trying to seize these war criminals is like holding lighted match over bucket of gasoline." He paused and looked at me to let it sink in, then continued, "Besides, I told you at Dayton, what was magic word. Do you remember?"

"I do, Mr. President," I responded. "You advised that we must be even-handed."

— Account by Gen. Wesley K. Clark in *Waging Modern War* 2001, 82

Why do some peace agreements last while others fail? Similarly, why are some agreements implemented successfully while others are challenged and sometimes abandoned altogether? While there are many reasons why agreements may fail,[1] in many cases successful implementation of the peace agreement seems to depend critically on the ability to marginalize or neutralize potential spoiler groups (Stedman 1997). Spoilers do not benefit from the peace agreement and therefore have strong incentives to undermine it if they can. Without effective management, spoilers can sometimes ruin a peace process even if the majority on both sides prefers to implement the agreement rather than return to war (Stedman 1997; Jones 1999; Kydd and Walter 2002).

Given that the belligerents themselves often are unlikely to have the resources or ability to neutralize spoiler groups, several authors have concluded that strong third-party enforcement is a necessary (if not sufficient) condition for successful implementation of peace agreements in the presence of spoiler groups (Walter 1997; Stedman 1997; Walter 2002). In many cases, third parties are uniquely qualified to manage the threat that spoilers pose. Third parties have the resources to monitor effectively spoiler groups and sanction them if they attempt to disrupt the peace process. Without third-party enforcement, the peace process is unlikely to succeed. As Stedman (1997:6) succinctly summarizes,

> The crucial difference between the success and failure of spoilers is the role played by international actors as custodians of peace. Where international custodians have created and implemented coherent, effective strategies for protecting peace and managing spoilers, damage has been limited and peace has triumphed. Where international custodians have failed to develop and implement such strategies, spoilers have succeeded at the cost of hundreds of thousands of lives.

Such accounts suggest that we need look no further than the lack of will or resolve on the part of the international community to explain many instances of failed implementation.

Although ensuring the capacity and will of third parties is no easy task, we argue that successful third-party enforcement is plagued by other problems as well. The management of spoiler groups presents unique problems for the would-be third-party enforcer. While spoiler groups (by definition) would destroy the agreement if they *could*, most spoiler groups do not have the capabilities or the numbers to directly threaten the peace agreement. Instead, their power rests in their ability to create conditions that undermine the majority's support for the agreement. As others have argued, the ultimate ability of spoiler groups to wreck the peace process depends critically on the successful radicalization of moderate elements (de Figueiredo and Weingast 1999; Kydd and Walter 2002). While spoiler groups can harass the peace process unilaterally, the peace process continues so long as the moderate elements remain committed to it and refuse to renew the war. In contrast, if the moderates join forces with the extremists, implementation fails. Maintaining the commitment of the moderates to the peace process is thus a key priority for any peacekeeping force. The rub for many peacekeeping troops, however, is that the very strategies that marginalize spoiler groups can, under some circumstances, serve to radicalize the moderate elements. As the leading quote of this chapter suggests, President Miloševic raised this very possibility with General Wesley Clark as NATO attempted to strengthen its enforcement presence in Bosnia-Herzegovina. After warning General Clark to be "even-handed" and to stop pursuing Serb war criminals, Clark recounts that Miloševic continued, "General Clark, please believe me. You must not continue actions like this or *Serb people* will view you as army of occupation. And occupying armies have not done well historically" (Clark 2001, 82, italics added). As General Clark was well aware, this was a threat; pursuing the Serb extremists was a double-edged sword. On the one hand, such operations had the possibility of marginalizing the spoiler groups and thus strengthening the peace process. On the other hand, such operations could also turn Serb moderates against NATO, the "occupying force," and encourage them to abandon the peace agreement altogether.

In this chapter, we attempt to capture this double-edged sword, by modeling the implementation of peace agreements as a four-actor game between a spoiler group S, a moderate group M, an opposition group O, and a third-party enforcer E. We assume that during the war M and S were allied against O. The peace agreement, however, represents a deal to share power between M and O that does not serve the interests of S. S then can be viewed as an extremist group—like the CDR in Rwanda, the Pale-based Serbs in Bosnia, or the Khmer Rouge in Cambodia—that prefers to return to war rather than implement the agreement. To simplify the analysis, we assume that O speaks with a unified voice and is not split between moderate and extremist factions. In reality, the difficulties for enforcement may be even more acute as *both* sides may be plagued by internal divisions.

We introduce the moderates' concerns regarding whether or not the third party will be even-handed by assuming that they are uncertain about whether the third-party enforcer is neutral or biased. Neutral enforcers sanction any attempts to circumvent the obligations of the peace agreement regardless of the source. Biased enforcers, in contrast, only sanction challenges by spoiler groups. While the moderates are willing to remain committed to the peace process so long as they anticipate that the third party is neutral and will sanction defections on both sides, they abandon the peace process and return to war if they anticipate that the third party will not be even-handed.

The model suggests that third parties often find it very hard to marginalize effectively extremists groups who would like to "spoil" the peace process even when the third party is capable and willing to do so. This is true for two reasons. First, if spoiler groups anticipate robust enforcement, they can lay low so as to avoid punishment and potential marginalization. By doing so, spoilers retain their ability to disrupt the peace at some later date when enforcement wanes. Second, even though a third party may be willing and able to sanction any attempts by extremists to disrupt the peace process, it may choose not to do so because it anticipates that doing so would radicalize the moderates. Moderates abandon the peace process when spoilers are sanctioned if they are sufficiently fearful that the third party is biased in favor of the opposition and so will not enforce each side's treaty obligations in an even-handed manner. Under these conditions, in order to avoid a resumption of the war, third parties are forced to be "even-handed" by not sanctioning anyone. The model thus suggests that successful implementation of the original terms of the agreement depends on far more than simply the capacity and willingness of the third party. Moderates also must be sufficiently confident that the third-party enforcer is neutral and thereby willing to sanction infractions by either side.

The chapter proceeds as follows. First, we discuss the growing literature on spoilers and review proposed suggestions for effectively managing such groups. Second, we introduce the model and discuss its equilibrium predictions. We then consider the implications of the model and derive specific testable hypotheses. Finally, we conclude with some suggestions for future research.

SPOILERS, THIRD PARTIES, AND THE PEACE PROCESS

The commitment problem provides one of the strongest explanations for bargaining failure (Fearon 1995). While both parties may prefer to reach (or implement) a negotiated agreement rather than fight a costly war (or return to a costly war), they may fail to do so because at least one side cannot credibly commit to implement the terms of the agreement. Traditionally, scholars have focused on incentives the parties themselves may have to renege on the terms of the deal. Posen (1993), for instance, highlights the difficulties created by offensive advantages. When offense dominates, it is difficult for the parties to commit credibly to maintain the agreement since the party that defects first enjoys a significant advantage. In a similar vein, Walter (1997) argues persuasively that civil wars are particularly difficult to terminate short of a total military victory because the vulnerability created by disarmament makes it difficult for either belligerent to promise credibly not to attack once disarmament begins. Fearon (1998) poses the issue more generally and suggests that implementation of an agreement often creates incentives for the parties to renege because the implementation process itself can shift the bargaining leverage between the parties. If the process does provide one side with additional leverage, then that side is unable to promise credibly not to take advantage of this newfound power to demand even greater concessions. Anticipating such actions, the weaker side eschews agreement.

While the possibility of such voluntary defections clearly affects the prospects for peace, Stedman (1997) also fruitfully highlights the important possibility that a commitment problem may arise even if the key signatories of the peace have no unilateral incentive to renege on the terms. Even if the signatories themselves have every incentive to maintain the terms of the agreement, the credibility of their commitment may come into doubt if they are not in complete control of implementation. Such "involuntary defection" arises when there are spoiler groups that do not benefit from the agreement and have the capacity to disrupt the peace process. Israel, for instance, finds it difficult to strike a deal with the Palestinian Authority (PA) at least in part because the PA cannot ensure implementation of key terms since it cannot or will not control such groups as Hamas (Kydd and Walter 2002). The prospects for such involuntary defection add another layer of difficulty to the already challenging process of maintaining peace.

De Figueiredo and Weingast (1999) and Kydd and Walter (2002) explore the ability of spoiler groups to disrupt the peace process. Central to their analyses is the shared assumption that spoilers can succeed only if they are able to persuade moderate groups, who would otherwise prefer to implement a peace agreement rather than return to war, to abandon the peace process. For de Figueiredo and Weingast, moderates may side with the extremists because they fear that the opposition may be aggressive and ultimately wish the destruction of their entire group. De Figueiredo and Weingast argue that extremist leaders can effectively play on these fears by intentionally scuttling the agreement. Since moderates cannot discern the true cause of failure—either their own leaders' intransigence or the aggressiveness of the opposition, the failure of the agreement can reinforce the moderates' fears regarding the opposition's aggressiveness and encourage them to side with their extremist leader even though the moderates desired peace. Here, extremist leaders can succeed even if their followers desire peace if they can take advantage of the "causal ambiguity" as to why negotiations failed to enflame the moderates' fears. In Kydd and Walter, a similar dynamic is at work. Uncertainty regarding the true intent of the opposing side allows extremists to persuade moderates that peace is too risky. Here, the existence of continued violence perpetuated by the extremists serves as a noisy signal of the *moderates'* commitment to the peace process. Especially if the moderates on Side A are perceived as capable of controlling the extremists, a successful act of terrorism can convince the moderates on Side B that the moderates on Side A are not truly committed to the peace process and encourage the moderates on Side B to abandon the process. The dynamic suggested by this work is discouraging. The extremists need not have the capacity unilaterally to disrupt the peace process to be successful. Rather, extremists need only successfully play on moderates' fears regarding the true intent of the moderates on the other side. Under certain conditions, extremists can effectively spoil what would otherwise be a robust peace agreement with very little violence.

Given that in these scenarios it is assumed that the majority of the population desires peace and prefers the terms of the negotiated peace to a continuation of the violence, this seems to be an especially opportune time for third-party intervention. While third parties are understandably reluctant to intervene when there is no peace to keep or when the commitment of the parties to peace is in doubt, in these scenarios the vast majority of the population is anxious to implement the terms of settlement. Given the considerable power asymmetry often enjoyed by third parties vis-à-vis potential spoiler groups, it also appears to be a situation in which third parties could make a significant difference at relatively little cost.

Most case studies of third-party intervention, however, suggest more often than not, opportunities lost rather than opportunities seized. Although UN forces in Cambodia successfully marginalized the Khmer Rouge, they were much less effective against the SOC (State of Cambodia) and its attempts to spoil the peace process (Stedman 1997; Doyle 1999). As Stedman (1997:33-35) reports, "For the most part, UNTAC [United Nations Transitional Authority in Cambodia] restrained from attempting to enforce compliance with its administrative directives." Enforcement against SOC was so lax in fact that "Akashi and UNTAC did not [even] insist that the political outcome of the election accurately reflect the electoral outcome." Similarly, in Bosnia, despite a 60,000-strong intervention force from thirty-four countries, enforcement especially during the first two years was extremely unreliable. Particularly noteworthy was the failure of the NATO-led Implementation Force (IFOR) commanders to arrest known Serb war criminals that had been indicted by the International Criminal Tribunal (Woodward 1999, Daalder 2000; Clark 2001). Although these cases should not be seen as total failures—after all both states have avoided a new war—neither should they be seen as clear success stories. Rather, despite a strong commitment by the international community to keep the peace and support the peace agreements that it helped to craft, violations of key provisions were allowed to occur with few consequences. Under what conditions can an interested and concerned third party effectively sanction violators and help to ensure a durable peace? Why might third parties fail to enforce key provisions of a peace agreement or take action that could marginalize extremists groups? While financial constraints and lack of interest provide part of the explanation for numerous failures to guarantee peace on the part of the international community, failure may also be due in part to the delicate balancing act the third party must maintain between its attempts to marginalize extremists and its desire to keep the moderates on board.

THE MODEL

In order to explore the ability of third parties to guarantee a peace agreement in the presence of spoiler groups, we model the implementation phase of a peace agreement between two former belligerents. While one side, the *Opposition (O)*, speaks with a unified voice, the other side is split between a majority group that favors the agreement, the *Moderates (M)*, and a minority group that does not support the agreement, the *Spoilers (S)*. The fourth and final actor in the model is a third party, the *Enforcer (E)*, tasked with the job of guaranteeing the peace agreement. In the implementation of the Dayton Peace Accords, for example, one might depict the Bosnians led by President Izetbegovic as *O*, the Serbs based in Banja Luka and their followers as *M*, the Serbs based in Pale and their followers as *S*, and IFOR as *E*.

The structure of the game is depicted in figure 10.1. The game begins with *S* choosing whether or not to challenge the agreement. A challenge is envisioned as some action that can sway the agreement in *S*'s favor if executed successfully but does not inherently undermine the entire agreement. *S* is not given the choice here to undermine the entire agreement because we assume that as a minority group *S* cannot unilaterally do so. So long as the moderates remain on board, the basic outlines of the agreement stands. In the implementation of the Dayton Accords, for example, the forced removal of moderate Serbs from Sarajevo or the harassment of returning refugees to Serb-controlled areas by Serb extremists are examples of the kinds of challenges that we hope to capture. While such challenges can effectively skew the implementation of the agreement in the Serbs favor, such actions do not scuttle the peace process entirely. In response to such challenges, *E* can choose whether or not to sanction *S*. We assume that if *E* does choose to

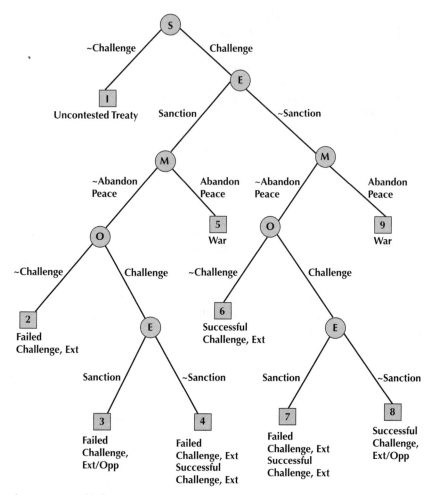

Figure 10.1.   Third-Party Enforcement and Treaty Implementation with Complete In-formation

sanction, then its efforts are completely effective and the terms of the origi-nal agreement are implemented as intended. If *E* chooses not to sanction, then at a minimum the implemented agreement is weakened to *S*'s benefit. After witnessing *E*'s choice to sanction or not, *M* must choose whether to abandon the peace process or not. If *M* abandons the peace process, then the belligerents return to war. If *M* chooses to support the peace process, then *O* can choose whether to challenge the peace agreement or not. As was the case for *S*, *O*'s choice is not whether or not to reject the peace agreement alto-gether. Rather, *O* chooses whether to take some relatively minor action that begins to skew the implemented agreement increasingly in its favor. In the Dayton example once again, the Bosnians can undermine the agreement on the edges by challenging the original presumption of parity in power-sharing arrangements and instead attempt to alter electoral rules in regions where they have a numeric advantage. In response to such infractions, E again must choose between sanctioning the offender or not.

The possible outcomes of this game are depicted in table 10.1. The outcomes can differ in three regards. The first key differentiation is whether war resumes as in Outcomes 5 and 9, or whether some sort of agreement is implemented. If some agreement is implemented, the second key differentiation is the type of agreement that is actually implemented. In Outcomes 1, 2, and 3, the original agreement is implemented as intended. In Outcomes 6 and 7, the agreement that is actually implemented favors the Spoiler and Moderate side more than was intended by the original agreement. In Outcome 4, the agreement that is actually implemented favors the Opposition side more than was intended by the original agreement. Finally, in outcome 8, the agreement that is actually implemented is a much weaker version of the original agreement as it reduces the obligations of both parties. The final differentiation between the outcomes depends on whether or not the third-party enforcer has sanctioned or not in response to challenges from either S or O.

Table 10.1. Outcomes and Payoffs of Implementation Game

Players	Outcomes Spoilers	Moderates	Opposition	Third-Party Enforcer
(1) Uncontested Treaty	T_s	T_m	T_o	T_e
(2) Failed Challenge (Sp)	$T_s - s$	$T_m + s$	$T_o + s$	$T_e + s - c$
(3) Failed Challenge (Sp, Opp)	$T_s - s + o$	$T_m + s + o$	$T_o + s - o$	$T_e + s - o - 2c$
(4) Failed Challenge (Sp), Successful Challenge (Opp)	$OT_s - s$	$OT_m + s$	$OT_o + s$	$OT_e + s - c$
(5) War	W_s	W_m	W_o	$W_e - c$
(6) Successful Challenge (Sp)	ST_s	ST_m	ST_o	ST_e
(7) Successful Challenge (Sp), Failed Challenge (Opp)	$ST_s + o$	$ST_m + o$	$ST_o - o$	$ST_e - o - c$
(8) Successful Challenge (Sp, Opp)	SOT_s	SOT_m	SOT_o	SOT_e
(9) War	W_s	W_m	W_o	W_e

The payoffs for the parties similarly depend on whether an agreement is implemented, what type of agreement is implemented, and whether or not the third party chooses to sanction or not. Payoffs for a return to war are denoted, W_s, W_m, W_o, W_e, respectively, for *Spoilers*, *Moderates*, *Opposition*, and *Enforcer*. Payoffs for an implemented agreement are denoted, T_s, T_m, T_o, T_e, if the original treaty was implemented, ST_s, ST_m, ST_o, ST_e, if a skewed agreement favoring S and M's side was implemented, OT_s, OT_m, OT_o, OT_e, if a skewed agreement favoring O was implemented, and SOT_s, SOT_m, SOT_o, SOT_e, if an agreement with weaker obligations for both S and M's side and O's side was implemented. If E chooses to sanction a challenge, E pays a cost c for each sanctioning episode. We also assume that the effect of the sanction is to weaken or marginalize the party that is being sanctioned. As a result, depending on one's position, a sanctioning episode can confer a benefit or a cost. If S is sanctioned, S pays the cost s but all other actors benefit by s. Here we assume that all actors, even M, benefit from a situation in which the spoiler group is marginalized. In contrast, if O is sanctioned, we assume that O pays a cost o, M and S receive a benefit o, but E pays a cost o. While M and S benefit from a weaker O, the third party enforcer does not. Sanctioning O then implies for the third party a direct cost for the sanction itself as well as an indirect cost for weakening or discrediting O.

Table 10.2. Preference Orderings for Spoilers, Moderates, Opposition, Neutral, and Biased Third-Party Enforcers

	Outcomes			Neutral	Biased
Players	Spoilers	Moderates	Opposition	Enforcer	Enforcer
(1) Uncontested Treaty	6	3	3, 4	2, 3	3, 4
(2) Failed Challenge (Sp)	8	2	2	1	2
(3) Failed Challenge (Sp, Opp)	7	1	3, 4	2, 3	3, 4
(4) Failed Challenge (Sp), Successful Challenge (Opp)	9	8	1	4	1
(5) War	2	7	6	9	9
(6) Successful Challenge (Sp)	4	5	8	5	6
(7) Successful Challenge (Sp), Failed Challenge (Opp)	3	4	9	6	7
(8) Successful Challenge (Sp, Opp)	5	6	5	7	5
(9) War	1	7	7	8	8

The assumed preference ordering for each player is depicted in table 10.2. Significantly, the game is stacked in favor of successful implementation; with the exception of S, all parties prefer the agreement as originally negotiated to returning to war and actually benefit from the marginalization of S. For M, outcomes in which the agreement as originally negotiated is implemented are preferred to all other outcomes (Outcomes 1, 2, and 3). Among the outcomes in which the agreement is implemented as intended, M prefers those outcomes that involve the sanctioning of O and/or S (Outcome 3 > Outcome 2 > Outcome 1). After these outcomes of successful implementation, M prefers the implementation of agreements that favor its side to those that weaken in any way the obligations of O (Outcomes 1, 2, 3 > Outcome 7 > Outcome 6 > Outcome 4). While M prefers all of these outcomes to war, M does prefer war to the implementation of an agreement skewed to favor only O (Outcomes 5, 9 > Outcome 4). M thus strongly favors peace but is willing to return to war if O is favored in the actual implementation of the agreement.

For O the most preferred outcome is one in which S is marginalized and the agreement is implemented in a way favorable to its interests (Outcome 4 > All Other Outcomes). Next best, however, are the outcomes in which the treaty as originally negotiated is implemented especially when S is marginalized (Outcome 2 > Outcomes 1, 3). O is also a strong advocate for peace because it too prefers a weakened treaty to war (Outcome 8 > Outcomes 5, 9). Like M, however, O prefers war if the implementation heavily favors the opposing side at its expense (Outcomes 5, 9 > Outcomes 6, 7). Thus, just like M, O only prefers war if it anticipates that the agreement will be implemented in such a way as to reduce the obligations of the other side but not its own obligations.

In contrast to M and O, S benefits most from a return to violence (Outcomes 5, 9 > All Other Outcomes). Short of war, S prefers an agreement implemented to favor its side to an agreement that weakens the obligations on both parties, but prefers a weakened agreement to one that is implemented as originally conceived especially if S has been sanctioned in the process (Outcomes 6, 7 > Outcome 8 > Outcome 1, 3 > Outcome 2). The worst outcome for S is a situation in which the agreement is implemented in a manner that favors O (All Other Outcomes > Outcome 4).

For the third-party enforcer, we assume a strong commitment to the peace process. For E, the least preferred outcome is a return to violence (All Other Outcomes > Outcomes 5 and 9). E strongly prefers implementation of the original agreement to an agreement that has weakened the obligations of both sides (Outcomes 1, 2, and 3 > Outcome 8). We further assume that the benefit E obtains from marginalizing S exceeds the cost of sanctioning so that E has clear incentives to sanction S (Outcome 2 > Outcomes 1 and 3). At this point, however, we differentiate between two types of third-party enforcers, a neutral enforcer and a biased enforcer. The neutral enforcer prefers outcomes associated with the implementation of the original agreement to any outcome that weakens the agreement even if the agreement is weakened to favor O (Outcomes 1, 2, 3 > Outcomes 4, 6, 7 > Outcome 8). When pushed, *Neutral E* will sanction O to ensure implementation of the agreement. The biased enforcer, in contrast, prefers an outcome in which the implementation process favors O to any of the outcomes associated with the implementation of the original agreement (Outcome 4 > Outcomes 1, 2, 3 and Outcome 8 > Outcome 7)). This preference ordering means that if called upon to enforce the original terms of the treaty against encroachments by O, *Biased E* will choose to let such infractions slide either because he actually prefers an agreement that favors O and/or because he does not want to discredit O or pay the costs to sanction O.[2]

IMPLEMENTATION UNDER COMPLETE INFORMATION

If all parties are certain regarding the preferences of the other players, then the game can be solved by backwards induction. If the third party is known to be neutral, that is it is willing to enforce compliance by both sides, then the predicted outcome of the game is an Uncontested Treaty (Outcome 1). The Subgame Perfect Nash Equilibrium is {~Challenge; ~Abandon Peace, ~Abandon Peace; ~Challenge, ~Challenge; Sanction, Sanction, Sanction} where the equilibrium is read {S Strategy; M Strategy if S sanctioned, M Strategy if S ~sanctioned; O Strategy if S sanctioned, O Strategy if S ~sanctioned; E Strategy if S challenges, E Strategy if O challenges and E has sanctioned S, E Strategy if O challenges and E has not sanctioned S}. In this instance, S chooses not to challenge because doing so invites reprisals from the international community and does not create the possibility that M will abandon the peace process. M chooses not to abandon the peace process because it is confident that the third party will sanction defections by both sides and thus knows that the terms of the original treaty will be honored, an outcome that M strongly prefers to a renewed war. While the credible promise to enforce the agreement in an even-handed fashion ensures that the agreement is not weakened, it does not result in any actor's most preferred outcome. Instead, by choosing not to challenge, S eliminates the possibility that it will be marginalized by stringent enforcement by E. The agreement is implemented, but all parties save the spoilers accept it as a second-best outcome because S remains a potential threat to the peace process in the future.

The outcome is very different, however, if E is known to be biased toward O. In this instance, the anticipated outcome is the implementation of a treaty that significantly weakens the obligations of both sides (Outcome 8). The Subgame Perfect Nash Equilibrium is {Challenge; Abandon Peace, ~Abandon Peace; Challenge, Challenge; ~Sanction, ~Sanction, ~Sanction} where the strategies are read as above. Interestingly, although the third party is completely willing and capable of sanctioning defections by S, E chooses not to do so and instead allows S to defect with impunity. The causal logic is straightforward. Since E cannot credibly threaten to sanction defections by O as a consequence of his bias, M anticipates that if E sanctions S in response to a challenge by S, then the outcome of the peace process will be the implementation of an agreement skewed to favor O. Given this, M chooses to abandon the peace process and return to war rather than accept a skewed peace agreement. However, if E does not sanction S in response to a violation by S, then the worst outcome from M's perspective is the implementation of an agreement that weakens the obligations of *both* sides. Although M would prefer to see the original agreement implemented, it prefers a weakened agreement to a renewal of the war. Thus, in this instance, M chooses not to abandon the peace process. E then must choose between sanctioning S and radicalizing M or not sanctioning S and accepting a weakened treaty. Given these unfortunate choices, E forgoes sanctioning S and accepts a treaty that is significantly weaker than originally intended. The rub of this outcome is that all players, with the exception of the spoilers, prefer implementation of the original treaty to the weakened treaty that is actually implemented. Such a mutually preferred outcome eludes them, however, because the third party cannot credibly commit to sanctioning infractions by the opposition as well. Absent such a credible commitment, the only way for E to be even-handed and retain the support of the moderates is for E to sanction neither side.

IMPLEMENTATION UNDER INCOMPLETE INFORMATION

We assume in what follows that M is not certain whether E is neutral and thus willing to sanction infractions regardless of whether the challenge was launched by S or O or whether E is biased and only willing to sanction infractions by S.[3] We denote the prior probability that E is neutral by η and the prior probability that E is biased by $1-\eta$. We denote M's updated beliefs about E's neutrality after observing whether or not E sanctions S as η^* and η^{**}, respectively.

Ideally, what we would like to occur is for E to be able to signal effectively its type to M if E is in fact neutral. If possible, E could effectively sanction S in response to violations rather than being forced to allow S to violate the terms of the agreement in order to avoid radicalizing M.[4] What we find instead is that all equilibria are pooling—neutral and biased enforcers always choose the same strategy. As a result, M is never able to update her beliefs regarding E's type in response to E's sanctioning behavior. This leads to several inefficient outcomes. In particular, the model anticipates that the demand for "even-handedness" often forces third parties to converge on the lowest common denominator and punish no one, even if they were willing and able to punish infractions by both sides.

Since we are assuming that only M is uncertain about E's type, the decisions made by O and E's response to O's challenge are determined completely by E's type. If E is neutral, then E sanctions any defection by O and, anticipating the credible commitment, O chooses not to challenge. Conversely, if E is biased, then E does not sanction if O defects and, anticipating the incredibility of the commitment to sanction, O challenges. M's decision is more complicated because M is not certain whether E's commitment to sanction O is credible or not because he does not know with certainty whether E is neutral or biased. Consider first M's decision if E did not sanction S when S challenged the agreement. On the one hand, M could choose to abandon the peace process and ensure itself the payoff W_m or it could remain committed to the peace process. If E is the neutral type, then M anticipates that E will sanction any defections by O and therefore expects the payoffs associated with outcome 6, ST_m. If E is the biased type, then M anticipates that E will not sanction O and therefore expects the payoffs associated with Outcome 8, SOT_m. Significantly, M prefers either of these outcomes to a renewal of war. Therefore, if E has not sanctioned S, then M has a dominant strategy not to abandon the peace process.

M's decision to remain committed to the peace process or abandon it is more complicated if E has in fact sanctioned S. In this case, M can again ensure itself the payoff W_m by abandoning the peace process regardless of E's type or it can gamble on the peace process and eschew violence. If M does not abandon the peace process and E is in fact neutral, then M expects to receive $T_m + s$, the payoff associated with the implementation of the original treaty and the benefit that comes with successful marginalization of S. However, if M does not abandon the peace process and E is in fact biased, then M expects to receive $OT_m + s$, the payoff associated with M's least preferred outcome, implementation of a biased agreement that favors O. Given that E has sanctioned S, M is only willing to gamble on the peace process if M is sufficiently confident that E is actually neutral and that the risk of getting its worst outcome is outweighed by the potential that the original treaty will be implemented as intended. M is sufficiently confident about E's neutrality if and only if, $\eta^* \geq \dfrac{W_m - OT_m - s}{T_m - OT_m}$ where η^* denotes M's belief that E is neutral after seeing E sanction.

Assume that this condition is in fact met, such that if E sanctions S, M remains committed to the peace process. How might we expect E to respond? The model suggests that regardless of whether E is in fact neutral or biased, E chooses to sanction S. Recall that both types of E prefer to sanction S. In the complete information case, the biased enforcer chooses not to sanction S only because it anticipates that M will abandon the peace process if it does. If E anticipates that M will not abandon the peace process because M believes that E's threat to sanction O is credible, then a biased enforcer is pleased to take advantage of such mistaken beliefs and mimic the neutral enforcer's sanctioning behavior. Since both types of E pool on sanctioning S in this instance, M is not able to learn anything about E's type from E's decision to sanction. Therefore, M's posterior belief regarding E's neutrality is equal to its prior belief, $\eta = \eta^*$. Anticipating that a challenge will be met by tough sanctioning regardless of E's type, resulting at best in an outcome in which the original treaty is implemented and its power marginalized, S chooses not to challenge the treaty.

The Perfect Bayesian Equilibrium (PBE) then is {~Challenge, ~Challenge; ~Abandon, ~Abandon; ~Challenge, ~Challenge, Challenge, Challenge; Sanction, Sanction, Sanction; Sanction, ~Sanction, ~Sanction: $\eta \geq \dfrac{W_m - OT_m - s}{T_m - OT_m}$},

where the strategies are read as {S strategy if E is neutral, S strategy if E is biased; M strategy if E sanction, M strategy if E ~sanction; O strategy if E is neutral, O strategy if E is biased; *Neutral E's strategy; Biased E's strategy*}. The good news is that if S believes that M is confident that E will enforce compliance in an even-handed way, then S gains nothing and risks a lot by challenging the agreement. The bad news is that S's strategic compliance precludes the possibility of stringent third-party enforcement and the eventual marginalization of S. Empirically, we would see two possible outcomes. If the third party is in fact neutral, the original treaty will be enforced as intended. If the third party is biased, then the treaty that is ultimately implemented will favor O at the expense of M and S.

Now consider the possibility that M is not sufficiently confident that E is neutral so that it does not trust that E will enforce compliance in an even-handed way, $\eta^* < \dfrac{W_m - OT_m - s}{T_m - OT_m}$. As before, if E does not sanction S, M has a dominant strategy to remain committed to the peace process. At worst, M anticipates that the outcome will be the implementation of an agreement in which the obligations of both sides are weakened and this outcome is preferred to a renewal of the war. If $\eta < \dfrac{W_m - OT_m - s}{T_m - OT_m}$, however, M prefers to abandon the peace process when E sanctions S. M does so because she is sufficiently confident that E is biased and thus will not implement the agreement in an even-handed fashion. To protect itself against its least preferred outcome, a skewed agreement that benefits O, M abandons the peace process.

If E anticipates that M will abandon the peace process if E sanctions S, then both neutral and biased enforcers forego sanctioning S. Although such a choice eliminates the possibility of marginalizing S, it also avoids radicalizing M. In this instance, the neutral enforcer is forced to mimic the behavior of the biased enforcer because failure to do so risks a complete breakdown of the peace process. If M believes strongly enough that E is biased, then the only way to eliminate M's fears of exploitation is not to sanction S. S's strategy in this case is clear. Since both types of E do not sanction violations by S, then S will choose to challenge the agreement regardless of E's type.

The Perfect Bayesian Equilibrium in this instance is {Challenge, Challenge; Abandon, ~Abandon; ~Challenge, ~Challenge, Challenge, Challenge; ~Sanction, Sanction, Sanction; ~Sanction, ~Sanction, ~Sanction: $\eta <$ $\frac{W_m - OT_m - s}{T_m - OT_m}$}, where the strategies are read as above. This combination of strategies suggests two possible outcomes depending on whether E is in fact neutral or biased. If E is biased, then the agreement that is actually implemented will be significantly weakened from its original version since the defections of neither S nor O will be sanctioned (Outcome 8). In contrast, if E is neutral, the third party will be in the unenviable position of tolerating defections by S, but credibly threatening to sanction violations by O (Outcome 6). In this instance, spoilers are richly rewarded because their ability to exploit the fears of the moderates ties the hands of the third party and ensures that the implementation of the agreement is skewed in their favor.

On the upside, in neither equilibria is peace abandoned altogether. The third party's ability to anticipate the radicalization of the moderates enables it to adapt its strategy to avoid a return to war. On the downside, neither equilibria ensures that the original treaty will be enforced as intended. In the first equilibrium, the original agreement may be enforced if the third party is in fact neutral, but will not be if the third party in fact favors O. In the second equilibrium, the original agreement is never implemented as originally intended. Instead, the agreement that is actually implemented weakens the obligations of one or both sides.

Perhaps even more unfortunately, the spoilers are never sanctioned in either equilibrium, despite stacking the deck in favor of this outcome. In the first equilibrium, spoilers strategically comply with the terms of the agreement because they anticipate robust enforcement. In the second equilibrium, the third-party enforcer is unable to sanction the spoilers because doing so radicalizes the moderates who are unwilling to risk the possibility that remaining committed to the peace process will result in a skewed agreement favoring the other side. This result suggests the possibility that in some instances a third party's failure to enforce an agreement may be due in part to strategic considerations rather than merely a lack of will or capacity as is frequently charged.

COMPARATIVE STATISTICS

While neither equilibrium is ideal, the second is decidedly inferior for those who value a strong, stable agreement. Under what conditions is it likely for this equilibrium to arise? It becomes more likely that $\eta < \dfrac{W_m - OT_m - s}{T_m - OT_m}$ and M prefers to abandon the peace process if E sanctions S as W_m increases and as T_m, OT_m, and s decrease. Recall that M can assure itself the value of war, W_m by abandoning the peace process, but by remaining committed it faces a gamble between a very good outcome in which the original treaty is implemented and S is marginalized, and its worst outcome of skewed implementation in favor of O. As W_m increases, then M must have stronger beliefs that E is neutral for it to be willing to gamble on not abandoning the peace process. In contrast, as M's value for the original agreement increases, the gamble of remaining committed to the peace process is less risky. As a result, M can be less optimistic about the chances that E is neutral and still be willing to gamble on peace. In contrast, if M only marginally prefers the original agreement to returning to war, then M must be very confident that E is neutral for it to be willing to gamble on peace.

This suggests that third parties may be able to enhance the durability of peace on the back end by carefully crafting the agreement on the front end. If the belligerents recognize that one side is afflicted with extremists that intend to disrupt the peace process, it may be in everyone's best interests to skew the original agreement in favor of that side. Note that the intent of doing so is not to placate the extremists. Rather, by skewing the agreement, it should increase the moderates' willingness to gamble on peace and thereby increase the third party's ability effectively to sanction the extremist groups without radicalizing the moderates. The fact that the terms of the Arusha Accords in Rwanda were skewed, not in favor of the moderate Hutus but instead in favor of the Tutsis, likely contributed to its failure. If the agreement itself had been more favorable, the Hutu moderates may have been more impervious to radicalization by the extremists and instead allowed third parties and their own government to weaken extremist groups that were committed to violence.

M also becomes less likely to abandon the peace process and more willing to gamble on peace when E sanctions S as OT_m increases or as M's fears of the agreement O would implement decrease. In contrast, if M really fears an agreement skewed in O's favor, M will be much less willing to allow E to sanction S. This implies that the third party's flexibility to sanction Spoilers and enforce the terms of the treaty depend very much on the Moderates' perception of what the Opposition will do if left unchecked. What does the original treaty obligate the Opposition to do? Ironically, the weaker the obligations, the smaller the difference between the original treaty and a treaty skewed to favor the Opposition and the more likely it is that the Moderates would be willing to gamble on peace.

Finally, as the benefits to M of marginalizing S increase, M can be less confident in E's neutrality and still be willing to gamble on peace. This last factor may explain in part why IFOR became more effective over time. In Bosnia, as the Serb moderates in Banja Luka increased in power, they increasingly saw the Pale-based Serbs as their primary competitors. While tension between both groups of Serbs and the Bosnian government remained high, the moderate Serbs increasingly felt that the extremists posed more of a threat to their power base than the Bosnians. In this instance, as s rose, the Serb moderates were more willing to side with IFOR and support a stronger implementation program. We summarize these hypotheses below:

H1: The terms of the original agreement are more likely to be implemented, as the Moderates' value for war decreases.

H2: The terms of the original agreement are more likely to be implemented, as the Moderates' value for the peace agreement increases.

H3: The terms of the original agreement are less likely to be implemented, as the Moderates' value for a peace agreement skewed in favor of the Opposition decreases.

H4: The terms of the original agreement are more likely to be implemented, as the Moderates' value for marginalizing Spoilers increases.

IMPLICATIONS

The key implication of this analysis is that while the failure of third-party guarantors to act in the face of clear violations may appear to result from incompetence or a failure of will, such failures may in fact be a result of strategic constraints. In order to ensure successful implementation of a peace agreement, third-party enforcers ideally want to exploit the split between moderates and extremists and empower moderates while marginalizing extremists. Sanctioning extremists at the slightest provocation is one way to do so. The analysis here, however, suggests that such a strategy can be very difficult to implement. While moderates want the extremists neutralized they also want to make sure that the third party is "even-handed" and does not allow the opposition to skew the agreement in its favor. If the moderates doubt that the enforcer will be even-handed, then sanctioning the extremists creates the possibility that the moderates will be exploited. In response to such fears, the enforcer is forced to demonstrate that it is "even-handed" by not sanctioning anyone.

Even if the moderates are convinced that the enforcer will prosecute in an even-handed fashion, the peace process remains shaky. In this instance, the extremists avoid being marginalized by laying low and not provoking retaliation by the third party. However, for third parties committed to the maintenance of peace this leaves them between a rock and a hard place. Unable to neutralize the spoilers because of their strategic compliance, third parties are also unable to withdraw because they recognize that the extremists will re-emerge as soon as a credible sanctioning threat disappears. The peace is secure only so long as the third party remains. This seems to provide at least a partial explanation for the inability of third parties to easily extract from such places as Bosnia. Despite serious efforts to implement the agreement, spoiler groups remain that continue to pose a real threat to future peace.

Although this latter situation is not ideal, it does seem to offer more hope for a lasting peace than instances where the third party must stand by as the original peace agreement is continuously eroded by challenges on all sides. This suggests that it is generally in the third party's best interests to create the perception of neutrality. If a third party is able to convince the moderates that its promise to sanction not only the extremists but the opposition as well is credible, then the peace process should be much more secure. There is, of course, an extensive if often contradictory literature on the benefits of third-party neutrality and bias.[5] Most of the literature on peacekeeping highlights as we do the importance of a neutral third party (Diehl 1993; Hampson 1996).[6] Without the enforcement authority granted by Chapter VII of the UN Charter, to be effective at managing minor infractions and facilitating communication between former belligerents, neutrality is essential. Without the cloak of neutrality, peacekeepers will be unable to generate the trust necessary to report credibly violations on either side or act as a mediator as new issues arise. Our model assumes, however, that the third party does have enforcement powers either granted unilaterally or under Chapter VII (of the United Nations Charter). We show that even in this instance when the third party comes in with strong enforcement powers, the perception of neutrality is still important. Unless the belligerents believe that the third-party enforcer will be even-handed in its enforcement, there will be no peace to keep as the moderates will abandon the agreement.

Third parties that come in as enforcers, however, may have considerable problems creating perceptions of neutrality. Enforcers do not simply monitor compliance and attempt to resolve disputes. Instead, they are given the much broader responsibility of enforcing the terms of the settlement and sanctioning those that violate the agreement. Countries that assume such extensive responsibilities are rarely disinterested. They often want peace but may also have their own interests regarding the terms of peace that are most preferable. Throughout the Bosnian war, for instance, NATO revealed a strong preference for the Bosnian Muslims over the Bosnian Serbs. Information that NATO intended to "train and equip" the Muslims despite agreements to reduce the size of the federation and republic's armies only reinforced the impression that the Muslims would be given much greater latitude during the implementation stage than the Serbs. Particularly in situations in which the enforcer played a non-neutral role during the war, as NATO did during the Bosnian War, it will be especially difficult to persuade key moderates that the same force will now pursue neutral implementation policies. Such concerns may provide yet another justification for why peacemaking forces and peacekeeping forces should be separate and come from different sources. The inclusion of Russian troops in IFOR, for instance, likely significantly reduced Serb fears that implementation would be biased. Fears of biased enforcement also likely explain why President Milošević attempted to get UN troops, rather than NATO troops, to secure the peace in Kosovo. Given the importance of perceptions of a neutral peacekeeping force, two additional hypotheses may be suggested:

> *H5*: The original terms of agreement are less likely to be implemented if the peacekeeping force includes members that fought with or assisted one belligerent at the expense of the other during the conflict.
>
> *H6*: The original terms of the agreement are more likely to be implemented if the peacekeeping force includes members that were not actively involved while the conflict was ongoing.

The analysis also suggests the importance of the relationship between the so-called Moderates and Extremists. In this analysis, we assumed that the moderates and spoilers were on the same side but differed significantly in their value for peace over war. This relationship between moderates and spoilers seems to characterize the relationship between moderate Hutus committed to the Arusha Accords and Hutu extremists like the CDR that were committed to the overthrow of Arusha. However, it is possible that those committed to peace and those opposed may not be on the same side. In Cambodia, for instance, while the Khmer Rouge is often depicted as spoilers, moderate groups in Cambodia that supported the peace process were not affiliated with the Khmer Rouge and instead represented completely different interests. In this instance, there were several different sides with fairly distinct interests, not two sides that were split into multiple factions. If spoilers and moderates are not on the same "side," it is not clear why moderate groups would be threatened when spoiler groups are sanctioned. The flexibility of third parties to sanction spoilers then may depend critically on whether or not spoiler groups represent a minority of one faction or represent an entirely different group. This implication is summarized in hypothesis seven:

H7: The original terms of the agreement are more likely to be implemented and spoilers sanctioned if the spoiler groups are not affiliated with any of the moderate groups that support the peace process.

A final implication is worth considering. In this analysis, we distinguished between biased and neutral enforcers (see footnote 2). Biased enforcers preferred agreements that favored one side over the other, while neutral enforcers preferred agreements that were consistent with the terms originally negotiated. However, both types of enforcers preferred any type of agreement to a return to war. These enforcers were truly *peace*-keepers first and foremost. Much of the strategy in the game in fact involved the enforcers adopting second-best strategies (i.e., not sanctioning spoilers) in order to avoid a return to war. Another type of enforcer could be envisioned. Rather than being committed to maintaining peace and willing to "sell-out" to ensure its continuation, the enforcer could instead be committed to enforcing the original terms of the agreement. In this case, the "*treaty*-keeper" would prefer a resumption of the war to at least some types of agreements that could be implemented.

Significantly, the distinction made here between peace-keeper and treaty-keeper may in some ways be more consistent with the distinction many scholars draw between neutral and biased third parties (Princen 1992). For many, neutral third parties are not only disinterested (i.e. they do not favor one side over another) but they value peace in any guise over war. Biased third parties, in contrast, only prefer certain limited terms that favor them and their side over war. It is clearly possible, however, that a third party could be neutral and committed to peace on any terms or it could be neutral and willing to abandon peace under certain conditions. The tendency to conflate these two dimensions may explain some of the confusion that pervades this literature.

While we have demonstrated here that third-party neutrality is important to a third party's ability to sanction spoilers, we anticipate that whether or not the third party is a "peace-keeper" or a "treaty-keeper" is also likely significantly to affect how this game will be played. An enforcer that is willing to risk a return to war in order to blackmail the belligerents into compliance may improve the odds that the terms of the original treaty are implemented but may do so by increasing the risk that the belligerents abandon the agreement altogether and return to war. In contrast, an enforcer that is committed to peace on any terms may ensure that war does not resume (as suggested by this model) but at the same time may accomplish this by allowing the terms of settlement to be so degraded that the peace that is enforced is worth very little. Further research on the impact of neutrality thus should be careful to distinguish between a third party's preference for one side over the other (partial vs. impartial) and its preference for peace under different conditions to a resumption of war (peace-keeper vs. treaty-keeper).

CONCLUSION

While this analysis represents a useful point of departure to begin thinking about the strategic constraints faced by third-party enforcers and the ability to guarantee a peace agreement in the presence of spoilers, there are several useful modifications and extensions that should be considered. One extension would be to consider how these dynamics might change over time. Is it possible for a third party to convince skeptical moderates that their threat to enforce the obligations of the treaty in an even-handed manner is credible? If the moderates were allowed to learn from the third party's behavior to the opposition, would it be possible for a neutral enforcer to create sufficient trust over time so that it could ultimately be able to sanction spoilers even if it was unable to do so initially? More generally, under what conditions could neutral third parties effectively signal their type to moderate groups? A second extension would be to consider how these dynamics work within a state. We have conceptualized the enforcer as an outsider—a third party. The enforcer, however, might very well be one side's government and the moderate's may be that government's constituents. In this instance, the government may worry that by cracking down on the extremists, it will encourage the moderates to abandon the government and throw their support behind the extremists. Whether and how these dynamics change if the enforcer is an insider or an outsider is worthy of investigation. Finally, this analysis suggests several testable hypotheses. Empirical evaluation will help us to determine whether or not the strategic incentives identified here do in fact impact the durability and nature of the peace.

While we intend to consider these extensions and others, the chapter reiterates a similar theme recently explored by Kydd and Walter (2002). Extremists need not be capable of unilaterally disrupting the peace process to be effective. Instead, they can undermine the peace process by playing the moderates' fears that they might be exploited. While savvy third parties can avoid the worst outcome of a renewal of war by ensuring moderates of even-handedness by sanctioning no one, such diversion ensures that the original peace agreement is weakened. The parties may not return to war, but the security of the peace remains in doubt.

NOTES

1. See particularly Werner (1999) and Fortna (2003a and 2003b).

2. Note that our definition of neutrality is focused on the preference orderings of agreements instead of merely on a desire for peace (Princen 1992). In designing this model, we struggled to reconcile what neutrality actually means and how it is used in the literature. We found neutrality meant many different things to many different people. The early mediation literature generally describes the concept we are trying to capture as impartiality, meaning no bias toward one side or the other. Neutrality is treated separately, almost in an early-twentieth-century sense, as noninvolvement (Bercovitch and Rubin 1992). Neutrality is defined by others in terms of actions, "even-handedness" or simply suggest it as a characteristic particular to "disinterested parties" who will be "fair" (Diehl 1993). But as Smith and Stam (2003b) point out, even parties that are solely interested in peace regardless of its terms and conditions may not be appropriately described as "disinterested." A third party's desire for peace may in fact encourage them to do things to bring about peace that are not necessarily "fair" (Smith and Stam, forthcoming). In our model, both biased and neutral enforcers prefer peace to war. They differ only over their preference for different types of peaceful outcomes, relating most closely to the idea of "impartiality."

3. Adding the additional complexity of uncertainty by S regarding E's type provides no additional leverage on the implementation dynamic because S's behavior depends completely on M's beliefs about E's type.

4. Since both types of enforcers prefer any peace agreement to war, signaling is not effective because the signal (sanctioning) is equally costly for both types.

5. Within the mediation literature, an extensive debate is ongoing regarding the relative effectiveness of neutrality over partiality for mediators. Some argue that a mediator can only be successful if both sides have confidence in the mediator (see Jackson 1952, Young 1967 and Northedge and Donelan 1971). Bercovitch, Anagnoson, and Wille (1991) argue that neutrality is less important than leverage, referring to a resource or piece of territory that one or both sides value that the mediator controls. Recently, Kydd (2003) has argued that biased mediators are the most effective because mediators play an informational role, so a biased mediator is most credible under certain conditions (see also Calvert 1985). The literature is similarly divided regarding the benefits of neutrality over partiality for third parties that intervene with force to end the conflict. Regan (2002) argues that neutrality creates a balance of capabilities that

should shorten the war. His empirical results, however, contradict this argument. Betts (1994) makes the opposite argument. He argues that since neutrality creates more balanced capability ratios, intervention prolongs conflicts. He also suggests that indecisiveness and a failure to address the real issues hinder neutral intervention because the focus is on fairness and justice, concepts wholly independent of and sometimes in conflict with peace (see also Luttwak 2001).

6. Peacekeeping refers to situations where lightly armed troops are inserted, usually during a lull in fighting or after a cease-fire. Peacekeeper functions include monitoring, providing humanitarian aid, maintaining law and order, and interposition (Diehl 1993).

11

Are Leaders Susceptible to Negative Political Advice? An Experimental Study of High-Ranking Military Officers

Alex Mintz

Are leaders susceptible to negative political advice? I report the results of a computerized process-tracing experiment with high-ranking officers of the U.S. Air Force in which the effect of negative political information on leaders' decisions is assessed in familiar and unfamiliar decision settings. Results support the basic tenet of poliheuristic theory: leaders are sensitive to negative political advice, which is often noncompensatory. To avoid "major political loss" they first focus on a few key dimensions, and then shift to analytic processing in evaluating "surviving" alternatives and making decisions.

In this chapter, I examine the effect of negative political advice on decision making of high-ranking military officers using computerized, process-tracing technology. I then test the effect of familiarity with the decision task on national security decisions. Specifically, I examine whether unfamiliar decision tasks lead to more changes in strategies of decision during a decision process than a familiar decision problem. I use a process-tracing experimental methodology via the Decision Board simulator to test the effect of negative political information and familiarity on strategy selection. I do so in the context of the poliheuristic theory of decision (Mintz 1993, 2003, 2004a; Mintz and Geva 1997; Mintz et al. 1997).

Brule and Mintz have recently (2004) found that positive support (>50%) for the use of force by the United States during the time period 1949–2001 led presidents to reject the Do Nothing, no-force alternative in favor of a more proactive, use force, Do Something policy. According to these authors, in a crisis, the president is not getting a "blank check" from the public to choose whatever option he wants, but, instead, is getting "marching orders" from the public to discard nonforce options and use force. Brule and Mintz (2004) also showed empirically that widespread opposition to the use of force often restricts presidents from employing force in a crisis. DeRouen (2003) pointed out that President Eisenhower rejected the use of force option in Dien Bien Phu because of negative public support for this policy. Eisenhower closely tracked public opinion which showed that over 68 percent of the population was opposed to U.S. involvement in Indochina (ibid, 18). The president considered public support of his broad foreign policy agenda as critical and he felt that "the public's support of a foreign policy was necessary for it to be successful" (quoted in DeRouen 2003, 18). Redd (2001) claimed that strong opposition (>60%) to the use of ground forces by the United States in Kosovo led President Clinton to reject the "deploy ground forces" option. Farnham (2000) found that domestic factors played a significant role in President Roosevelt's decision making during the Munich crisis. Goertz (2004, 27) claimed that presidents Eisenhower and Nixon and Secretary of State Kissinger "considered using nuclear weapons in war but were constrained by public opinion."

The effect of political factors on leaders' decisions to use force is not unique to the United States or even to democracies. Sathasivam (2003) reported that political pressure on Pakistan's prime minister, Nawaz Sharif, from the public, the military, and the political opposition forced Sharif to reject the Do Nothing option following the nuclear weapons tests by India in May 1998 and led to the adoption of the Do Something, test nuclear weapons, option. According to Sathasivam (2003, 65), a Gallup poll taken in February 1996 indicated that "80 percent of Pakistanis support a Pakistani nuclear test, if India tests first." Mintz (2004a) claimed that widespread public opposition significantly influenced the Turkish parliament's March 2003 decision to veto a proposed deployment of 62,000 U.S. troops to Turkey as a launching pad for a possible attack against Iraq. Former Israeli foreign minister Ben-Ami (2002) pointed out that the lack of public support, prior to the Israeli elections of 2001, for Israeli concessions to the Palestinians in Taba was a major reason why concessions were not even considered officially by the Israeli government. Recently the Israeli chief of staff, Moshe Ya'alon, revealed that the Israeli leadership takes public opinion into consideration in deciding on retaliatory and targeted assassinations of terrorists (Ya'alon 2004). These examples show that leaders take into account the political ramifications of their decisions, and they avoid alternatives that are likely to harm them politically or personally.

Kinne (2004) showed that "avoiding major political loss" principle is not unique to democratic regimes. According to Kinne (2004, 16), it is applicable to single-party autocracies, personalist autocracies, and military dictatorships. However, it varies according to the type of the autocracy: leaders of single-party systems eliminate alternatives that "do not sufficiently appease the interest of the party"; leaders in personalist autocracies "eliminate decision alternatives that do not satisfy the leader's need to maintain political status"; whereas leaders of military regimes eliminate alternatives that "do not sufficiently appease the ruling military cabal or *junta.*"

Mintz (2004c) found that Saddam Hussein's decision not to withdraw from Kuwait in 1990–1991 even in face of a mighty coalition can be explained by his fear of losing face, political legitimacy, and power. Kinne documented Pakistan's decision not to send troops to Iraq in 2003, Saddam's decision to stay in Kuwait in 1991, and former Soviet president Mikhail Gorbachev's foreign policy "revolution" of the 1980s as motivated by the same, "avoid major political loss," principle. One reason Yasser Arafat did not bow to U.S. and Israeli pressure at Camp David 2000 was because there was no support for Palestinian concessions among his constituencies (Mintz and Mishal 2003). There is therefore overwhelming anecdotal and empirical support for the thesis that leaders reject the no-force, Do Nothing alternative when the public wants them to use force and reject the Do Something, use-force alternative if the public constraints them from using force. Thus, a political analyst's warning of a politically harmful consequence of a policy is often noncompensatory (Brule and Mintz 2004).

The second aspect of this study is concerned with the effect of familiarity with the decision task on national security decisions. Klein (2002, 272) pointed out that most critical decisions we make are based on intuition: "although sometimes difficult to explain, intuition is important in making decisions and is based on the ability to recognize patterns and interpret cues, i.e., it develops through experience," and familiarity with the decision problem. Khong (1992) found that American policymakers repeatedly have invoked the lessons of history when making decisions about military campaigns. Khong argued that leaders use analogies to perform specific cognitive and information-processing tasks essential to decision making. Familiarity with the decision problem based on previous experience is used as a decision aid in making decisions. Geva, Mintz, and Redd (2000) found familiarity to affect decision making when alternatives or dimensions (attributes) are added to the choice set or dimension set in a dynamic way during a crisis. Extending the argument presented in Mintz 2004b, I examine the effect of negative political advice on decision making in familiar versus unfamiliar situations.

DO LEADERS AVOID MAJOR POLITICAL LOSS?
AN EXPERIMENTAL ASSESSMENT

Poliheuristic theory (PH) suggests that policymakers switch from one decision strategy (i.e., dimension based) to another (i.e., alternative based) during the decision process. In other words, in reaching a decision, policymakers first focus on dimensions and then on alternatives. Does familiarity or lack of familiarity with a decision task affect decision strategy change in foreign policy? Does negative political information affect choice?

Poliheuristic theory attempts to bridge between the rational choice school of decision making and the cognitive psychology school. A major proposition of poliheuristic theory is that decisionmakers use a variety of decision strategies in a two-stage process and that different decision strategies are employed at different stages of the decision process (Mintz 1993; Payne, Bettman, and Johnson 1993).

Mintz et al. (1997) posit that in the first stage of the poliheuristic decision process, the decisionmaker simplifies the decision task by using a heuristic-based search. In the second stage, the decisionmaker uses an analytic, alternative-based search on the narrowed choice set in an attempt to maximize gains and minimize costs. One heuristic often employed by leaders is avoiding negative political loss.

Leaders are sensitive to negative political advice. I test whether avoiding political loss is noncompensatory. I also test whether national security decision makers change strategies of decision during the decision process under familiar versus unfamiliar decision tasks and with ambiguous versus unambiguous information.

Poliheuristic theory has implications for the analysis of how foreign policy decisionmakers process political information and cope with unfamiliar versus familiar choice situations. Consistent with the theory, state leaders use decision heuristics such as the avoid-major-loss, noncompensatory decision principle to simplify the decision task in the first stage of the decision process. One way in which this is accomplished, as pointed out by Russo and Dosher (1983; see also Geva, Driggers, and Mintz 1997), is for the decisionmaker to use a more dimension-based analysis, which is cognitively less demanding and, therefore, aids in coping with the lack of familiarity of the decisionmaker with the decision task. A key dimension that state leaders focus on in the first stage of the decision is domestic politics (DeRouen 2003; Mintz 1993; 2003).

Political advice is more likely to be noncompensatory in familiar rather than in unfamiliar settings. This is because in familiar settings leaders can better judge the political consequences of different options, while in an unfamiliar setting, leaders are typically faced with a greater uncertainty about the consequences of their actions, have to deal with more issues and dimensions, and are often surprised by new circumstances. Poliheuristic theory postulates that dimension-based heuristics simplify the decision process. It therefore implies, indirectly, that in unfamiliar settings that characterize numerous foreign policy decisions, policymakers will tend to rely in the first stage of the decision process on dimension-based heuristics; that is, they will focus on the dimensions or attributes of the decision. Once the decision task becomes more manageable and simplified, the decisionmaker switches to an alternative-based strategy.

HYPOTHESES

The following hypotheses are tested in this study, using a computerized process-tracing methodology and the Decision Board simulator with senior military officers:

Hypothesis 1: Consistent with poliheuristic theory, leaders are sensitive to negative political information, which is often noncompensatory. This is more pronounced in familiar decision situations than in unfamiliar situations.

Hypothesis 2: Consistent with poliheuristic theory, decisionmakers use more than one decision strategy during the decision process. Specifically, they switch from dimension-based analysis in the first stage of the PH process to alternative-based calculations in the second stage of the process.

Hypothesis 3: The familiarity of decisionmakers with the decision task affects strategy *change* during the decision process. Specifically, the poliheuristic shift from a dimension-based strategy to an alternative-based strategy is more likely to occur in an unfamiliar situation than in a familiar setting.

Hypothesis 4: There is an interaction effect between familiarity and ambiguity on choice.

To test these hypotheses, I use the Decision Board simulator and a decision process-tracing experimental methodology in a study of high-ranking officers of the U.S. Air Force.

COMPUTERIZED DECISION PROCESS TRACING

There is a wide use of theoretical ideas from cognitive and social psychology in the study of foreign policy decision making. These ideas are not easily tested using historical case studies alone. George (1980) advocated the use of process tracing in the late 1970s. The methodology has not yet been rigorously used in the study of foreign policy decision making (but see Astorino-Courtois 2000; Mintz et al. 1997; Redd 2002). The main strength of the process-tracing methodology is its ability to identify specific decision rules and decision models used by decision makers and to test theoretically derived implications of situational and personal variables on the decision process and its outcome.

Ford et al. (1989) explain that process tracing directly identifies what information was accessed to form a judgment and the order in which the information was accessed. This information can then be used to make inferences about what decision strategies have been employed in arriving at a choice. According to Ford et al., the examination of the decisionmaker's pattern of information search can "identify alternative models or strategies used in making a decision" (p. 77). Three groups of scholars in political science use process-tracing techniques: "(1) Taber and Steenbergen (1995) focus on tracing the cognitive algebra in political decision making; (2) Riggle and Johnson (1996) employ protocol-tracing techniques to investigate age-related differences in strategies used to evaluate political candidates; (3) Lau and Redlawsk (1992) use information boards to trace compensatory and noncompensatory strategies of decision (Mintz et al. 1997, 556).

THE DECISION BOARD SIMULATOR

The core structure of the Decision Board platform, which is depicted in table 11.1, is a matrix of alternatives and dimensions on which the alternatives are evaluated (see Mintz et al. 1997). The computerized board records key features of the decision-making process. These features are subsequently used to identify decision strategies of policymakers.[1] A major category of these features relates to the sequence in which the information is accessed by the decisionmaker. Version 4.0 of the Decision Board is available at www.decision board.org/academic.

A decision problem typically consists of the selection of an alternative from a set of available alternatives. "The choice set is evaluated along single or, more typically, multiple dimensions. The 'values' in the matrix represent the evaluation of a given alternative on a given dimension. These information bins can be opened to reveal their contents by the click of the mouse, whereas decisions are made by clicking on the choice box of a desired alternative" (Mintz et al. 1997). "The computerized Decision Board records (*a*) the sequence in which decisionmakers acquire the information, (*b*) the number of items that respondents view for every alternative along every dimension, and (*c*) the amount of time that elapses from the time respondents begin the task until they make their choice" (ibid). Version 4.0 of the Decision Board also

Table 11.1. The Decision Board Platform

Dimensions	Alternatives			
	Blockade	*Sanctions*	*Use of Force*	*Do Nothing*
Political	Implications	Implications	Implications	Implications
Military	Implications	Implications	Implications	Implications
Economic	Implications	Implications	Implications	Implications
Diplomatic	Implications	Implications	Implications	Implications
Your choice:	_____	_____	_____	_____

displays the "decision portraits" of decisionmakers and calculates holistic versus nonholistic search patterns and maximizing versus satisficing decision rules. Using the process-tracing technique, one can identify the strategy selection and decision model of leaders and other decisionmakers.

To enhance the robustness of this experiment, we used two foreign policy scenarios. One context (the "familiar scenario") dealt with a military dispute that erupted between two small islands because of a rivalry over control of a large uranium field. Subsequently, one nation invaded the other. The invasion also resulted in the invading country holding foreign citizens as hostages. In this scenario, the decisionmaker was presented with four alternatives (Geva et al 1997):

- use of force
- blockade
- sanctions
- do nothing

A second scenario (the "unfamiliar scenario") dealt with the choice of a hypothetical site for a new naval base in the Pacific. The alternatives in this scenario consisted of four fictitious islands that were unknown to the officers: Alpha, Beta, Charlie, and Delta (see Mintz et al. 1997). Whereas the values used in both scenarios were identical, the statements that preceded the numerical values were modified to reflect the specific context of each case (Geva, Driggers, and Mintz 1997).

The dimensions that were employed in both scenarios represent decision criteria that were found to be relevant in other studies of foreign policy decisions in international relations (see James and Oneal 1991; Morgan and Bickers 1992; Ostrom and Job 1986). Hence, the dimensions included in the Decision Board were the following:

- political
- economic

- military
- diplomatic

Following the definition of the four alternatives and four dimensions, the values were inserted in the decision matrix. These values "consisted of a descriptive statement and a summarizing numeric value (on a scale from -10 to $+10$). For instance, the decisionmaker can speculate, on the basis of her or his stored beliefs" (Taber and Steenbergen 1995), "on the impact of the use of force on the political dimension. He or she may evaluate the use-of-force option in terms of public approval and decide that it is too costly" (Mintz et al. 1997). Converting such an evaluation to a scale, the political dimension is assigned a negative score (-10, -9, or -8) on the use-of-force alternative. The values in the matrix can also stem, of course, from an external source to the decisionmaker (Redd 2002). A credible source, such as the chief economic adviser, "may tell the chief executive that "do nothing" can be very beneficial to the nation's trade deficit, implying a high positive score (e.g., a score of 9) for this alternative on the economic dimension" (Geva, Driggers, and Mintz 1997). Naturally, the extent of advisers' influence on these scores may represent various factors associated with the leaders' expertise and susceptibility to influence (Redd 2002). Thus, as in Mintz et al. (1997) and Redd (2002), the alternatives and their values in the Decision Board were presented as being provided by chief advisers to the decisionmaker: "the chairman of the Joint Chiefs of Staff," "the secretary of state," the "chief political adviser," and the "chief economic adviser."

To test the robustness of the findings, we introduced ambiguity to the decision task, by inserting *ranges* of values into the information bins (see below). To assess the effect of negative political information on choice, a score of -8 was assigned to the political implications of the alternative with the highest value overall (A4). I expect the officers to process information in a two-stage process as predicted by the theory and to view negative political advice as noncompensatory. The extent of familiarity with the alternatives is expected to affect the decisionmaker's dependence on the information in the Decision Board. The "unfamiliar scenario" is assumed to make the decision task cognitively more demanding. Consequently, I expect that respondents will access more information in the unfamiliar case and use more dimension-based processing in the first stage of the unfamiliar case than in the familiar situation.

METHOD[2]

Subjects

Seventy-two high-ranking military officers from the U.S. Air Force Academy at Colorado Springs participated in this experiment. The respondents included one brigadier general, three colonels, eleven lieutenant colonels, and other officers. They are members of the command and instructional staff at the U.S. Air Force Academy. The air force commanders were randomly assigned to the different experimental conditions.[3]

Design

The basic structure of the experiment was a between-groups factorial design. The factors were: familiarity with the choice set (unfamiliar vs. familiar alternatives) and ambiguity (no ambiguity, mid-level ambiguity, and high-level ambiguity). Various values were inserted in the political bin for A4—the alternative with the highest overall value (see table 11.2). We also randomized the sequence of alternatives in the choice set.

Dependent Variables

The dependent variable in this study consisted of two process-tracing parameters of decision making: information search pattern and the choices respondents made. Previous studies of process tracing (e.g., Ford et al. 1989; Payne, Bettman, and Johnson 1993) "depict two "pure" modes of information acquisition that are often used as a key dependent variable in studies using the process-tracing methodology" (Mintz et al. 1997). The first pattern is known as the *alternative-based* strategy, whereby the decisionmaker reviews sequentially all items for a given alternative across different dimensions—and then continues the search process by reviewing information for another alternative across dimensions. The second strategy, *dimension based*, implies a process whereby the decisionmaker focuses on a given dimension and reviews all the alternatives along this dimension and repeats the process for another dimension. The moves were compared and measured in our study using the Billings and Scherer (1988) search index (SI) (see Mintz et al. 1997 for a similar operationalization). The index is used to quantify the search sequence. It ranges from -1 (purely dimensional processing) to $+1$ (purely alternative-based processing). Obviously, a change of sign in this process indicator represents a change in the decision strategy (ibid.).

The scoring of the moves followed Billings and Scherer's (1988, 10) definition: "Each move to a new piece of information which was within the same alternative and across dimensions was classified as an inter-dimensional move (alternative-based), while a move within a dimension and across alternatives was labeled as intra-dimensional (dimension-based). Moves to both a different alternative and a different dimension were labeled shifts. The search pattern variable is defined as the number of alternative-based moves minus the number of dimensional moves divided by the sum of these two numbers."

The index tallies the number of dimensional moves (d), alternative moves (a), and shifts (s) (moves that are not alternative or dimension based) and uses the equation $SI = (a-d)/(a+d)$ to define the search index. Positive numbers imply more alternative-based moves, and negative numbers imply dimensional moves. Shifts are disregarded from this index.

To identify the change in decision strategy, we compared the search pattern that the air force officers used for the first six items of information with the search pattern of the remaining items that respondents reviewed during the crisis (Geva, Driggers, and Mintz 1997). We chose six items as the cutoff point because this represents half of the mean number of items reviewed by the respondents. Sensitivity analysis consistently demonstrated this as well.

Material

It is well documented that the cognitive demands imposed by the decision task affect strategy selection (Russo and Dosher 1983; Maoz 1997). Specifically, the heavier the cognitive load, the more likely it is that decisionmakers will use simplifying heuristics. In this project, variations in cognitive demand were introduced by (a) manipulating the familiarity of decisionmakers with the decision task and (b) manipulating the level of ambiguity of information.

Manipulation of familiarity. As pointed out above, two foreign policy scenarios were used. One dealt with a military dispute between two small islands. Previous experiments (see Mintz et al. 1997; Geva et al. 1997) demonstrated that such a scenario was *familiar* to the respondents; that is, they held a priori beliefs about what such alternatives entailed, and they had a priori preferences for certain alternatives (the preference-over-preference phenomenon). The second scenario—the unfamiliar case—consisted of four fictitious islands unfamiliar to the respondents and involved the choice of a site for a new naval base in the Pacific. The respondents analyzing this scenario were asked to choose among these islands. Our manipulation check showed that respondents in the unfamiliar scenario used considerably more information than in the familiar condition in the experiment. They accessed more decision cells (information) on the Decision Board, an indication that this scenario was less familiar to them. In the unfamiliar scenario, decision makers had no a priori preferences for certain alternatives.

Manipulation of ambiguity of information. The second manipulation used in this study is for ambiguity. *Ambiguity* is defined as a situation in which the outcome associated with each alternative in a choice set can be represented only as *a range* of possible outcomes. As originally reported in Geva, Driggers, and Mintz (1997), the numerical evaluations of the alternatives along the four dimensions were altered to reflect increasing levels of ambiguity. This was done by increasing the range of the numerical evaluations presented to the respondent. In the no-ambiguity condition, the evaluation of each alternative was represented by a single numerical evaluation. In the medium-ambiguity condition, the evaluations were presented as a range of 2 in the values. For example, the single numerical value of 5 was expressed as a value that is "somewhere between 4 and 6." In the high-ambiguity condition, the range between the lowest rating and the highest number was 4. Under this condition, the sentence read, "I would rate this alternative somewhere between 3 and 7" (Geva, Driggers, and Mintz 1997). Moreover, the same ranges of values were kept constant across the two different scenarios in the experiment. Table 11.2 shows the values used in this experiment to evaluate the four alternatives along four dimensions.

Political information. To assess the effect of negative political information on choice, a negative/positive score was assigned to the political dimension on different alternatives and compared across familiar and unfamiliar conditions.

To control for any bias introduced by the order in which the alternatives were presented, the design included four different sequences of the alternatives (A C B D, B D C A, C A D B, and D B A C).

Because many foreign policy and national security decisions are made under time and informational constraints, we introduced in this experiment a time constraint cued by occasional beeps by the computer. No other time limit was imposed on the respondents (ibid.).

Procedure

The experiment was administered at the computer labs of the U.S. Air Force Academy, where each respondent was able to operate individually on a computer. The instructions and decision scenarios were displayed on the computer

Table 11.2. Values in the Decision Matrix

	Alpha	Beta	Charlie	Delta
Political	0	7	1	−8
Military	−7	0	6	5
Economic	2	−6	4	6
Diplomatic	8	2	−8	2

Note: The numbers in the matrix correspond to the "no-ambiguity" condition. The values for mid-level ambiguity have a range of 2. The values for high-level ambiguity have a range of 4 (Geva, Driggers, and Mintz 1997).

screen. The instructions to the officers were straightforward. They were told that they would be exposed to a specific international scenario and were then presented with a decision matrix that contained action alternatives relevant to the decision and their consequences on different dimensions. The instructions to the decisionmakers also mentioned that the "quality of decision you make in the context of the simulation will suggest your ability to comprehend national-level decision making." Previous studies (e.g., Mintz et al. 1997) indicate that portraying a decision task in these terms increases the motivation of the respondents to perform the task seriously, without contaminating or confounding the salience of a particular decisional dimension.

Prior to performing the foreign policy decision, a simple practice session was administered to familiarize the officers with the Decision Board simulator. When a decision was made, a post-decision questionnaire was administered, followed by a debriefing (Geva, Mintz, and Redd 2000; Mintz et al. 1997).

RESULTS

The Susceptibility of Leaders to Negative Political Advice

The experiment with the air force commanders revealed that they followed the noncompensatory principle of political decision making, especially in the familiar condition: Faced with negative information about the political consequences of selecting the "best" alternative, two-thirds of the officers rejected the "best" alternative, even though this alternative had the highest overall score among all alternatives. When given a negative evaluation on the political implications of the alternative with the highest overall score, three-fourths of the officers in the familiar condition and almost 6 in 10 officers in the unfamiliar condition rejected this alternative.

In the unfamiliar condition, when the information about the political consequences of the alternative was unambiguous, negative, and clear, as many as 83.33 percent of the officers rejected the "best" alternative, despite the fact that it yielded the highest overall score. However, as the information presented became vague and less negative (in the mid-level and high level of ambiguity), there was less evidence for the elimination of the "correct" alternative based on negative political advice.

A key result of this chapter is, therefore, that leaders avoid major political loss by rejecting even the most promising alternative if it scores negatively on the political dimension. Negative political loss in noncompensatory. Public opposition to the use of force, a negative assessment of the political implications of a particular policy by a political adviser, regime survival, domestic political opposition, intraparty rivalry, the prospects of an electoral defeat if force is used, may lead to the rejection of such an alternative. Leaders are likely to pursue alternatives that may not be the "best" overall, but that do *not* damage them politically or personally.

The Effects of Familiar and Unfamiliar Settings on Information Processing and Choice

The results also show support for the two-stage poliheuristic decision process. As in previous studies, changes in strategy were identified by comparing the search pattern (search index) for the first items of information reviewed (stage 1) with the search pattern of the remaining items of information (stage 2). The results of this test show that there is a statistically significant difference, $F(1, 66) = 7.508$ ($p < .01$), between the stage 1 search index ($M = -.254$) and the stage 2 search index ($M = -.038$), suggesting a decrease in dimension-based processing between the stages (Geva, Driggers, and Mintz 1997). This pattern supports hypothesis 2 and a key tenet of poliheuristic theory, that is, a two-stage foreign policy decision process. In other words, in making decisions, policymakers first use dimensions to simplify the complex decision problem and then evaluate "surviving" alternatives.

The experiment also showed significantly more dimension-based processing in the unfamiliar condition than in the familiar condition, as demonstrated by the strong effect of familiarity on the search index, $F(1, 66) = 4.103$ ($p < .03$). Specifically, when the decision task was unfamiliar to the officers, they tended to use more dimensional search ($M = -.293$) than under conditions of familiarity ($M = .130$). In attempting to deal with increased complexity, leaders apparently employ the simplifying heuristic of dimension-based processing (ibid.).

The proportion of subjects who changed from a dimension-based to an alternative-based strategy when the decision task is unfamiliar and the information is ambiguous supports hypothesis 3, except for the mid-level of ambiguity. Specifically, 50 percent and 58 percent of the respondents in the unfamiliar condition switched strategies in the predicted direction under high and low levels of ambiguity, respectively, whereas only 25 percent and 33 percent of the subjects in the familiar setting switched strategies in low and high levels of ambiguity, respectively (50 percent of the subjects switched strategies in the mid-level of ambiguity in the familiar condition). The results thus show stronger evidence for a poliheuristic process in the unfamiliar condition, at low and high levels of ambiguity, than in familiar situations. The Analysis of Variance test showed, however, that neither ambiguity nor familiarity alone had significant effects on *changes* in decision strategy (Geva, Driggers, and Mintz 1997). Therefore, hypothesis 3 is only partially supported.

When one examines the specific search index scores at each processing phase, it is evident that when significant strategy changes occur, they consistently reflect a shift from a dimension-based to an alternative-based search. This is consistent with the theory. In the unfamiliar choice set, the changes in the high and low levels of ambiguity reflected the same pattern—less dimension-based processing in the second phase of information acquisition. Specifically, in the high-ambiguity condition, the SI score goes from $M = -164$ (dimension-based search) to $M = .218$ (alternative-based search). In the familiar choice set, where most of the strategy changes are associated with the medium level of ambiguity, decisionmakers also increased alternative-based processing at the second phase ($M = .224$) compared with the first phase ($M = -.043$). This result lends support to poliheuristic theory (Geva, Driggers, and Mintz 1997). In addition, the ANOVA yielded a significant interaction effect of familiarity and ambiguity on choice, $F(2, 66) = 2.584$ ($p < .05$), supporting hypothesis 4 of this study.

The results thus showed strong evidence for a noncompensatory elimination process when decisionmakers are given negative political advice about the political consequences of a particular alternative as well as dimension-based search in the first phase of the decision process especially in the unfamiliar condition with low or high ambiguity.

Multimethod analyses of the effects of negative political information on choice corroborate the main finding of this chapter. Brule and Mintz (2004, for example, use statistical analysis to show that public opinion is often noncompensatory. Mintz (1993) used a case study to illustrate the noncompensatory thesis in the context of the U.S. decision to attack Iraq in 1991, while Redd (2003), who surveyed the experimental evidence on poliheuristic theory, found strong evidence for dimension-based, noncompensatory processing of information. The consistent results of a noncompensatory principle, based on such multimethod tests, add to the robustness of the findings reported in this chapter.

CONCLUSION

This study tested, using air force commanders and the Decision Board simulator, whether negative political information is noncompensatory and whether unfamiliarity with the decision task affects strategy *change* during the decision-making process.

The results support the noncompensatory principle of poliheuristic theory: Negative political advice led officers to eliminate the "best" alternative, due to the noncompensatory, "avoid-major-political-loss" principle. Leaders might be sensitive to negative political information even more than to bureaucratic/organizational advice (see Christensen and Redd 2004). This is particularly evident in familiar settings. In unfamiliar situations, this is evident only when the political advice that is given is clear and unambiguous.

The results provide strong support for other aspects of poliheuristic theory as well. Specifically, the experiment found that decisionmakers change decision strategy in the course of the decision task, as predicted by the theory (Mintz 1993, 2003, 2004a; Mintz et al. 1997). Unfamiliar decision problems with ambiguous information about the decision's consequences also have a significant impact on a two-stage poliheuristic process, although familiarity and ambiguity alone did not affect strategy change during the decision process. It is still a two-stage process.

Ford et al. (1989) have noted that the selection of a particular strategy affects the ultimate choice. They have shown that choices made while processing information by alternatives are often very different from choices made while relying on dimensions. Herek, Janis, and Huth (1987) have also found significant correlations between the decision process and the decision outcome. Ford et al. (1989) found that the use of simplifying heuristics often led to suboptimal outcomes, whereas alternative-based strategies produce outcomes that lead to better consequences. Using high-ranking commanders of the U.S. Air Force, we showed that even national security decisionmakers reject promising alternatives when they are presented with negative information on the political consequences of these alternatives. The use of such heuristics in decision making may lead to suboptimal foreign policy or national security decisions.

NOTES

This is a revised and expanded version of an article entitled, "Foreign Policy Decision Making in Familiar and Unfamiliar Settings: An Experimental Study of High-Ranking Military Officers," originally published in the *Journal of Conflict Resolution* 48, no. 1 (February 2004).

1. The Decision Board simulator is a computerized tool for decision process tracing that allows the observation and recording of an individual's choice strategy. It allows researchers to identify the patterns in which decisionmakers acquire information and make decisions. The Decision Board 4.0 has been utilized in research, teaching, and training:

Research: to test theories of decision making (expected utility, prospect theory, cybernetic theory, poliheuristic theory); to assess the effect of framing and affect on decision making; for modeling voting games and electoral campaigns; for process tracing of political and economic trends and events.

Teaching: in courses in international relations, public policy and public administration, and management. The board has been used at twelve universities, including the University of Michigan; the University of Connecticut, National Defense University; University of Canterbury, New Zealand; China Foreign Affairs University in Beijing, China; Tel Aviv University, Israel; the University of Wisconsin–Milwaukee; U.S. Air Force Academy; School of Management and Department of Political Science at Yale University; and the Program in Foreign Policy Decision Making and the George Bush School of Government and Policy, Texas A&M University.

Training: in emergency response decision making, bargaining, negotiation, mediation, and analysis of a variety of crisis situations.

2. This experiment was first reported in Geva, Driggers, and Mintz (1997). Also see Mintz et al. (1997).

3. Russell Driggers administered the experiment at the U.S. Air Force Academy.

Bibliography

Achen, Christopher, and Duncan Snidal. "Rational Deterrence Theory and Comparative Case Studies." *World Politics* 41, no. 2 (January 1989): 413–69.

Adeola, F. "Military Expenditures, Health, and Education: Bedfellows or Antagonists in Third World Development?" *Armed Forces and Society* 22, no. 3 (Spring 1996): 441–55.

Altfeld, Michael. "Arms Races?—And Escalation? A Comment on Wallace." *International Studies Quarterly* 27, no. 2 (June 1983): 225–31.

Anand, Sudhir and Kara Hanson. "Disability-Adjusted Life Years: A Critical Review." *Journal of Health Economics* 16, no. 6 (December 1997): 685–702.

Anselin, Luc. *Spatial Econometrics: Methods and Models.* Dordrecht: Kluwer, 1988.

Archer, D., and R. Gartner. "Violent Acts and Violent Times: A Comparative Approach to Postwar Homicide Rates." *American Sociological Review* 41, no. 6 (December 1976): 937–63.

Armstrong, Scott J. "Combining Forecasts: The End of the Beginning or the Beginning of the End?" *International Journal of Forecasting* 5, no. 4 (1989): 585–88.

Ashford, Oliver M. *Prophet—or Professor? The Life and Work of Lewis Fry Richardson.* Boston: Hilger, 1985.

Astorino-Courtois, Allison. "The Effects of Stakes and Threat on Foreign Policy Decision Making." *Political Psychology* 21, no. 3 (September 2000): 489–510.

Astorino-Courtois, Allison, and Brittani Trusty. "Degrees of Difficulty: The Effect of Israeli Policy Shifts on Syrian Peace Decisions." *Journal of Conflict Resolution* 44, no. 3 (June 2000): 359–77.

Auerswald, D. "Domestic Institutions and Military Conflicts." *International Organization* 53, no. 3 (Summer 1999): 469–504.

———. *Disarmed Democracies: Domestic Institutions and the Use of Force.* Ann Arbor: University of Michigan Press, 2000.

Auerswald, D., and P. Cowhey. "Ballotbox Diplomacy: The War Powers Resolution and the Use of Force." *International Studies Quarterly* 41, no. 3 (September 1997): 505–28.

239

Ball, N. *Security and Economy in the Third World.* Princeton, N.J.: Princeton University Press, 1988.

Barbieri, Katherine. "Economic Interdependence: A Path to Peace or Source of Interstate Conflict?" *Journal of Peace Research* 33, no.1 (February 1996): 29–49.

Barbieri, Katherine, and Jack Levy. "Sleeping with the Enemy: The Impact of War on Trade." *Journal of Peace Research* 36, no. 4 (July 1999): 463–79.

Barro, Robert. "Economic Growth in a Cross Section of Countries." *Quarterly Journal of Economics* 106, no. 2 (May 1991): 407–43.

Bates, Darrell. *The Fashoda Incident of 1898: Encounter on the Nile.* London: Oxford University Press, 1984.

Bates, R.H. *Ethnicity, Capital Formation, and Conflict* (Working Paper No. 27). Cambridge, Mass.: Harvard University, Center for International Development, 1999.

Bavaud, Francois. "Models for Spatial Weights: A Systematic Look." *Geographical Analysis* 30, no. 2 (April 1998): 153–71.

Beck, Nathaniel. "The Illusion of Cycles in International Relations: Do Goldstein's Long Cycles Really Exist?" *International Studies Quarterly* 35, no. 4 (December 1991): 455–76.

Beck, Nathaniel, and Richard M. Tucker. "Conflict in Space and Time." Typescript, Department of Political Science, University of California San Diego, 1996.

Belsley, David A., Edwin Kuh, and Roy E. Welsch. *Regression Diagnostics: Identifying Influential Data and Sources of Collinearity.* New York: Wiley, 1980.

Ben-Ami, Shlomo. Interview with Alex Mintz, Tel Aviv, Israel 2002.

Bennett, D. Scott. "Integrating and Testing Models of Rivalry." *American Journal of Political Science* 42, no. 4 (October 1998): 1200–32.

Bennett, D. Scott, and Allan C. Stam. (a). "EUGene: A Conceptual Manual." *International Interactions* 26, no. 2 (April–June 2000): 179–204.

———. (b). "Research Design and Estimator Choices in the Analysis of Interstate Dyads: When Decisions Matter." *Journal of Conflict Resolution* 44, no. 5 (October 2000): 653–85.

———. *The Behavioral Origins of War.* Ann Arbor: University of Michigan Press, 2004.

Bennett, D. Scott., and T. Nordstrom. "Foreign Policy Substitutability and Internal Economic Problems in Enduring Rivalries." *Journal of Conflict Resolution* 44, no. 1 (February 2000): 33–61.

Benoit, Kenneth. "Democracies Really Are More Pacific (in General): Reexamining Regime Type and War Involvement." *Journal of Conflict Resolution* 40, no. 4 (December 1996): 636–57.

Bercovitch, Jacob, J. J. Anagnoson, and D. Wille. "Some Conceptual Issues and Empirical Trends in the Study of Successful Mediation in International Relations." *Journal of Peace Research* (Special Issue on International Mediation) 28, no. 1 (February 1991): 7–17.

Bercovitch, Jacob, and Karl DeRouen Jr. "Assessing Mediation Strategies in Ethnic Conflict."*Armed Forces and Society* (forthcoming).

Bercovitch, Jacob, and Jeffrey Z. Rubin. *Mediation in International Relations: Multiple Approaches to Conflict Management.* New York: St. Martin's Press, 1992.

Bertin, Jacques. *Semiology of Graphics: Diagrams, Networks, Maps.* Madison: University of Wisconsin Press, 1983.

Betts, Richard K. "The Delusion of Impartial Intervention." *Foreign Affairs* 73, no. 6 (November–December 1994): 20–33.

Billings, Robert S., and Lisa L. Scherer. "The Effects of Response Mode and Importance on Decision-Making Strategies: Judgment versus Choice." *Organizational Behavior and Human Decision Processes* 41, no. 1 (February 1988): 1–19.

Binder, Sarah. "The Dynamics of Legislative Gridlock, 1947–96." *American Political Science Review* 93, no. 3 (September 1999): 519–34.

———. *Stalemate: Causes and Consequences of Legislative Gridlock.* Washington, D.C.: Brookings Institution Press, 2003.

Bivand, Roger S. "Using the R Statistical Data Analysis Language on GRASS 5.0 GIS Data Base Files." *Computers and Geosciences* 26, nos. 9–10 (1 November 2000): 1043–52.

Blainey, Geoffrey. *The Causes of War.* London: The MacMillan Press, 1973.

———. *The Causes of War.* 3d ed. New York: Free Press, 1988.

Blechman, B., and S. Kaplan. *Force without War: U.S. Armed Forces as a Political Instrument.* Washington, D.C.: Brookings Institution Press, 1978.

Bond, J., and R. Fleisher. *Polarized Politics: Congress and the President in a Partisan Era.* Washington, D.C.: CQ Press, 2000.

Bracken, P., and C. Petty. *Rethinking the Trauma of War.* London: Save the Children, 1998.

Brady, D., J. Cooper, and P. Hurley. "The Decline of Party in the U.S. House of Representatives: 1886–1968." *Legislative Studies Quarterly* 4, no. 3 (August 1979): 381–407.

Brams, Steven J. "Transaction Flows in the International System." *American Political Science Review* 60, no. 4 (December 1966): 880–98.

———. "The Structure of Influence Relationships in the International System." Pp. 583–99 in *International Politics and Foreign Policy*, 2d ed., edited by James N. Rosenau. New York: Free Press, 1969.

———. *Superpower Games.* New Haven, Conn.: Yale University Press, 1985.

Brandt, P., and J. Williams. "A Linear Poisson Autoregressive Model: The Poisson AR(p) Model." *Political Analysis* 9, no. 2. (February 2001): 164–84.

Braveman, P., A. Meyers, T. Schlenker, and C. Wands. "Public Health and War in Central America." Pp. 238–54 in *War and Public Health*, updated ed., edited by B.S. Levy, and V.W. Sidel. Washington, D.C.: American Public Health Association, 2000.

Brecher, Michael. "Reflections on a Life in Academe." Paper presented at the annual meeting of the International Studies Association, Chicago Ill., February 1995.

Brecher, Michael, and Jonathan Wilkenfeld. *A Study of Crisis.* Ann Arbor: University of Michigan Press, 2000.

Bremer, Stuart. "The Contagiousness of Coercion: The Spread of Serious International Disputes, 1900–1976. " *International Interactions* 9, no. 1 (1982): 29–55.

———. "Dangerous Dyads: Conditions Affecting the Likelihood of Interstate War, 1816–1965." *Journal of Conflict Resolution* 36, no. 2 (June 1992): 309–41.

————. "Democracy and Militarized Interstate Conflict, 1816–1965." *International Interactions* 18, no. 3 (February 1993): 231–49.

Brennan, Geoffrey, and Francis Castles. "Introduction." Pp. 1–24 in *Australia Reshaped: 200 Years of Institutional Transformation*, edited by G. Brennan and F. Castles. Cambridge, U.K.: Cambridge University Press, 2002.

Brewer, Cynthia A. (a). "Color Use Guidelines for Mapping and Visualization." Pp. 123–47 in *Visualization in Modern Cartography*, edited by A.M. MacEachren and D.R.F. Taylor. Tarrytown, N.Y.: Elsevier Science, 1994.

————. (b)."Guidelines for Use of the Perceptual Dimensions of Color for Mapping and Visualization." Pp. 54–63 in *Color Hard Copy and Graphic Arts III: Proceedings of the International Society for Optical Engineering (SPIE)*, edited by J. Bares. San Jose, Calif.: February 1994.

Brody, R. *Assessing the President: The Media, Elite Opinion, and Public Support.* Stanford, Calif.: Stanford University Press, 1991.

Brody, R., and C. Shapiro. "A Reconsideration of the Rally Phenomenon in Public Opinion." Pp. 77–102 in *Political Behavior Annual*, edited by Samuel Long. Boulder, Colo.: Westview, 1989.

Brogan, Patrick. *World Conflicts: Why and Where They Are Happening.* London: Bloomsbury, 1989.

Brule, David, and Alex Mintz. "Public Opinion and the Presidential Use of Force." Paper presented at the annual meeting of the International Studies Association, Montreal, Canada, March 2004.

Bueno de Mesquita, Bruce. *The War Trap.* New Haven, Conn.: Yale University Press, 1981.

Bueno de Mesquita, Bruce, and David Lalman. "Empirical Support for Systemic and Dyadic Explanations of International Conflict." *World Politics* 41, no. 1 (October 1988): 1–20.

————. *War and Reason: Domestic and International Imperatives.* New Haven, Conn.: Yale University Press, 1992.

Bueno de Mesquita, B., J. Morrow, R. Siverson, and A. Smith. (a). "Policy Failure and Political Survival: The Contribution of Political Institutions." *Journal of Conflict Resolution* 43, no. 2 (April 1999): 131–45.

————. (b). "An Institutional Explanation of the Democratic Peace." *American Political Science Review* 93, no. 4 (December 1999): 791–807.

————. "Political Institutions, Political Survival, and Policy Success." Pp. 59–84 in *Governing for Prosperity*, edited by B. Bueno de Mesquita, and H. Root. New Haven, Conn.: Yale University Press, 2000.

Bueno de Mesquita, Bruce, Alastair Smith, Randolph Siverson, and James Morrow. *The Logic of Political Survival.* Cambridge, Mass.: M.I.T. Press, 2003.

Buhaug, Halvard, and Scott Gates. "The Geography of Civil War." *Journal of Peace Research* 39, no. 4 (July 2002): 417–33.

Burnett, D. Graham, Matthew Edney, Mary G. Sponberg Pedley, and David Woodward, eds. *History of Cartography, Volume 4: Cartography in the European Enlightenment.* Chicago: University of Chicago Press, forthcoming.

Calvert, Randall L. "The Value of Biased Information: A Rational Choice Model of Political Advice." *Journal of Politics* 47, no. 2 (June 1985): 530–56.

Canes-Wrone, B. *Who Leads Whom? The Policy Effects of Presidents' Relationship with the Masses.* Unpublished manuscript, forthcoming.

Carment, David, and Frank P. Harvey. *Using Force to Prevent Ethnic Violence: An Evaluation of Theory and Evidence, Praeger Studies on Ethnic and National Identities in Politics.* Westport, Conn.: Praeger, 2001.

Carter, James. *Keeping Faith: Memoirs of a President.* New York: Bantam Books, 1982.

Cederman, Lars-Erik. *Emergent Actors in World Politics: How States and Nations Develop and Dissolve.* Princeton, N.J.: Princeton University Press, 1997.

Cederman, Lars-Erik, and Kristian Skrede Gleditsch. "Conquest and Regime Change: An Evolutionary Model of the Spread of Democracy and Peace." *International Studies Quarterly* (2004).

Centers for Disease Control and Prevention. "Famine-Affected, Refugee, and Displaced Populations: Recommendations for Public Health Issues." *Morbidity and Mortality Weekly Report* 41, no. RR-13 (24 July 1992): 1–76.

Chernoff, Fred. *The Power of International Theory.* London: Routledge, 2005.

Christensen, Eben J., and Steven B. Redd. "Bureaucrats vs. the Ballot Box in Foreign Policy Decision Making: An Experimental Analysis of the Bureaucratic Politics Model and the Poliheuristic Theory." *Journal of Conflict Resolution* 48, no. 1 (February 2004): 69–90.

Christensen, Thomas J., and Jack Synder. "Chain Gangs and Passed Bucks: Predicting Alliance Patterns in Multipolarity." *International Organization* 44, no. 2 (Spring 1990): 137–68.

Clark, D. "Trading Butter for Guns: Domestic Imperatives for Foreign Policy Substitution." *Journal of Conflict Resolution* 45, no. 5 (October 2001): 636–60.

Clark, General Wesley K. *Waging Modern War.* New York: Public Affairs, 2001.

Clausewitz, Carl von. *On War.* Translated by Michael Howard and Peter Paret. Princeton, N.J.: Princeton University Press, 1976 [1832].

Cleveland, William S. *Visualizing Data.* Murray Hill, N.J.: Hobart, 1993.

———. *Elements of Graphing Data.* Pacific Grove, Calif.: Wadsworth, 1994.

Cliff, Andrew D., and J. Keith Ord. *Spatial Autocorrelation.* London: Pion, 1973.

Cobban, Helena. *The Superpowers and the Syrian-Israeli Conflict: Beyond Crisis Management?* New York: Praeger, 1991.

Cohen, William. "The Wrong Target. " *Newshour.* (10 May 1999). Transcript available: http://www.pbs.org/newshour/bb/europe/jan-june99/bombing_5-10.html.

Coleman, J. "Unified Government, Divided Government, and Party Responsiveness." *American Political Science Review* 93, no. 4 (December 1999): 821–35.

Collier, Paul. "On the Economic Consequences of Civil War." *Oxford Economic Papers* 51, no. 1 (January 1999): 168–83.

Collier, Paul., and A. Hoeffler. *Greed and Grievance in Civil War* (Policy Research Paper 2355). Washington, D.C.: World Bank, 2000.

———. "Regional Military Spillovers." Paper presented at the Annual World Bank Conference on Development Economics, Washington, D.C., May 2001.

Cooper, P. *By Order of the President*. Lawrence: University Press of Kansas, 2002.

Cornes, Richard, and Todd Sandler. *The Theory of Externalities, Public Goods, and Club Goods*. Cambridge, U.K.: Cambridge University Press, 1996.

Cortright, David, and Carnegie Commission on Preventing Deadly Conflict. *The Price of Peace: Incentives and International Conflict Prevention, Carnegie Commission on Preventing Deadly Conflict Series*. Lanham, Md.: Rowman & Littlefield Publishers, 1997.

Coser, Lewis. *The Functions of Social Conflict*. New York: Free Press, 1956.

Cox, Gary, and Matthew McCubbins. *Legislative Leviathan: Party Government in the House*. Berkeley, Calif.: University of California Press, 1993.

Cressie, Noel. *Statistics for Spatial Data*. New York: Wiley, 1991.

Daalder, Ivo H. *Getting to Dayton*. Washington D.C.: Brookings Institution Press, 2000.

Dahl, Robert. *Polyarchy: Participation and Opposition*. New Haven, Conn.: Yale University Press, 1971.

Dasgupta, P. *An Inquiry into Well-Being and Destitution*. New York: Oxford University Press, 1993.

Davis, D., and J. Kuritsky. "Violent Conflict and Its Impact on Health Indicators in Sub-Saharan Africa, 1980 to 1997." Paper presented at the annual meeting of the International Studies Association, New Orleans, La., March 2002.

Deaton, A. "Policy Implications of the Gradient of Health and Wealth." *Health Affairs* 21, no. 2 (March–April 2002): 13–30.

De Figueiredo, Rui J. P., and Barry R. Weingast. "The Rationality of Fear: Political Opportunism and Ethnic Conflict." Pp. 261–302 in *Civil Wars, Insecurity, and Intervention*, edited by Barbara F. Walter and Jack Snyder. New York: Columbia University Press, 1999.

DeRouen, Karl. "The Indirect Link: Economics, Politics and the Use of Force." *Journal of Conflict Resolution* 39, no. 4 (December 1995): 671–96.

——. (a). "The Guns-Growth Relationship in Israel." *Journal of Peace Research* 37, no. 1 (January 2000): 69–84.

——. (b)."Presidents and the Diversionary Use of Force: A Research Note." *International Studies Quarterly* 44, no. 2 (June 2000): 317–28.

——. "The Decision Not to Use Force at Dien Bien Phu: A Poliheuristic Perspective." Pp.11–28 in *Integrating Cognitive and Rational Theories of Foreign Policy Decision Making*, edited by A. Mintz. New York: Palgrave Macmillan, 2003.

DeRouen, K., and J. Peake. "The Dynamics of Diversion: The Domestic Implications of Presidential Use of Force." *International Interactions* 28, no. 2 (January 2002): 191–211.

Desch, M.C. "Democracy and Victory: Why Regime Type Hardly Matters." *International Security* 27, no. 2 (Fall 2002): 5–47.

Deutsch, Karl, and J. David Singer. "Multipolar Power Systems and International Stability." *World Politics* 16, no. 3 (April 1964): 390–406.

Diehl, Paul. "Arms Races and Escalation: A Closer Look." *Journal of Peace Research* 20, no. 3 (September 1983): 205–12.

———. "Geography and War: A Review and Assessment of the Empirical Literature." Pp.121–37 in *The New Geopolitics*, edited by Michael D. Ward. Philadelphia: Gordon and Breach, 1992.

———. *International Peacekeeping*. Baltimore, Md.: Johns Hopkins University Press, 1993.

———. *A Road Map to War: Territorial Dimensions of International Conflict*. Nashville, Tenn: Vanderbilt University Press, 1999.

Diehl, Paul F., and Gary Goertz. *War and Peace in International Rivalry*. Ann Arbor: University of Michigan Press, 2000.

Dixon, William J. "Democracy and the Management of International Conflict." *Journal of Conflict Resolution* 37, no. 1 (March 1993): 42–68.

———. "Democracy and the Peaceful Settlement of International Conflict." *American Political Science Review* 88, no. 1 (March 1994): 14–32.

Domke, William, Richard Eichenberg, and Catherine Kelleher. "The Illusion of Choice: Defense and Welfare in Advanced Industrial Democracies, 1948–1978." *American Political Science Review* 77, no. 1 (March 1983): 19–35.

Doyle, Michael W. "War and Peace in Cambodia." Pp. 181–220 in *Civil Wars, Insecurity, and Intervention*, edited by Barbara F. Walter and Jack Snyder. New York: Columbia University Press, 1999.

Doyle, Michael W., and Nicholas Sambanis. *Making War and Building Peace: The United Nations after the Cold War*, forthcoming.

Easterly, William, and Ross Levine. "Troubles with the Neighbours: Africa's Problem, Africa's Opportunity." *Journal of African Economies* 7, no. 1 (March 1998): 120–42.

Edwards, G. *On Deaf Ears: The Limits of the Bully Pulpit*. New Haven, Conn.: Yale University Press, 2003.

Elbadawi, I., and N. Sambanis. "How Much War Will We See? Explaining the Prevalence of Civil War." *Journal of Conflict Resolution* 46, no. 3 (June 2002): 307–34.

Elman, Colin, and Miriam Elman, eds. *Progress in International Relations Theory*. Cambridge, Mass.: MIT Press, 2003.

Enterline, Andrew J., and Kristian S. Gleditsch. "Threats, Opportunity, and Force: Externalization of Domestic Pressure, 1946–82." *International Interactions* 26, no. 1 (June 2000): 21–53.

Enterline, Andrew, and David Sobek. "Fruits of Force? Domestic and Interstate Responses to Domestic Threats and the Fate of Political Leaders." Unpublished Ms., 2001.

European Commission, Joint Research Centre. N.D. www.sensitivityanalysis.jrc.cec.eu.int/default2.asp?page=sa (21 October 2003).

Evans, D.B., A. Tandon, C.J.L. Murray, and J.A. Lauder. *The Comparative Efficiency of National Health Systems in Producing Health: An Analysis of 191 Countries* (GPE Discussion Paper No. 29). Geneva, Switzerland: World Health Organization, 2000.

Evans, D.B., L. Bendib, A. Tandon, K. Lauer, S. Ebenezer, R.C.W. Hutubessy, et al. *Estimates of Income Per Capita, Literacy, Educational Attainment, Absolute Poverty, and Income Gini Coefficients for the World Health Report 2000* (GPE Discussion Paper No. 7). Geneva, Switzerland: World Health Organization, 2000.

Farnham, Barbara. *Roosevelt and the Munich Crisis: A Study of Political Decision-Making.* Princeton, N.J.: Princeton University Press, 2000.

Faust, Katherine, and John Skvoretz. "Comparing Networks across Space and Time, Size and Species." *Sociological Methodology* 32, no. 1 (January 2002): 267–99.

Feachem, R., D. Jamison, and E. Bos. "Changing Patterns of Disease and Mortality in Sub-Saharan Africa." Pp. 3–27 in *Disease and Mortality in Sub-Saharan Africa*, edited by R. Feachem and D. Jamison. New York: Oxford University Press, 1991.

Fearon, James. "Counterfactuals and Hypothesis Testing in Political Science." *World Politics* 43, no. 2 (January 1991): 169–95.

——. (a). "Signaling versus the Balance of Power and Interests." *Journal of Conflict Resolution* 38, no. 2 (June 1994): 236–69.

——. (b). "Domestic Political Audiences and the Escalation of International Disputes." *American Political Science Review* 88, no. 3 (September 1994): 577–92.

——."Rationalist Explanations for War." *International Organization* 49, no. 3 (Summer 1995): 379–414.

——. "Signaling Foreign Policy Interests: Tying Hands versus Sinking Costs." *Journal of Conflict Resolution* 41, no.1 (February 1997): 68–90.

——. "Commitment Problems and the Spread of Ethnic Conflict." Pp. 107–26 in *The International Spread of Ethnic Conflict: Fear, Diffusion, and Escalation*, edited by David Lake and Donald Rothchild. Princeton, N.J.: Princeton University Press, 1998.

Filmer, D., and L. Pritchett. "The Impact of Public Spending on Health: Does Money Matter?" *Social Science and Medicine* 49, no. 10 (November 1999): 1309–23.

Filson, Darren, and Suzanne Werner. "A Bargaining Model of War and Peace: Anticipating the Onset, Duration, and Outcome of War." *American Journal of Political Science* 46, no. 4 (October 2002): 819–37.

Fisher, L. "Deciding on War against Iraq: Institutional Failures." *Political Science Quarterly* 118, no. 3 (Fall 2003): 389–410.

Foege, W. "Arms and Public Health: A Global Perspective." Pp. 3–11 in *War and Public Health*, updated ed., edited by B.S. Levy and V.W. Sidel. Washington, D.C.: American Public Health Association, 2000.

Ford, J. Kevin, Neal Schmitt, Susan L. Schechtman, Brian M. Hults, and Mary L. Doherty. "Process Tracing Methods: Contributions, Problems, and Neglected Research Questions." *Organizational Behavior and Human Decision Processes* 43, no. 1 (February 1989): 75–117.

Fordham, B. (a). "Partisanship, Macroeconomic Policy, and U.S. Uses of Force, 1949–1994." *Journal of Conflict Resolution* 42, no. 4 (August 1998): 418–39.

——. (b). "The Politics of Threat Perception and the Use of Force: A Political Economy Model of U.S. Uses of Force, 1949–1994." *International Studies Quarterly* 42, no. 3 (September 1998): 567–90.

——. "Another Look at 'Parties, Voters, and the Use of Force Abroad.'" *Journal of Conflict Resolution* 46, no. 4 (August 2002): 572–96.

Fordham, B., and C. Sarver. "Militarized Interstate Disputes and United States Uses of Force." *International Studies Quarterly* 45, no. 3 (September 2001): 455–66.

Fortna, Page. (a). "Scraps of Paper? Agreements and the Durability of Peace." *International Organization* 57, no. 2 (Spring 2003): 337–72.

——. (b). "Inside and Out: Peacekeeping and the Duration of Peace after Civil and Interstate Wars." Pp. 97–114 in *Dissolving Boundaries*, edited by Suzanne Werner, David Davis, and Bruce Bueno de Mesquita. New York: Blackwell Publishers, 2003.

Fourth Freedom Forum. *Morbidity and Mortality among Iraqi Children from 1990 through 1998.* http://www.fourthfreedom.org/php/t-si-index.php?hinc=garf-index .hinc (30 March 2004).

Freedman, L., and E. Karsh. *The Gulf Conflict, 1990–1991: Diplomacy and War in the New World Order.* Princeton, N.J.: Princeton University Press, 1993.

Garrett, L. "The Return of Infectious Disease." Pp. 183–94 in *Plague and Politics*, edited by A.T. Price-Smith. New York: Palgrave, 2001.

Gartner, Scott Sigmund, and Randolph M. Siverson. "War Expansion and War Outcome." *Journal of Conflict Resolution* 40, no. 1 (March 1996): 4–15.

Gartzke, Erik, and Quan Li. "All's Well That Ends Well: A Reply to Oneal, Barbieri, & Peters." *Journal of Peace Research* 40, no. 2 (November 2003): 727–32.

Gaubatz, K. "Election Cycles and War." *Journal of Conflict Resolution* 35, no. 2 (June 1991): 212–44.

Gawrych, George. *The Albatross of Decisive Victory: War and Policy between Egypt and Israel in the 1967 and 1973 Arab-Israeli Wars.* Westport, Conn.: Greenwood Press, 2000.

Gelpi, Christopher. "Democratic Diversions: Governmental Structure and the Externalization of Domestic Conflict." *Journal of Conflict Resolution* 41, no. 2 (April 1997): 255–82.

——. "Alliances as Instruments of Intra-Allied Control." Pp. 107–39 in *Imperfect Unions: Security Institutions over Time and Space*, edited by Helga Haftendorn, Robert O. Keohane, and Celeste A. Wallander. New York: Oxford University Press, 1999.

Gelpi, Christopher, and M. Griesdorf. "Winners or Losers? Democracies in International Crisis, 1918–94." *American Political Science Review* 95, no. 3 (September 2001): 633–47.

George, Alexander L. *Presidential Decision Making in Foreign Policy: The Effective Use of Information and Advice.* Boulder, Colo.: Westview, 1980.

——. "Strategies for Preventative Diplomacy and Conflict Resolution: Scholarship for Policy Making." *Cooperation and Conflict* 34, no. 1 (1999): 9–19.

Gerosi, F., and G. King. *Short Term Effects of War Deaths on Public Health in the U.S.* (working paper). Cambridge, Mass.: Harvard University, Center for Basic Research in the Social Sciences, 2002.

Geva, Nehemia, Karl DeRouen, and Alex Mintz. "The Political Incentive Explanation of 'Democratic Peace': Evidence from Experimental Research." *International Interactions* 18, no. 3 (1993): 215–29.

Geva, Nehemia, Russell Driggers, and Alex Mintz. "Effects of Ambiguity on Strategy and Choice in Foreign Policy Decision Making: An Analysis Using the Decision Board Platform." Paper presented at the annual meeting of the American Political Science Association, San Francisco, Calif., September 1997.

Geva, Nehemia, Alex Mintz, and Steven B. Redd. "Structure and Process in Foreign Policy Decision-Making." Discussion paper, Program in Foreign Policy Decision Making, Texas A&M University, 2000.

Ghobarah, H., P. Huth, and B. Russett. "Civil Wars Kill and Maim People—Long After the Shooting Stops." *American Political Science Review* 97, no. 2 (May 2003): 189–202.

——. "Comparative Public Health: The Political Economy of Human Misery and Well-Being." *International Studies Quarterly* 48, no. 1 (March 2004): 73–94.

Gibler, Douglas M., and Meredith Sarkees. "Measuring Alliances: The Correlates of War Formal Interstate Alliance Data Set, 1816–2000." *Journal of Peace Research*, 41, no. 2 (March 2004): 211–22.

Gilpin, Robert. *War and Change in World Politics*. New York: Cambridge University Press, 1981.

Gleditsch, Kristian S. *All International Politics Is Local: The Diffusion of Conflict, Integration, and Democratization*. Ann Arbor: University of Michigan Press, 2002.

——. "A Revised List of Wars between and within Independent States, 1816–2001." *International Interactions* (forthcoming 2004).

Gleditsch, Kristian S., and Michael D. Ward. "Double Take: Reexamining Democracy and Autocracy in Modern Polities." *Journal of Conflict Resolution* 41, no. 3 (June 1997): 361–83.

——. "War and Peace in Time and Space: The Role of Democratization." *International Studies Quarterly* 44, no. 1 (March 2000): 1–29.

——. "Measuring Space: A Minimum Distance Database." *Journal of Peace Research* 38, no. 6 (November 2001): 749–68.

——. "The Diffusion of Democracy and the International Context of Democratization." Typescript, Department of Political Science, University of California, San Diego, 2003.

Gleditsch, Nils Petter, and Håvard Hegre."Peace and Democracy: Three Levels of Analysis." *Journal of Conflict Resolution* 41, no. 2 (April 1997): 283–310.

Gochman, Charles S. "Status, Conflict, and War: The Major Powers, 1920–1975." Ph.D. diss., University of Michigan, 1975.

Goemans, Hein. *War and Punishment: The Causes of War Termination and the First World War*. Princeton, N.J.: Princeton University Press, 2000.

Goemans, Hein, and Scott de Marchi. "Is Jerusalem Divisible? Preference Landscapes and Issue Indivisibility." Paper presented at the Political Economy of Conflict Conference, Yale University, New Haven, Conn., March 23–24, 2001.

Goertz, Gary. "Constraints, Compromises and Decision Making." *Journal of Conflict Resolution* 48, no. 1 (February 2004): 14–37.

Goldstein, Joshua. "Kondratieff Waves as War Cycles." *International Studies Quarterly* 29, no. 4 (December 1985): 411–44.

Goodin, Bob. *The Theory of Institutional Design*. Cambridge, U.K.: Cambridge University Press, 1996.

Goodman, Hirsh, and W. Seth Carus. *The Future Battlefield and the Arab-Israeli Conflict*. London: Transaction Publishers, 1990.

Gowa, Joanne. "Politics at the Water's Edge: Parties, Voters, and the Use of Force Abroad." *International Organization* 52, no. 2 (Spring 1998): 307–24.

——. *Ballots and Bullets: The Elusive Democratic Peace*. Princeton, N.J.: Princeton University Press, 1999.

Gray, Colin S. *Modern Strategy*. Oxford: Oxford University Press, 1999.

Green, Donald, and Ian Shapiro. *Pathologies of Rational Choice Theory*. New Haven, Conn.: Yale University Press, 1994.

Grimmett, Geoffrey, and David Stirzaker. *Probability and Random Processes*. London: Clarendon Press, 1992.

Grimmett, R. "Congressional Use of Funding Cutoffs since 1970 Involving U.S. Military Forces and Overseas Deployments." Congressional Research Service Report for Congress. Order Code RS20775. Washington, D.C., 2001

Grobar, L.M., and S. Gnanaselvam. "The Economic Effects of the Sri Lankan Civil War." *Economic Development and Cultural Change* 41, no. 2 (January 1993): 395–405

Gurr, T.R. *Peoples versus States: Minorities at Risk in the New Century*. Washington, D.C.: United States Institute of Peace, 2000.

Gustafson, P., V. Gomes, C. Veiira, H. Jaensen, R. Seng, R. Norberg, et al. "Tuberculosis Mortality during a Civil War in Guinea-Bissau." *Journal of the American Medical Association* 286, no. 5 (1 August 2001): 599–603.

Hall, David K. "The Laotian War of 1962 and the Indo-Pakistani War of 1971." Pp. 135–221 in *Force without War*, edited by B. Blechman and S. Kaplan. Washington, D.C.: Brookings Institution Press, 1978.

Hampson, Fen Osler. *Nurturing Peace: Why Peace Settlements Succeed or Fail*. Washington, D.C.: U.S. Institute of Peace Press, 1996.

Harary, Frank, Robert Z. Norman, and Dorwin Cartright. *Structural Models: An Introduction to the Theory of Directed Graphs*. New York: Wiley, 1965.

Harley, J. Brian, and David Woodward, eds. *History of Cartography, Volume 2, Book 1: Cartography in the Traditional Islamic and South Asian Societies*. Chicago: University of Chicago Press, 1992.

——, eds. *History of Cartography, Volume 2, Book 2: Cartography in the Traditional East and Southeast Asian Societies*. Chicago: University of Chicago Press, 1994.

Hartman, S.W. "The Impact of Defense Expenditure on the Domestic American Economy, 1964–1972." *Public Administration Review* 33, no. 4 (July–August 1973): 379–90.

Hegre, H., T. Ellingsen, S. Gates, and N.P. Gleditsch. "Toward a Democratic Civil Peace? Democracy, Political Change, and Civil War, 1816–1992." *American Political Science Review* 95, no. 1 (March 2001): 33–48.

Henderson, Errol A., and J. David Singer. "Civil War in the Post-colonial World: 1946–92." *Journal of Peace Research* 37, no. 3 (May 2000): 275–99.

Hensel, Paul R. "Territory: Theory and Evidence on Geography and Conflict." Pp. 57–84 in *What Do We Know about War?* edited by John A. Vasquez. Lanham, Md.: Rowman & Littlefield Publishers, 2000.

Herek, Gregory, Irvin Janis, and Paul Huth. "Decision Making during International Crises: Is Quality of Process Related to Outcome?" *Journal of Conflict Resolution* 31, no. 2 (June 1987): 203–26.

Hess, Gregory D. "An Introduction to Lewis Fry Richardson and His Mathematical Theory of War and Peace." *Conflict Management and Peace Science* 14, no. 1 (Spring 1995): 77–113.

Hewitt, Joseph, and Michael Wilkenfeld. "Democracies in International Crisis." *International Interactions* 22, no. 2 (1996): 123–42.

Hinckley, B. *Less Than Meets the Eye: Foreign Policy Making the Myth of the Assertive Congress*. Chicago: University of Chicago Press, 1994.

Holbrook, Richard. *To End a War*. New York: The Modern Library, 1999.

Howell, W. *Power without Persuasion: The Politics of Direct Presidential Action*. Princeton, N.J.: Princeton University Press, 2003.

Howell, W., S. Adler, C. Cameron, and C. Riemann. "Divided Government and the Legislative Productivity of Congress, 1945–1994." *Legislative Studies Quarterly* 25, no. 2 (May 2000): 285–312.

Howell, W., and J. Pevehouse. "Presidents, Congress, and the Use of Force." *International Organization* (forthcoming).

Humphreys, R. Stephen. *Between Memory and Desire: The Middle East in a Troubled Age*. Berkeley, Calif.: University of California Press, 1999.

Huntington, Samuel. *The Clash of Civilizations and the Remaking of World Order*. New York: Simon & Schuster, 1996.

Huth, Paul K. *Extended Deterrence and the Prevention of War*. New Haven, Conn.: Yale University Press, 1988.

——. "Major Power Intervention in International Crises, 1918–1988." *Journal of Conflict Resolution* 42, no. 6 (December 1998): 744–70.

——. "Deterrence and International Conflict: Empirical Findings and Theoretical Debates." *Annual Review of Political Science* 2 (June 1999): 25–48.

Huth Paul K., and T. Allee. *The Democratic Peace and Territorial Conflict in the Twentieth Century*. Cambridge, U.K.: Cambridge University Press, 2002.

Huth, Paul K., and Bruce Russett. "What Makes Deterrence Work? Cases from 1900 to 1980." *World Politics* 36, no. 4 (July 1984): 496–526.

——. "Deterrence Failure and Crisis Escalation." *International Studies Quarterly* 32, no. 1 (March 1988): 29–45.

Ibrahim, Saad Eddin. (a). "An Islamic Alternative in Egypt: The Muslim Brotherhood and Sadat." Pp. 128–67 in *Egypt, Islam and Democracy: Twelve Critical Essays*. Cairo: The American University in Cairo Press, 1996.

——. (b). "Anatomy of Egypt's Militant Islamic Groups: Methodological Notes and Preliminary Findings." Pp. 256–74 in *Egypt, Islam and Democracy: Twelve Critical Essays*. Cairo: The American University in Cairo Press, 1996.

Isham, Valerie. "An Introduction to Spatial Point Processes and Markov Random Fields." *International Statistical Review* 49, no.1 (April 1981): 21–43.

Jackson, Elmore. *Meeting of Minds: A Way to Peace through Mediation*. New York: McGraw-Hill, 1952.

Jaggers, Keith, and Ted R. Gurr. "Tracking Democracy's Third Wave with the Polity III Data." *Journal of Peace Research* 32, no. 4 (November 1995): 469–82.

——. "Polity III: Regime Change and Political Authority, 1800–1994," 2d release. Boulder, Colo.: Keith Jaggers/College Park, Md.: Ted Robert Gurr, producers. Ann

Arbor, Mich.: Inter-University Consortium for Political and Social Research, distributor, 1996.

James, Patrick, and John R. Oneal. "The Influence of Domestic and International Politics on the President's Use of Force." *Journal of Conflict Resolution* 35, no. 2 (June 1991): 307–32.

Jones, Charles. *Presidency in a Separated System*. Washington, D.C.: Brookings Institution Press, 1994.

Jones, Daniel M., Stuart A. Bremer, and J. David Singer. "Militarized Interstate Disputes, 1816–1992: Rationale, Coding Rules, and Empirical Patterns." *Conflict Management and Peace Science* 15, no. 2 (Fall 1996): 163–213.

Kacowicz, Arie M. *Zones of Peace in the Third World: South America and West Africa in Comparative Perspective*. Albany: State University of New York Press, 1998.

Karnow, Stanley. *Vietnam: A History*. New York: Penguin, 1983.

Karol, D. "Divided Government and U.S. Trade Policy: Much Ado about Nothing?" *International Organization* 54, no. 4 (Autumn 2000): 825–44.

Kennedy, P. *A Guide to Econometrics*. 3d ed. Cambridge, Mass.: MIT Press, 1992.

Khong, Yuen Foong. *Analogies at War: Korea, Munich, Dien Bien Phu and the Vietnam Decisions of 1965*. Princeton, N.J.: Princeton University Press, 1992.

King, Gary, Robert Keohane, and Sidney Verba. *Designing Social Inquiry: Scientific Inference in Qualitative Research*. Princeton, N.J.: Princeton University Press, 1994.

Kinne, Brandon. "Decision Making in Autocratic Regimes: A Poliheuristic Perspective." Unpublished manuscript, Yale University, New Haven, Conn., 2004.

Kinsella, David. "No Rest for the Democratic Peace." *American Political Science Review* 99 (forthcoming).

Kjellén, Rudolf. *Staten som Lifsform* [The state as an organism]. Stockholm: Hugo Geber, 1916.

Klein, Gary. *Intuition at Work*. New York: Bantam Dell, 2002.

Knoke, David. *Political Networks: The Structural Perspective*. New York: Cambridge University Press, 1990.

Krause, K. "Military Statecraft: Power and Influence in Soviet and American Arms Transfer Relationships." *International Studies Quarterly* 35, no. 3 (September 1991): 313–36.

Krehbiel, K. "Where's the Party?" *British Journal of Political Science* 23, no. 2 (April 1993): 235–66.

Krug, E., L. Dahlberg, J. Mercy, A. Zwi, and R. Lozano, eds. *World Report on Violence and Health*. Geneva, Switzerland: World Health Organization, 2002.

Kuhn, Thomas S. *The Structure of Scientific Revolutions*. Chicago: University of Chicago Press, 1962.

Kydd, Andrew. "Which Side Are You On? Bias, Credibility, and Mediation." *American Journal of Political Science* 47, no. 4 (October 2003): 597–611.

Kydd, Andrew, and Barbara F. Walter. "The Politics of Extremist Violence." *International Organization* 56, no. 2 (Spring 2002): 263–96.

Lai, Brian. "Rational Explanations of the Externalization of Internal Conflict." Paper presented at Annual Meeting of the American Political Science Association, Atlanta, Ga., 1999.

Lake, David A., and Patrick Morgan, eds. *Regional Orders: Building Security in a New World*. State College: Pennsylvania State University Press, 1997.

Lake, David A., and Matthew A. Baum. "The Invisible Hand of Democracy: Political Control and the Provision of Public Services." *Comparative Political Studies* 34, no. 6 (August 2001): 587–621.

Larson, Deborah W. "Good Judgment in Foreign Policy." Pp. 3–23 in *Good Judgment in Foreign Policy*, edited by S. Renshon and D. Larson. Lanham, Md.: Rowman & Littlefield Publishers, 2003.

Lau, Richard R., and David P. Redlawsk. "How Voters Decide: A Process Tracing Study of Decision Making during Political Campaigns." Paper presented at the annual meeting of the American Political Science Association, Chicago, Ill., September 1992.

Lee, S.C., Robert G. Muncaster, and Dina A. Zinnes. "The Friend of My Enemy Is My Enemy: Modeling Triadic International Relationships." *Synthese* 100, no. 3 (September 1994): 333–58.

Leeds, Brett Ashley. (a). "Do Alliances Deter Aggression? The Influence of Military Alliances on the Initiation of Militarized Interstate Disputes." *American Journal of Political Science* 47, no. 3 (July 2003): 427–39.

———. (b)."Alliance Reliability in Times of War: Explaining State Decisions to Violate Treaties." *International Organization* 57, no. 4 (October 2003): 801–27.

Leeds, Brett Ashley, and David R. Davis. "Domestic Political Vulnerability and International Disputes." *Journal of Conflict Resolution* 41, no. 6 (December 1997): 814–34.

Leeds, Brett Ashley, Andrew G. Long, and Sara McLaughlin Mitchell. "Re-evaluating Alliance Reliability: Specific Threats, Specific Promises." *Journal of Conflict Resolution* 44, no. 5 (October 2000): 686–99.

Leeds, Brett Ashley, Jeffrey M. Ritter, Sara McLaughlin Mitchell, and Andrew G. Long. "Alliance Treaty Obligations and Provisions, 1815–1944." *International Interactions* 28, no. 3 (January 2002): 261–84.

Lemke, Douglas, and William Reed. "The Relevance of Politically Relevant Dyads." *Journal of Conflict Resolution* 45, no. 1 (February 2001): 126–44.

Lesch, Ann Mosley, and Mark A. Tessler. *Israel, Egypt and the Palestinians: From Camp David to Intifada*. London: Midland Books, 1989.

Levy, Jack. "Alliance Formation and War Behavior: An Analysis of the Great Powers, 1495–1975." *Journal of Conflict Resolution* 25, no. 4 (December 1981): 581–613.

———. "The Diversionary Theory of War: A Critique." Pp. 259–88 in *The Handbook of War Studies*, edited by M. Midlarsky. Boston, Mass.: Unwin Hyman, 1989.

Lewis, David. *Presidents and the Politics of Agency Design*. Stanford, Calif.: Stanford University Press, 2003.

Lian, B., and J. Oneal. "Presidents, the Use of Military Force and Public Opinion." *Journal of Conflict Resolution* 37, no. 2 (June 1993): 277–300.

Lindsay, J. *Congress and the Politics of U.S. Foreign Policy*. Baltimore, Md.: Johns Hopkins University Press, 1994.

Lindsay, J., and R. Ripley. "How Congress Influences Foreign and Defense Policy." Pp. 17–45 in *Congress Resurgent: Foreign and Defense Policy on Capitol Hill*, edited by R. Ripley and J. Lindsay. Ann Arbor: University of Michigan Press, 1993.

Lohmann, S., and S. O'Halloran. "Divided Government and U.S. Trade Policy: Theory and Evidence." *International Organization* 48, no. 4 (Autumn 1994): 595–632.

Long, J.S. *Regression Models for Categorical and Limited Dependent Variables.* Thousand Oaks, Calif.: Sage Publications, 1997.

Luttwak, Edward N. "The Curse of Inconclusive Intervention." Pp. 265–72 in *Turbulent Peace*, edited by Chester A. Crocker, Fen Osler Hampson, and Pamela Aall. Washington, D.C.: United States Institute for Peace Press, 2001.

Mackinder, Halford J. "The Geographical Pivot of History." *Geographical Journal* 23, no. 4 (April 1904): 421–44.

Mahan, Alfred Thayer. *The Influence of Sea Power upon History, 1660–1783.* Boston, Mass.: Little, Brown, 1890.

Mansfield, Edward. "Distribution of Wars over Time." *World Politics* 41, no. 1 (October 1988): 21–51.

———. *Power, Trade, and War.* Princeton, N.J.: Princeton University Press, 1994.

Mansfield, Edward, and Jon Pevehouse. "Trade Blocs, Trade Flows, and International Conflict." *International Organization* 54, no. 4 (Autumn 2000): 775–808.

Maoz, Zeev. *National Choices and International Processes.* Cambridge, U.K.: Cambridge University Press, 1990.

———. *Domestic Sources of Global Change.* Ann Arbor: University of Michigan Press, 1996.

———. "Decisional Stress, Individual Choice and Policy Outcomes: The Arab-Israeli Conflict." Pp.163–81 in *Decision Making on War and Peace: The Cognitive-Rational Debate*, edited by N. Geva and A. Mintz. Boulder, Colo.: Lynne Rienner. 1997.

———. Dyadic MID Dataset (1999). http://spirit.tau.ac.il/zeevmaoz/dyadmid.html.

———. "The Street-Gangs of World Politics: The Origins, Management, and Consequences of International Alliances, 1816–1986." Pp. 111–44 in *What Do We Know about War?* edited by John A. Vasquez. Boulder, Colo.: Rowman & Littlefield Publishers, 2000.

———. "Democratic Networks: Connecting National, Dyadic, and Systemic Levels-of-Analysis in the Study of Democracy and War." Pp. 141–88 in *War in a Changing World*, edited by Zeev Maoz and Azar Gat. Ann Arbor: University of Michigan Press, 2001

———. "An Index of Network Polarization." Mimeographed. Tel Aviv University, April 2003.

———. "Pacifism and Fightaholism in International Politics: A Structural History of National and Dyadic Conflict, 1816–1992." *International Studies Review* (forthcoming 2005).

Maoz, Zeev, and Nasrin Abdolali. "Regime Types and International Conflict, 1816–1976." *Journal of Conflict Resolution* 33, no. 1 (March 1989): 3–35.

Maoz, Zeev, Alex Mintz, T. Clifton Morgan, Glenn Palmer, and Richard Stoll, eds. *Multiple Paths to Knowledge: Methodology in the Study of Conflict Management and Conflict Resolution*. Lanham, Md.: Lexington Books, 2004.

Maoz, Zeev, and Ben D. Mor. *Bound by Struggle: The Strategic Evolution of Enduring Rivalries*. Ann Arbor: University of Michigan Press, 2002.

Maoz, Zeev, and Bruce Russett. "Alliances, Contiguity, Wealth, and Political Stability: Is the Lack of Conflict among Democracies a Statistical Artifact?" *International Interactions* 17, no. 3 (Spring 1992): 245–67.

———. "Normative and Structural Causes of Democratic Peace: 1946–1986." *American Political Science Review* 87, no. 3 (September 1993): 624–38.

Maoz, Zeev, Lesley Terris, and Ranan Kuperman. "International Networks and System Stability." Paper presented at the annual meeting of the International Studies Association, New Orleans, La., March 24–27, 2002.

Maoz, Zeev, Lesley Terris, Ranan Kuperman, and Ilan Talmud. "International Networks and the Evolution of the International System, 1816–1990." Paper presented at the Peace Science Society (International), Tucson, Ariz., October 28–30, 2002.

March J.G., and J.P. Olsen. "Institutional Perspectives on Political Institutions." *Governance* 9, no. 3 (July 1996): 247–64.

Marshall, Monty G., and Keith Jaggers. "Polity IV Project: Political Regime Characteristics and Transitions, 1800–2002." http://www.cidcm.umd.edu/inscr/polity/ (September 2003).

Martin, L. *Democratic Commitments: Legislatures and International Cooperation*. Princeton, N.J.: Princeton University Press, 2000.

Mathers, C., R. Sadana, J. Salomon, C.J.L. Murray, and A. Lopez. *Estimates of DALE for 191 Countries: Methods and Results* (GPE Working Paper No. 16). Geneva, Switzerland: World Health Organization, 2000.

Mayer, K. *With the Stroke of a Pen*. Princeton, N.J.: Princeton University Press, 2001.

Mayhew, David. *Divided We Govern*. New Haven, Conn.: Yale University Press, 1991.

Mearsheimer, John. "Back to the Future: Instability in Europe after the Cold War." *International Security* 15, no. 1 (Summer 1990): 5–56.

Mechanic, D. "Disadvantage, Inequality, and Social Policy." *Health Affairs* 21, no. 2 (March–April 2002): 48–59.

Meernik, J. "Presidential Support in Congress: Conflict and Consensus on Foreign and Defense Policy." *Journal of Politics* 55, no. 3 (August 1993): 569–87.

———. "Presidential Decision Making and the Political Use of Military Force." *International Studies Quarterly* 38, no. 1 (March 1994): 121–38.

———. "Modeling International Crises and the Political Use of Military Force by the USA." *Journal of Peace Research* 37, no. 5 (September 2000): 547–62.

Meernik, James, and Peter Waterman. "The Myth of Diversionary Use of Force by American Presidents." *Political Research Quarterly* 49, no. 3 (September 1996): 573–90.

Midlarsky, Manus I. *On War: Political Violence in the International System*. New York: Free Press, 1975.

Miers, Anne C., and T. Clifton Morgan. "Multilateral Sanctions and Foreign Policy Success: Can Too Many Cooks Spoil the Broth?" *International Interactions* 28, no. 2 (April–June 2002): 117–36.

Miller, Ross A. "Regime Type, Strategic Interaction, and the Diversionary Use of Force." *Journal of Conflict Resolution* 43, no. 3 (June 1999): 388–402.

Milner, H. *Interests, Institutions, and Information*. Princeton, N.J.: Princeton University Press, 1997.

Mintz, Alex. "Guns versus Butter: A Disaggregated Analysis." *American Political Science Review* 83, no. 4 (December 1989): 1285–93.

——. "The Decision to Attack Iraq: A Noncompensatory Theory of Decision Making." *Journal of Conflict Resolution* 37, no. 4 (December 1993): 595–618.

——, ed. *Integrating Cognitive and Rational Theories of Foreign Policy Decision Making*. New York: Palgrave Macmillan, 2003.

——(a). "How Do Leaders Make Decisions? A Poliheuristic Perspective." *Journal of Conflict Resolution* 48, no. 1 (February 2004): 3–13.

——(b). "Foreign Policy Decision Making in Familiar and Unfamiliar Settings: An Experimental Study of High-Ranking Military Officers." *Journal of Conflict Resolution* 48, no. 1 (February 2004): 91–104.

——(c). "How Leaders Make Decisions." Unpublished manuscript, United Nations Studies at Yale, 2004.

Mintz, Alex, and Nehemia Geva. "The Poliheuristic Theory of Foreign Policy Decision-Making." Pp. 81–101 in *Decision Making on War and Peace: The Cognitive-Rational Debate*, edited by N. Geva and A. Mintz. Boulder, Colo.: Lynne Rienner, 1997.

Mintz, Alex, Nehemia Geva, Steven Redd, and Amy Carnes. "The Effect of Dynamic and Static Choice Sets on Political Decision Making: An Analysis Using the Decision Board Platform." *American Political Science Review* 91, no. 3 (September 1997): 553–66.

Mintz, Alex, and Chi Huang. "Defense Expenditures, Economic Growth, and the 'Peace Dividend'" *American Political Science Review* 84, no. 4 (December 1990): 1283–93.

——. "Guns versus Butter: The Indirect Link." *American Journal of Political Science* 35, no. 3 (August 1991): 738–57.

Mintz, Alex, and Shaul Mishal. "Decision Matrixes and Outcomes: Arafat and Sharon's Policy Alternatives and Considerations in the Intifada." Paper presented at the Gilman Conference on New Directions in International Relations. Yale University, New Haven, Conn., February 2003.

Mintz, Alex, and Michael D. Ward. "The Political Economy of Military Spending in Israel." *American Political Science Review* 83, no. 2 (June 1989): 521–33.

Mitchell, S., and W. Moore. "Presidential Uses of Force during the Cold War: Aggregation, Truncation, and Temporal Dynamics." *American Journal of Political Science* 46, no. 2 (April 2002): 438–53.

Modelski, George. "Long Cycles, Kondratieffs and Alternating Innovations: Implications for US Foreign Policy." Pp. 63–83 in *Political Economy of Foreign Affairs*

Behavior, edited by C.W. Kegley and P. McGowan. Beverly Hills, Calif.: Sage, 1981.

Monmonier, Mark, and David Woodward, eds. *History of Cartography, Volume 6: Cartography in the Twentieth Century*. Chicago: University of Chicago Press, forthcoming.

Moon, B. *The Political Economy of Basic Human Needs*. Ithaca, N.Y.: Cornell University Press, 1991.

Moore, Will H. "The Repression of Dissent." *Journal of Conflict Resolution* 44, no.1 (February 2000): 107–27.

Moore, W., and D. Lanoue. "Domestic Politics and U.S. Foreign Policy: A Study of Cold War Conflict Behavior." *Journal of Politics* 65, no. 2 (May 2003): 376–97.

Moran, Patrick A.P. "A Test for Serial Independence of Residuals." *Biometrika* 37, nos. 1/2 (June 1950): 178–81.

Morgan, T. Clifton, and C. J. Anderson. "Domestic Support and Diversionary External Conflict in Great Britain, 1950–1992." *Journal of Politics* 61, no. 3 (August 1999): 799–814.

Morgan, T. Clifton, and Kenneth N. Bickers. "Domestic Discontent and the External Use of Force." *Journal of Conflict Resolution* 36, no. 1 (March 1992): 25–52.

Morgan, T. Clifton, and S. Campbell. "Domestic Structure, Decisional Constraint, and War: So Why Kant Democracies Fight?" *Journal of Conflict Resolution* 35, no. 2 (June 1991): 187–211.

Morrow, James. "A Twist of Truth: A Reexamination of the Effects of Arms Races on the Occurrence of War." *Journal of Conflict Resolution* 33, no. 3 (September 1989): 500–29.

———. "Alliances, Credibility, and Peacetime Costs." *Journal of Conflict Resolution* 38, no. 2 (June 1994): 270–97.

Morton, Rebecca B. *Methods and Models: A Guide to the Empirical Analysis of Formal Models in Political Science*. Cambridge, U.K.: Cambridge University Press, 1999.

Moscicki, A.-B., N. Hills, S. Shiboski, K. Powell, N. Jay, E. Hanson, et al. "Risks for Incident Human Papillomavirus and Low-Grade Squamous Intrepithelial Lesion Development in Young Females." *Journal of the American Medical Association* 285, no. 23 (20 June 2001): 2995–3002.

Moul, William B. "Great Power Nondefense Alliances and the Escalation to War of Conflicts between Unequals, 1815–1939." *International Interactions* 15, no. 1 (January–March 1988): 25–43.

Mueller, Dennis. *Public Choice II*. New York: Cambridge University Press, 1989.

Mueller, J. *War, Presidents, and Public Opinion*. New York: Wiley Press, 1973.

Murdoch, J., and T. Sandler. "Economic Growth, Civil Wars, and Spatial Spillovers." *Journal of Conflict Resolution* 46, no. 1 (February 2002): 91–110.

Murdoch, James C., Todd Sandler, and Keith Sargent. "A Tale of Two Collectives: Sulfur versus Nitrogen Oxides Emission Reduction in Europe." *Economica* 64, no. 254 (May 1997): 281–301.

Murray, C.J.L., and A. Lopez, eds. *The Global Burden of Disease*. Cambridge, Mass.: Harvard University, School of Public Health, on behalf of the WHO and the World Bank, 1996.

———. "Progress and Directions in Refining the Global Burden of Disease Approach: A Response to Williams." *Health Economics 9*, no. 1 (January 2000): 69–82.

Murray, C.J.L., J. Salomon, C. Mathers, and A. Lopez. *Summary Measures of Population Health: Concepts, Ethics, Measurement, and Applications*. Geneva, Switzerland: World Health Organization, 2002.

Muthoo, Abhinay. *Bargaining Theory with Applications*. New York: Cambridge University Press, 1999.

Nemeth, R. J., and D.A. Smith. "International Trade and World System Structure." *Review 8*, no. 4 (Spring 1985): 517–60.

Neteler, Marcus, and Helena Mitasova. *Open Source GIS: A GRASS GIS Approach*. Dordrecht: Kluwer Academic, 1997.

Nicholson, Michael. "Lewis Fry Richardson and the Study of the Causes of War." *British Journal of Political Science 29*, no. 3 (June 1999): 541–63.

Nincic, Miroslav. "Loss Aversion and the Domestic Context of Military Intervention." *Political Research Quarterly 50*, no. 1 (March 1997): 97–120.

Northedge, F. S. and Michael D. Donelan. *International Disputes: The Political Aspects*. London: Europa, 1971.

O'Loughlin, John, Michael D. Ward, Corey L. Lofdahl, Jordin S. Cohen, David S. Brown, David Reilly, Kristian S. Gleditsch, and Michael Shin. "The Diffusion of Democracy, 1946–1994." *Annals of the Association of American Geographers 88*, no. 4 (December 1998): 545–74.

Olson, M. "Dictatorship, Democracy, and Development." *American Political Science Review 87*, no. 3 (September 1993): 567–76.

Oneal, John R. "Empirical Support for the Liberal Peace." Pp. 189–206 in *Economic Interdependence and International Conflict: New Perspectives on an Enduring Debate*, edited by Edward Mansfield and Brian Pollins. Ann Arbor: University of Michigan Press, 2003.

Oneal, John R., and James Ray. "New Tests for Democratic Peace Controlling for Economic Interdependence, 1950–1985." *Political Research Quarterly 50*, no. 4 (December 1997): 751–75.

Oneal, John R., and Bruce M. Russett. "The Classical Liberals Were Right: Democracy, Interdependence, and Conflict, 1950–1985." *International Studies Quarterly 41*, no. 2 (June 1997): 267–95.

Oneal, John R., and Jaroslav Tir. "Do Diversionary Uses of Force Threaten the Democratic Peace?" University of Alabama, Unpublished Ms., 2003.

Ord, J. Keith, and Arthur Getis. "Local Spatial Autocorrelation Statistics: Distributional Issues and an Application." *Geographical Analysis 27*, no. 4 (October 1995): 286–306.

Oren, Ido. "The War Proneness of Alliances." *Journal of Conflict Resolution 34*, no. 2 (June 1990): 208–33.

Østerud, Øyvind. "The Uses and Abuses of Geopolitics." *Journal of Peace Research 25*, no. 2 (June 1988): 191–99.

Ostrom, Charles W., and Brian L. Job. "The President and the Political Use of Force." *American Political Science Review* 80, no. 2 (June 1986): 541–66.

Ostrom, C., and D. Simon. "Promise and Performance: A Dynamic Model of Presidential Popularity." *American Political Science Review* 79, no. 2 (June 1985): 334–58.

Payne, John W., James R. Bettman, and Eric Johnson. *The Adaptive Decision Maker*. Cambridge, U.K.: Cambridge University Press, 1993.

Pedersen, D. "Political Violence, Ethnic Conflict, and Contemporary Wars: Broad Implications for Health and Well-Being." *Social Science and Medicine* 55, no. 2 (July 2002): 175–90.

Peterson, M. *Legislating Together: The White House and Capitol Hill from Eisenhower to Reagan*. Cambridge, Mass.: Harvard University Press, 1990.

Peterson, P. "The International System and Foreign Policy." Pp. 3–22 in *The President, the Congress, and the Making of Foreign Policy*, edited by P. Peterson. Norman: University of Oklahoma Press, 1994.

Pindyck, R., and D. Rubinfeld. *Econometric Models & Economic Forecasts*. New York: McGraw Hill, 1991.

Polachek, Solomon. "Why do Democracies Cooperate More and Fight Less: The Relationship between International Trade and Cooperation." *Review of International Economics* 5, no. 3 (August 1997): 295–309.

Pollack, Kenneth M. (a.) *The Threatening Storm: The Case for Invading Iraq*. New York: Random House, 2002.

———. (b). "Next Stop Baghdad?" *Foreign Affairs* 81, no. 2 (March–April 2002): 32–47.

Posen, Barry. "The Security Dilemma and Ethnic Conflict." Pp. 27–47 in *Ethnic Conflict and International Security*, edited by Michael E. Brown. Princeton, N.J.: Princeton University Press, 1993.

Pouillier, J.P., and P. Hernandez. *Estimates of National Health Accounts: Aggregates for 191 Countries in 1997* (GPE Discussion Paper No. 26). Geneva, Switzerland: World Health Organization, 2000.

Powell, Robert. "Crisis Bargaining, Escalation, and MAD." *American Political Science Review* 81, no. 3 (September 1987): 717–35.

———. *In the Shadow of Power*. Princeton, N.J.: Princeton University Press, 1999.

———. "The Inefficient Use of Power: Costly Conflict with Complete Information." Unpublished manuscript. Berkeley, Calif., 2003.

Price-Smith, A.T. *The Health of Nations: Infectious Disease, Environmental Change, and Their Effects on National Security and Development*. Cambridge, Mass.: MIT Press, 2002.

Princen, Thomas. *Intermediaries in International Conflict*. Princeton, N.J.: Princeton University Press, 1992.

Prins, B., and C. Sprecher. "Institutional Constraints, Political Opposition, and Interstate Dispute Escalation: Evidence from Parliamentary Systems, 1946–89." *Journal of Peace Research* 36, no. 3 (May 1999): 271–88.

Pritchett, L., and L. Summers. "Wealthier Is Healthier." *Journal of Human Resources* 31, no. 4 (Autumn 1996): 841–68.

Przeworski, A., M. Alvarez, J.A. Cheibub, and F. Limongi. *Democracy and Development: Political Institutions and Well-Being in the World, 1950–1990.* Cambridge, U.K.: Cambridge University Press, 2000.

Putnam, Robert. "Diplomacy and Domestic Politics: The Logic of Two-Level Games." *International Organization* 42, no. 3 (Summer 1988): 427–60.

Raiffa, Howard. *The Art and Science of Negotiation.* Cambridge, Mass.: Harvard University Press, 1982.

Ray, James L. "Status Inconsistency and War Involvement among European States, 1816–1970." Ph.D. diss., University of Michigan, 1974.

———. "Does Democracy Correlate With Peace?" Pp. 299–316 in *What Do We Know About War?* edited by John A. Vasquez. Lanham, Md.: Rowman & Littlefield Publishers, 2000.

———. "Integrating Levels of Analysis in World Politics." *Journal of Theoretical Politics* 13, no. 4 (October 1, 2001): 355–88.

Redd, Steven B. "The Influence of Advisors and Decision Strategies on Foreign Policy Choices: President Clinton's Decision to Use Force in Kosovo." Paper presented at the annual meeting of the International Studies Association, Chicago, Ill., February 2001.

———. "The Influence of Advisors on Foreign Policy Decision Making: An Experimental Study." *Journal of Conflict Resolution* 46, no. 3 (June 2002): 335–64.

——— "The Poliheuristic Theory of Foreign Policy Decision Making: Experimental Evidence." Pp. 101–26 in *Integrating Cognitive and Rational Theories of Foreign Policy Decision Making*, edited by A. Mintz. New York: Palgrave Macmillan, 2003.

Reed, William. "A Unified Statistical Model of Conflict Onset and Escalation." *American Journal of Political Science* 44, no. 1 (January 2000): 84–93.

Regan, Patrick M. *Civil Wars and Foreign Powers.* Ann Arbor: University of Michigan Press, 2000.

———. "Third-Party Interventions and the Duration of Intrastate Conflicts." *Journal of Conflict Resolution* 46, no. 1 (February 2002): 55–73.

Reiter, Dan. "Exploding the Power Keg Myth: Preemptive Wars Almost Never Happen." *International Security* 20, no. 2 (Autumn 1995): 5–34.

———. "Exploring the Bargaining Model of War." *Perspectives on Politics* 1, no. 1 (March 2003): 27–43.

Reiter, Dan, and Allan C. Stam. *Democracies at War.* Princeton, N.J.: Princeton University Press, 2002.

———. "Understanding Victory: Why Political Institutions Matter." *International Security* 28, no.1 (Summer 2003): 168–79.

Reiter, D., and E. Tillman. "Public, Legislative, and Executive Constraints on the Democratic Initiation of Conflict." *Journal of Politics* 64, no. 3 (August 2002): 810–27.

Richards, Diana, T. Clifton Morgan, Rick Wilson, Valarie Schwebach, and Garry Young. "Good Times, Bad Times, and the Diversionary Use of Force." *Journal of Conflict Resolution* 37, no. 3 (1993): 504–36.

Richardson, Lewis Fry. *Statistics of Deadly Quarrels.* Pittsburgh, Pa.: Quadrangle/Boxwood, 1960.

——. "The Problem of Contiguity: An Appendix to Statistics of Deadly Quarrels." [1942] *General Systems: Yearbook of the Society for General Systems Research* 6 (1961): 139–87.

Riggle, Ellen D. B., and Mitzi M. S. Johnson. "Age Difference in Political Decision Making: Strategies for Evaluating Political Candidates." *Political Behavior* 18, no. 1 (March 1996): 99–118.

Ripley, Brian D. *Statistical Inference for Spatial Processes*. Cambridge, U.K.: Cambridge University Press, 1988.

Roberts, L., C. Hale, F. Belyakdoumi, L. Cobey, R. Ondeko, M. Despines, et al. *Mortality in Eastern Democratic Republic of Congo*. New York: International Rescue Committee, 2001.

Rodrik, Dani. "Where Did All the Growth Go? External Shocks, Social Conflict, and Growth Collapses." *Journal of Economic Growth* 4, no. 4 (December 1999): 385–412.

Rosato, Sebastian. "The Flawed Logic of Democratic Peace Theory." *American Political Science Review* 97, no. 4 (November 2003): 585–602.

Rosenfeld, Richard. "The Case of the Unsolved Crime Decline." *Scientific American* 290, no. 2 (February 2004): 82–89.

Rousseau, David, C. Gelpi, D. Reiter, and Paul Huth. "Assessing the Dyadic Nature of the Democratic Peace." *American Political Science Review* 90, no. 3 (September 1996): 512–33.

Rubinstein, Ariel. "Perfect Equilibrium in a Bargaining Model." *Econometrica* 50, no. 1 (January 1982): 97–110.

Rudalevige, A. *Managing the President's Program*. Princeton, N.J.: Princeton University Press, 2002.

Rummel, R. J. "Democracy, Power, Genocide, and Mass Murder." *Journal of Conflict Resolution* 39, no. 1 (March 1995): 3–26.

——. *Power Kills: Democracy as a Method of Non-violence*. New Brunswick, N.J.: Transaction, 1997.

Russett, Bruce. *International Regions and the International System*. Chicago: Rand McNally, 1967.

——. "International Behavior Research: Case Studies and Cumulation." Pp. 425–43 in *Approaches to the Study of Political Science*, edited by Michael Hass and Henry Kariel. San Francisco, Calif.: Chandler, 1970.

——. "Defense Expenditures and National Well-Being." *American Political Science Review* 76, no. 4 (December 1982): 767–77.

——. "Economic Decline, Electoral Pressure, and the Initiation of Interstate Conflict." Pp. 123–140 in *Prisoners of War?* edited by C. Gochman and A. Sabrosky. Lexington, Mass.: D.C. Heath, 1990.

Russett, Bruce, and John R. Oneal. *Triangulating Peace: Democracy, Interdependence, and International Organizations*. New York: W.W. Norton, 2001.

Russo, J. Edward, and Barbara Anne Dosher. "Strategies for Multiattribute Binary Choice." *Journal of Experimental Psychology: Learning, Memory, and Cognition* 9, no. 4 (October 1983): 676–96.

Sachs, J. "Helping the World's Poorest." Policy paper, Harvard University, Center for International Development, 1999: www.cid.harvard.edu/cidinthenews/articles/sf9108 .html (11 Dec. 2003).

Salehyan, Idean, and Kristian Skrede Gleditsch. "Refugee Flows and the Spread of Civil War." Typescript, Department of Political Science, University of California, San Diego, 2003.

Sambanis, Nicholas. "Do Ethnic and Nonethnic Civil Wars Have the Same Causes? A Theoretical and Empirical Inquiry (Part I)." *Journal of Conflict Resolution* 45, no. 3 (June 2001): 259–82.

———. "A Review of Recent Advances and Future Directions in the Literature on Civil War." *Defence and Peace Economics* 13, no. 3 (June 2002): 215–44.

———. "Using Case Studies to Refine and Expand the Theory of Civil War." In *Economic Models & Case Studies of Civil War*," edited by Paul Collier and Nicholas Sambanis, forthcoming.

Sarkees, Meredith Reid. "The Correlates of War Data on War: An Update to 1997." *Conflict Management and Peace Science* 18, no. 1 (Fall 2000): 123–44.

Sass, J., and L. Ashford. *2002 Women of Our World*. New York: Population Reference Bureau, 2002.

Sathasivam, Kanishkan "No Other Choice: Pakistan's Decision to Test the Bomb." Pp. 55–76 in *Integrating Cognitive and Rational Theories of Foreign Policy Decision Making*, edited by A. Mintz. New York: Palgrave Macmillan, 2003.

Sayrs, Lois. "The Long Cycle in International Relations: A Markov Specification." *International Studies Quarterly* 37, no. 2 (June 1993): 215–37.

Schelling, Thomas. *The Strategy of Conflict*. London: Oxford University Press, 1960.

Schnietz, K. "The Reaction of Private Interests to the 1934 Reciprocal Trade Agreements Act." *International Organization* 57, no. 1 (Winter 2003): 213–38.

Schrodt, Philip A. "Detecting United States Mediation Styles in the Middle East, 1979–1998." Pp. 99–124 in *Multiple Paths to Knowledge: Methodology in the Study of Conflict Management and Conflict Resolution*, edited by Z. Maoz, A. Mintz, T. C. Morgan, G. Palmer, and R. Stoll. Lanham, Md.: Lexington Books, 2004.

Schrodt, Philip A., and Alex Mintz. "The Conditional Probability Analysis of Events Data." *American Journal of Political Science* 32, no. 1 (February 1988): 217–30.

Schultz, Kenneth A. "Domestic Opposition and Signaling in International Crises." *The American Political Science Review* 92, no. 4 (December 1998): 829–44.

———. *Democracy and Coercive Diplomacy*. Cambridge, U.K.: Cambridge University Press, 2001.

Sen, A. *Poverty and Famine*. New York: Oxford University Press, 1981.

Senese, Paul D. "Between Disputes and War: The Effect of Joint Democracy on Interstate Conflict Escalation." *Journal of Politics* 59, no. 1 (February 1997): 1–27.

Shah, G. *Public Health and Urban Development: The Plague in Surat*. London: Sage, 1997.

Shazly, Saad El. *Crossing the Sinai*. Washington, D.C.: American Middle East Research Association, 1980.

Sherman, R. "Delegation, Ratification, and U.S. Trade Policy: Why Divided Government Causes Lower Tariffs." *Comparative Political Studies* 35, no. 10 (December 2002): 1171–97.

Signorino, Curtis S., and Jeffery M. Ritter. "Tau-b or Not Tau-b: Measuring the Similarity of Foreign Policy Positions." *International Studies Quarterly* 43, no. 1 (March 1999): 115–44.

Singer, J. David. "The Level-of-Analysis Problem in International Relations." Pp. 77–92 in *The International System: Theoretical Essays*, edited by Klaus Knorr and Sidney Verba. Princeton, N.J.: Princeton University Press, 1961.

——. "The Incomplete Theorist: Insight without Evidence." Pp. 62–86 in *Contending Approaches to International Politics*, edited by K. Knorr and J. N. Rosenau. Princeton, N.J.: Princeton University Press, 1969.

——. "Reconstructing the Correlates of War Capabilities Dataset on Material Capabilities of States, 1816–1985." *International Interactions* 14, no. 2 (April–June 1988): 115–32.

——. "Cultural Composition of States Data, 1820–1990." Correlates of War Project, Department of Political Science, University of Michigan (1995).

Singer, J. David, Stuart Bremer, and John Stuckey. "Capability Distribution, Uncertainty, and Major Power War, 1820–1965." Pp. 19–48 in *Peace, War, and Numbers*, edited by Bruce Russett. Beverly Hills, Calif.: Sage, 1972.

Singer, J. David, and Thomas Cusack. "Periodicity, Inexorability, and Steersmanship in International War." Pp. 404–25 in *From National Development to Global Community*, edited by R. Merritt and B. Russett. London: Allen & Unwin, 1981.

Singer, J. David, and Melvin Small. "National Alliance Commitments and War Involvement, 1815–1945." *Peace Research Society (International) Papers* 5 (1966): 109–40.

——. "Alliance Aggregation and the Onset of War." Pp. 247–86 in *Quantitative International Politics: Insight and Evidence*, edited by J. David Singer. New York: Free Press, 1968.

——. *National Material Capabilities Dataset. Study No. 9903.* Ann Arbor, Mich.: Inter-University Consortium for Political and Social Research, 1993.

——. "National Material Capabilities Codebook," Correlates of War Project, University of Michigan. http://www.umich.edu/~cowproj/capabilities.html (September 2003).

Siverson, Randolph M., and Harvey Starr. *The Diffusion of War: A Study in Opportunity and Willingness*. Ann Arbor: University of Michigan Press, 1991.

Slantchev, Branislav. (a). "The Power to Hurt: Costly Conflict with Completely Informed States." *American Political Science Review* 97, no. 1 (February 2003): 123–33.

——. (b). "The Principle of Convergence in Wartime Negotiations." *American Political Science Review* 97, no. 1 (November 2003): 621–33.

Small, Melvin, and J. David Singer. *Resort to Arms*. Beverly Hills, Calif.: Sage Publications, 1982.

Smith, Alastair. "Alliance Formation and War." *International Studies Quarterly* 39, no. 4 (December 1995): 405–25.

——. "Diversionary Foreign Policy in Democratic Systems." *International Studies Quarterly* 40, no. 1 (March 1996): 133–54.

——. "The Nature of Warfare: Power, Bargaining, Super Weapons, Elections and the Democratic Peace." Paper presented at the Western regional meeting of the International Studies Association, Davis, Calif., October 1997.

——. (a)."Fighting Battles, Winning Wars." *Journal of Conflict Resolution* 42, no. 3 (June 1998): 301–20.

——. (b). "International Crises and Domestic Politics." *American Political Science Review* 92, no. 3 (September 1998): 623–38.

——. (c). "Extended Deterrence and Alliance Formation." *International Interactions* 24, no. 4 (October–December 1998): 315–43.

Smith, Alastair, and Allan C. Stam. (a). "Mediation and Peacekeeping in a Random Walk Model of War." *International Studies Review* 5, no. 4 (December 2003): 115–35.

——. (b). "Mediation and Peacekeeping in a Random Walk Model of Civil and Interstate War." Pp. 115–36 in *Dissolving Boundaries*, edited by Suzanne Werner, David Davis, and Bruce Bueno de Mesquita. New York: Blackwell Publishers, 2003.

——. "Bargaining and the Nature of War." *Journal of Conflict Resolution* (forthcoming October 2004).

Smith, Dan. *The Penguin Atlas of War and Peace*. East Rutherford, N.J.: Penguin USA, 2003.

Smith, Dan, and Michael Kidron. *The State of the World Atlas*. East Rutherford, N.J.: Penguin USA, 2003.

Snyder, David, and Edward L. Kick. "Structural Position in the World System and Economic Growth, 1955–1970." *American Journal of Sociology* 84, no. 4 (March 1979): 1096–126.

Solingen, Ethel. *Regional Orders at Century's Dawn: Global and Domestic Influences on Grand Strategy*. Princeton, N.J.: Princeton University Press, 1998.

Spiezio, K. Edward. "British Hegemony and Major Power War, 1815–1939: An Empirical Test of Gilpin's Model of Hegemonic Governance." *International Studies Quarterly* 34, no. 2 (June 1990): 165–81.

Spykman, Nicolas. *The Geography of Peace*. New York: Harcourt, Brace, 1944.

Starr, Harvey. *Anarchy, Order, and Integration: How to Manage Interdependence*. Ann Arbor: University of Michigan Press, 1997.

——. "Substitutability in Foreign Policy: Theoretically Central, Empirically Elusive." *Journal of Conflict Resolution* 44, no. 1 (February 2000): 128–38.

Starr, H., and G.D. Thomas. "The 'Nature' of Contiguous Borders: Ease of Interaction, Salience, and the Analysis of Crisis." *International Interactions* 28, no. 3 (January 2002): 213–35.

Stedman, Stephen John. "Spoiler Problems in Peace Processes." *International Security* 22, no. 2 (Fall 1997): 5–53.

Steiber, Steven. "The World System and World Trade: An Empirical Exploration of Conceptual Conflict." *Sociological Quarterly* 20, no. 1 (Winter 1979): 23–36.

Stein, A.A. *The Nation at War*. Baltimore: Johns Hopkins University Press, 1980.

Stein, Janice G., and David A. Welch. "Rational and Psychological Approaches to the Study of International Conflict: Comparative Strengths and Weaknesses." Pp. 51–77 in *Decision-Making on War and Peace: The Cognitive-Rational Debate*, edited by N. Geva and A. Mintz. Boulder, Colo.: Lynne Rienner Publishers, 1997.

Stein, Kenneth W. *Heroic Diplomacy: Sadat, Kissinger, Begin and the Quest for Arab-Israeli Peace*. New York: Routledge, 1999.

Stern, Eric. "Contextualizing and Critiquing the Poliheuristic Theory." *Journal of Conflict Resolution*. 48, no. 1 (February 2004): 105–26.

Stewart, F. "War and Underdevelopment: Can Economic Analysis Help Reduce the Costs?" *Journal of International Development* 5, no. 4 (July–August 1993): 357–80.

Stoll, Richard J. "The Guns of November: Presidential Reelections and the Use of Force, 1947–1982." *Journal of Conflict Resolution* 28, no. 2 (June 1984): 231–46.

———. "Conclusion: Multiple Paths to Knowledge? Integrating Methodology and Substance in the Study of Conflict Management and Conflict Resolution." Pp. 343–61 in *Multiple Paths to Knowledge: Methodology in the Study of Conflict Management and Conflict Resolution*, edited by Z. Maoz, A. Mintz, T. C. Morgan, G. Palmer, and R.J. Stoll. Lanham, Md.: Lexington Books, 2004.

Strauss, Michael A. "Reading the Blueprints of Creation." *Scientific American* 290, no. 2 (February 2004): 54–61.

Szayna, Thomas A., et al. *The Emergence of Peer Competitors: A Framework for Analysis*. Santa Monica, Calif.: Rand Corporation, 2001.

Szreter, S. "Economic Growth, Disruption, Deprivation, Disease, and Death." Pp. 76–116 in *Plague and Politics*, edited by A.T. Price-Smith. New York: Palgrave, 2001.

Taber, Charles. "An Artificial Mediator." Pp. 153–85 in *Multiple Paths to Knowledge: Methodology in the Study of Conflict Management and Conflict Resolution*, edited by Z. Maoz, A. Mintz, T.C. Morgan, G. Palmer, and R. Stoll. Lanham, Md.: Lexington Books, 2004.

Taber, Charles S., and Marco R. Steenbergen. "Computational Experiments in Electoral Behavior." Pp. 141–78 in *Political Judgment*, edited by M. Lodge and K. McGraw. Ann Arbor: University of Michigan Press, 1995.

Taylor, H., and S. Karlin. *An Introduction to Stochastic Modeling*. New York: Academic Press, 1994.

Telhami, Shibley. *Power and Leadership in International Bargaining: The Path to the Camp David Accords*. New York: Columbia University Press, 1990.

Tessler, Mark. *A History of the Israeli-Palestinian Conflict*. Indianapolis: Indiana University Press: 1994.

Thaler, Richard. *Quasi-rational Economics*. New York: Russell Sage Foundation, 1991.

Thomas, D. "Incomes, Expenditures, and Health Outcomes." Pp. 142–64 in *Intrahousehold Resource Allocation in Developing Countries: Models, Methods, and Policy*, edited by L. Haddad, J. Hoddinott, and H. Alderman. Baltimore: Johns Hopkins University Press, 1997.

Thompson, William. "Polarity, the Long Cycle, and Global Power War." *Journal of Conflict Resolution* 30, no. 4 (December 1986): 587–615.

———. *On Global War*. Columbia: University of South Carolina Press, 1988.

Toole, M.J. "Complex Emergencies: Refugee and Other Populations." Pp. 419–42 in *The Public Health Consequences of Disasters*, edited by E. Noji. New York: Oxford University Press, 1997.

———. "Displaced Persons and War." Pp. 197–212 in *War and Public Health*, updated ed., edited by B.S. Levy, and V.W. Sidel. Washington, D.C.: American Public Health Association, 2000.

Troester, Rod. *Jimmy Carter as Peacemaker*. Westport, Conn.: Praeger Series in Presidential Studies, 1996.

Tsebelis, G. *Veto Players: How Political Institutions Work*. Princeton, N.J.: Princeton University Press, 2002.

Tuchman, Barbara W. *The Guns of August*. New York: Bantam Books, 1962.

Tufte, Edward R. *The Visual Display of Quantitative Information*. Cheshire, Conn.: Graphics Press, 1983.

———. *Envisioning Information*. Cheshire, Conn.: Graphics Press, 1990.

———. *Visual Explanations: Images and Quantities, Evidence and Narrative*. Cheshire, Conn.: Graphics Press, 1997.

United Nations. *World Urbanization Prospects: The 1996 Revision*. New York: United Nations 1998.

United Nations Development Programme (UNDP). *Human Development Report 2002*. New York: Oxford University Press, 2002.

United States Institute of Peace (USIP). *Special Report: Aids and Violent Conflict in Africa*. Washington, D.C.: United States Institute of Peace, 2001.

Van Rossem, Ronan. "The World System Paradigm as General Theory of Development: A Cross-National Test." *American Sociological Review* 61, no. 3 (June 1996): 508–27.

Vasquez, John A. *The War Puzzle*. New York; Cambridge, U.K.: Cambridge University Press, 1993.

Vasquez, John A., and Colin Elman, eds. *Balancing of Power*. Boston: Rowman & Littlefield, 2002.

Wagner, R. Harrison. "Bargaining and War." *American Journal of Political Science* 44, no. 3 (July 2000): 469–84.

Wallace, Michael. "Arms Races and Escalation: Some New Evidence." *Journal of Conflict Resolution* 23, no. 1 (March 1979): 3–16.

———. "Armaments and Escalation: Two Competing Hypotheses." *International Studies Quarterly* 26, no. 1 (March 1982): 37–56.

Walt, Stephen M. *The Origins of Alliances*. Ithaca, N.Y.: Cornell University Press, 1987.

Walter, Barbara F. "The Critical Barriers to Civil War Settlement." *International Organization* 51, no. 3 (Summer 1997): 335–64.

———. *Negotiating Settlements to Civil Wars*. Princeton, N.J.: Princeton University Press, 2001.

———. Committing to Peace: The Successful Settlement of Civil Wars. Princeton, N.J.: Princeton University Press, 2002.

Waltz, Kenneth N. "The Stability of a Bipolar World." *Daedalus* 93, no. 4 (December 1964), 881–905.

———. *Theory of International Politics*. Reading, Mass.: Addison-Wesley, 1979.

———. "The Spread of Nuclear Weapons: More May Be Better." *Adelphi Paper #171*. London: International Institute of Strategic Studies, 1981.

Ward, Michael D., and Kristian S. Gleditsch. "War and Peace in Space and Time: The Role of Democratization." *International Studies Quarterly* 44, no. 1 (March 2000): 1–29.

———. "Location, Location, Location: An MCMC Approach to Modeling the Spatial Context of War and Peace." *Political Analysis* 10, no. 3 (Summer 2002): 244–60.

Ward, Michael D., John V. O'Loughlin, Jordin S. Cohen, Kristian S. Gleditsch, Corey L. Lofdahl, and Michael E. Shin. "The Spatial and Temporal Diffusion of Democracy, 1945–1994." Paper presented at the 37th Annual Convention of the International Studies Association, San Diego, Calif., 16–21 April 1996.

Wasserman, Stanley, and Katherine Faust. *Social Network Analysis: Methods and Applications.* New York: Cambridge University Press, 1994.

Wayman, Frank W. "Bipolarity and War: The Role of Capability Concentration and Alliance Patterns among Major Powers, 1816–1965." *Journal of Peace Research* 21, no. 1 (April 1984): 61–78.

Weede, Erich. "Arms Races and Escalation: Some Persisting Doubts." *Journal of Conflict Resolution* 24, no. 2 (June 1980): 285–87.

———. "Extended Deterrence, Superpower Control, and Militarized Interstate Disputes, 1962–1976." *Journal of Peace Research* 26, no. 1 (February 1989): 7–17.

Weissman, Stephen. *A Culture of Deference: Congress's Failure of Leadership in Foreign Policy.* New York: Basic Books, 1995.

Werner, Suzanne. "The Precarious Nature of Peace: Resolving the Issues, Enforcing the Settlement, and Renegotiating the Terms." *American Journal of Political Science* 43, no. 3 (July 1999): 912–34.

———. "Deterring Intervention: The Stakes of War and Third-Party Involvement." *American Journal of Political Science* 44, no. 4 (October 2000): 720–32.

Werner, Suzanne, and Douglas Lemke. "Opposites Do Not Attract: The Impact of Domestic Institutions, Power, and Prior Commitments on Alignment Choices." *International Studies Quarterly* 41, no. 3 (September 1997): 529–46.

Westwood, John. *The History of Middle East Wars.* London: JG Press, 2002.

Wildavsky, A. "The Two Presidencies." *Trans-Action* 4 (December 1966): 7–14.

Wilensky, Harold. *The Welfare State and Equality.* Berkeley: University of California Press, 1975.

Wilkinson, R. *Unhealthy Societies: The Afflictions of Inequality.* New York: Routledge, 1996.

Willer, David, ed. *Network Exchange Theory.* Westport, Conn.: Praeger, 1999.

Williams, A. "Calculating the Global Burden of Disease: Time for a Strategic Reappraisal?" *Health Economics* 8, no. 1 (February 1999): 1–8.

Winchester, Simon. *The Map That Changed the World: William Smith and the Birth of Modern Geology.* New York: HarperCollins, 2001.

Wittkopf, E., and M. Dehaven. "Soviet Behavior, Presidential Popularity, and the Penetration of Open Political Systems." Pp. 433–53 in *New Directions in the Study of Foreign Policy,* edited by C. Hermann, C. Kegley, and J. Rosenau. Boston: Unwin Hyman, 1987.

Wittman, Donald. "How a War Ends: A Rational Model Approach." *Journal of Conflict Resolution* 23, no. 4 (December 1979): 743–63.

———. "War or Peace?" Paper presented at the "Political Economy of Conflict Conference," Yale University, New Haven, Conn., March 23–24, 2001.

Wolfsfeld, Gadi. *Media and Political Conflict.* Cambridge, U.K.: Cambridge University Press, 1997.

Woodward, David, ed. (a). *History of Cartography, Volume 3: Cartography in the European Renaissance*. Chicago: University of Chicago Press, forthcoming.

——, ed. (b). *History of Cartography, Volume 5: Cartography in the Nineteenth Century*. Chicago: University of Chicago Press, forthcoming.

Woodward, David, and G. Malcolm Lewis, eds. *History of Cartography, Volume 2, Book 3: Cartography in the Traditional African, American, Arctic, Australian, and Pacific Societies*. Chicago: University of Chicago Press, 1998.

Woodward, Susan L. "Bosnia and Herzegovina: How Not to End Civil War." Pp. 73–115 in *Civil Wars, Insecurity, and Intervention*, edited by Barbara F. Walter and Jack Snyder. New York: Columbia University Press, 1999.

World Bank. *Breaking the Conflict Trap: Civil War and Development Policy*. Washington, D.C., 2003.

World Health Organization (WHO). The World Health Report 2000: Health Systems: Improving Performance. Geneva, Switzerland, 2000.

Ya'alon, Moshe. Interview in *Ha'aretz*. Tel Aviv, Israel, 2004.

Yapp, M.E. *The Near East since the First World War*. 2d ed. London: Pearson Education, 1996.

Young, Oran. *The Intermediaries: Third Parties in International Crises*. Princeton, N.J.: Princeton University Press, 1967.

Zagare, Frank. "Rationality and Deterrence." *World Politics* 42, no. 2 (January 1990): 238–60.

Zelikow, P. "The United States and the Use of Force: A Historical Summary." Pp. 31–81 in *Democracy, Strategy, and Vietnam*, edited by G. Osborn, et al. Lexington, Mass.: Lexington Books, 1987.

Zinnes, Dina. "Constructing Political Logic: The Democratic Peace Puzzle." *Journal of Conflict Resolution* 48, no. 3 (forthcoming June 2004).

Index

Page numbers in italic type refer to tables or figures.

About the Contributors

Karl DeRouen Jr. is an associate professor of political science at the University of Alabama. He received his Ph.D. in political science from Texas A&M University. His research interests are conflict processes and international political economy. His previous work has appeared in the *Journal of Politics*, *Journal of Conflict Resolution*, *British Journal of Political Science*, *International Interactions*, *Defence and Peace Economics*, *International Studies Quarterly*, and other journals. He is a co-investigator in a three-year project to study internal conflict in the Asia-Pacific region. Other ongoing projects include civil war outcome, duration and onset; the determinants of conflict management success; and strategic interaction in the Middle East.

Hazem Adam Ghobarah is project manager at Mathsoft, Inc. in Cambridge, Massachusetts. He has been research fellow at Harvard University's Weatherhead Center for International Affairs (2000-2002). Dr. Ghobarah has published on topics related to statistics, international relations, public health, and evolutionary psychology. His work has appeared in *Social Science & Medicine*, *International Studies Quarterly*, and the *American Political Science Review*.

Kristian Skrede Gleditsch is assistant professor of political science at the University of California, San Diego, and a research associate of the Centre for the Study of Civil War at the International Peace Research Institute, Oslo (PRIO), Norway. His research interests include conflict and cooperation, democratization, and spatial dimensions of social and political processes. He is the author of *All International Politics Is Local: The Diffusion of Conflict, Integration, and Democratization* (University of Michigan Press, 2002). His articles have appeared in the *American Journal of Political Science, American*

Political Science Review, Annals of the Association of American Geographers, International Interactions, Internasjonal Politikk, International Studies Quarterly, Journal of Conflict Resolution, Journal of Peace Research, Political Analysis, and *Political Psychology.*

Shaun Goldfinch is a senior lecturer in the School of Political Science and Communication at the University of Canterbury in Christchurch, New Zealand. He obtained his Ph.D. from the Department of Political Science, University of Melbourne, Australia, in 1999. He has previously worked as a policy analyst in the New Zealand Department of Justice and as a social scientist in the New Zealand Institute for Social Research and Development, and has held positions as visiting associate professor at the Center for National University Finance in Tokyo and visiting professor at Otemon University, Osaka, Japan. He is author of *Remaking New Zealand and Australian Economic Policy: Ideas, Institutions, and Policy Communities* (Georgetown University Press, 2000), and has published widely in academic journals including *Governance, Tijdschrift voor Economische en Sociale Geografie,* and *Political Science.* He won the Sam Richardson award for the most important/influential article in the 1999 volume of the *Australian Journal of Public Administration.* He is currently completing a book on e-government and information systems in the New Zealand public sector, which will be published by Otago University Press.

William Howell received his Ph.D. in political science from Stanford University in 2000, and is currently assistant professor of government at Harvard University. He has written widely on separation-of-powers issues and American political institutions, especially the presidency. He is the author of *Power without Persuasion: The Politics of Direct Presidential Action* (Princeton University Press, 2003), and *The Education Gap: Vouchers and Urban Schools* (with Paul Peterson, Brookings Institution Press, 2002). He has published articles in *International Organization, Journal of Politics, Journal of Policy Analysis and Management, Journal of Law, Economics, and Organization, Legislative Studies Quarterly,* and other journals. He is currently writing a book with Jon Pevehouse on Congress and the presidential use of force.

Paul Huth received his Ph.D. in political science in 1986 from Yale University. He is professor of political science at the University of Michigan and research professor at the Institute for Social Research. Professor Huth has published widely in leading journals on subjects related to the study of international conflict and war, including deterrence behavior, crisis decision making, territorial disputes, and the democratic peace. He is the recipient of numerous grants from the National Science Foundation. He is the author of *Extended Deterrence and the Prevention of War* (Yale University Press, 1988), *Standing Your Ground* (University of Michigan Press, 1996), and *The Democratic Peace and Territorial Conflict in the Twentieth Century* (Cambridge University Press, 2003).

Ranan D. Kuperman is lecturer in international relations, University of Haifa, Israel, and has held various visiting academic positions in Germany and New Zealand. His most recent book is entitled *Investment in Peace: The Politics of Economic Cooperation between Israel, Jordan, and the Palestinian Authority* (with Shaul Mishal and David Boas, Sussex Academic Press, 2001). His articles have been published in *International Interactions, Journal of Peace Research*, and the *Journal of Strategic Studies*.

Brett Ashley Leeds is associate professor of political science at Rice University. Her current research explores the formation, design, effectiveness, and influence of cooperative agreements and institutions in international politics. She is the principal investigator for a study on the politics of military alliances supported by the National Science Foundation. Her recent articles have appeared in the *American Journal of Political Science, International Organization*, and *Journal of Conflict Resolution*.

Zeev Maoz is professor of political science at the University of California, Davis. He is the author of several books and numerous articles on international conflict, strategy, decision making, and bargaining. His forthcoming book *Defending the Holy Land? A Critical Assessment of Israel's National Security and Foreign Policy, 1949–2003* will be published by the University of Michigan Press.

Alex Mintz is the Cullen-McFadden Professor of Political Science at Texas A&M University and Senior Fellow at U.N. Studies at Yale. Professor Mintz has received his Ph.D. from Northwestern University. He is the coeditor of the ISA-sponsored journal, *Foreign Policy Analysis*, and the associate editor for Experiments and Simulations of the *Journal of Conflict Resolution*.

Jon Pevehouse received his Ph.D. in political science from Ohio State University. His main research interests lie in international relations theory, foreign policy, international security, international political economy, and political methodology. He is the author of *Democracy from Above? Regional Institutions and Democratization*, forthcoming from Cambridge University Press. He has published articles in journals such as the *American Political*

Science Review, *American Journal of Political Science*, *International Organization*, *Journal of Politics*, and *Journal of Conflict Resolution*. He is currently writing a book with William Howell on Congress and the presidential use of force. His other current research areas include the politics behind the expansion of regional trade arrangements and the influence of international organizations in the post–Cold War era.

Bruce Russett is Dean Acheson Professor of International Relations and Political Science and director of United Nations Studies at Yale University. He has held visiting appointments at Columbia, Michigan, North Carolina, Harvard, the Free University of Brussels, the Richardson Institute in London, the Netherlands Institute for Advanced Study, the Tel Aviv University, and Tokyo University Law School. He has edited the *Journal of Conflict Resolution* since 1973. He is past president of the International Studies Association and of the Peace Science Society (International), and holds an honorary doctorate from Uppsala University. He has published 220 book chapters and journal articles, and 23 books including *The Once and Future Security Council* (1997) and *Triangulating Peace: Democracy, Interdependence, and International Organizations* (2001, with John Oneal).

Alastair Smith is associate professor of politics at New York University. He obtained his Ph.D. in political science from the University of Rochester in 1995. He has taught at Yale University and Washington University in St. Louis. He is the author of *The Logic of Political Survival* (with Bruce Bueno de Mesquita, Randolph Siverson, and James Morrow, MIT Press, 2003) and *Election Timing* (Cambridge University Press, 2004). His main research interests are formal models of international behavior.

Allan C. Stam is professor of government and the coordinator of the War and Peace Studies Program at Dartmouth College. He received his Ph.D. from the University of Michigan in 1993. Before attending college, he served in the U.S. Army Special Forces. His research appears in numerous political science journals. He has received several grants supporting his work, including three from the National Science Foundation, and received the International Studies Association's Karl W. Deutsch Award for 2004. His books include *Win, Lose or Draw* (University of Michigan Press, 1996), *Democracies at War* (Princeton University Press, 2002) and *The Behavioral Origins of War* (University of Michigan Press, 2003).

Ilan Talmud graduated from Columbia University (1992). He heads the Graduate Program at the Department of Sociology, University of Haifa, Israel. His research interests include: network analysis, economic and organizational sociology, models of competition, cooperation and knowledge transfer; privatization, the flexible labor market, and globalization. He is also interested in social stratification, gender, and political sociology.

Lesley G. Terris is a Ph.D. candidate in political science at Tel-Aviv University. Her research investigates international negotiation and mediation processes, while combining game theoretic modeling with quantitative and qualitative analyses. Her research interests also include the study of international politics through simulations and network analysis.

Michael D. Ward is professor of political science at the University of Washington. He is a founding member of the Center for Statistics and Social Sciences and a member of the Board of Directors of the Center for Spatially Informed Social Sciences. Most of his recent work deals with the analysis and presentation of data reflecting the inherent dependencies in international politics and economics.

Suzanne Werner is an associate professor in the Department of Political Science at Emory University. She received her Ph.D. from Vanderbilt University in 1993. She has published in several academic journals, including the *American Journal of Political Science*, *Journal of Conflict Resolution*, *International Studies Quarterly*, *Journal of Peace Research*, and *Political Research Quarterly*. Her research interests focus on the causes and consequences of international war. Most recently, her research focuses on modeling the process of negotiating and fighting that takes place during war. This research examines the onset, termination, and aftermath of war as a single conflict process and has as its goal improving our understanding of the conditions that affect the duration of war as well as the conditions that facilitate a lasting peace.

Amy Yuen is a graduate student in the Department of Political Science at Emory University. She completed her undergraduate work at Duke University. Her dissertation focuses on the role of third parties in conflict termination. She is particularly interested in the connections between the terms of settlement, often influenced by third parties, and the durability of peace agreements.